ASSOCIATION FOR SCO
NUMBER FII

POEMS BY A LADY

by Helen Craik

*

The ASSOCIATION FOR SCOTTISH LITERATURE aims to promote the study, teaching and writing of Scottish literature, and to further the study of the languages of Scotland. To these ends, ASL publishes works of Scottish literature (of which this volume is an example); literary criticism and in-depth reviews of Scottish books in *Scottish Literary Review*; and scholarly studies of language in *Scottish Language*. It also publishes *New Writing Scotland*, an annual anthology of new poetry, drama and short fiction, in Scots, English and Gaelic. ASL has also prepared a range of teaching materials covering Scottish language and literature for use in schools.

All the above publications are available as a single 'package' in return for an annual subscription. Enquiries should be sent to:

ASL, Scottish Literature, 7 University Gardens, University of Glasgow, Glasgow G12 8QH.
Telephone +44 (0)141 330 5309 or visit our website at **www.asls.org.uk**.

ASSOCIATION FOR SCOTTISH LITERATURE

POEMS BY A LADY

by

Helen Craik

edited from the Beinecke Manuscript

by

Rachel Mann and Patrick Scott

GLASGOW

2023

*

Published in Great Britain, 2023
by the Association for Scottish Literature
Scottish Literature
University of Glasgow
7 University Gardens
Glasgow G12 8QH

ASL is a registered charity no. SC006535
www.asls.org.uk

ISBN: 978-1-906841-56-0

A catalogue record for this book
is available from the British Library

Set in Sabon Pro
Typeset by ASL, Glasgow

Printed by Ashford Colour Press, Gosport

CONTENTS

List of illustrations:

PREFACE AND
ACKNOWLEDGEMENTS

THE SCOTTISH WRITER Helen Craik (1751–1825) has been drawing increased critical attention as a novelist, particularly for her five Gothic non-Scottish novels, but almost none of her poetry has ever been available in print. It was exciting therefore, in the fall of 2020, to come on a catalogue record for a 178-page manuscript of Craik's poetry that survives in the Beinecke Rare Book and Manuscript Library, Yale University. It is part of the library's James Marshall Osborn and Marie-Louise Osborn Collection, which was fully transferred only after Mr Osborn's death in 1976; the Craik manuscript, Beinecke MS Osborn c375, had probably been in the Osborn collection for some twenty years before that. This edition, transcribing and annotating the Beinecke manuscript, represents, we believe, the first opportunity ever for readers to see the range and nature of Craik's poetic work. These poems, written in Craik's twenties and thirties but almost all unpublished till now, cast new light on Craik's literary interests and Dumfriesshire connections, begin to dispel speculations about her mysterious early life, and add significantly to the available corpus of poetry by Scottish women writers in the Romantic era.

Given the limited available information about Craik's writing, life, and reading, much in the comments and notes here about the poems is necessarily preliminary. As well as giving headnotes on the background or sources of the longer poems, we have aimed to annotate names, places, and literary allusions. Craik's very occasional use of distinctively Scots words or turns of phrase is treated in the notes, rather than in a separate glossary. Craik's manuscript is her fair copy, and her few corrections are recorded in the notes, not in the text itself; where a blank line between verse-paragraphs in Craik's manuscript falls at the top of the printed page here, it is indicated by a ¶ in the left margin. We hope to see fuller critical and interpretative discussion of these poems from other scholars in the coming years, and we should be glad to hear from anyone who has additional background information on specific items or who knows the whereabouts of other Craik manuscripts.

We have been pleased at the interest shown by other scholars as we worked on this project, and we appreciate the assistance and encouragement we have received from librarians and scholars on both sides of the Atlantic. Most important has been the help of Natalia Sciarini and Matthew Rowe, at the Beinecke Library, Yale University, who answered our enquiries, provided photographs of the manuscript itself, and even checked pages for us from one of Craik's as-yet-undigitised novels; more recently, June Can at the Beinecke sent scans of the related provenance file. Patrick Scott first became interested in Helen Craik in connection with research on the Lilly manuscript of Robert Burns's song 'A red, red rose'. Sarah McElroy Mitchell and Maureen Maryanski, at the Lilly Library, Indiana University, sent him provenance material for that manuscript which pointed back to the Craiks as its original recipients and long-time owners. Soon after reporting that research, and repeating the general belief that Craik's own poems were missing, he noticed the Beinecke catalogue entry. Nearer at hand, we are indebted for ongoing assistance at the University of South Carolina from Elizabeth Sudduth, Associate Dean for Special Collections, Matt Hodge, Rob Smith, and others in the Irvin Department of Rare Books & Special Collections; from Sean King, Brian Barr, Bill Boland, and Amber Cook in Inter-Library Loans; and from Sharon Verba and her colleagues in Reference & Research Services.

In Scotland, during a period when archive access and research travel were limited, we were helped by a number of librarians and archivists: Allyson Carlisle, Elizabeth Course, and Alison Burgess, at the Ewart Library, Dumfries; Susan Taylor, at the Mitchell Library, Glasgow; Robert MacLean, Archives and Special Collections, Glasgow University Library; and Ralph McLean and Robert Betteridge, at the National Library of Scotland. In addition, we are grateful to Jamie Blackett of Arbigland for permission to use the estate map drawn by William Ferguson and for answering our questions about the house and estate. Valentina Bold kindly shared Dumfries area contacts, and Alice Rourke and Wendy Hampson, of the Kirkbean Parish Heritage Society, responded to other queries.

More generally, we are indebted to the pioneer research on Helen Craik by Adriana Craciun and, more recently, Marianna D'Ezio. It was a query from Andrew Calhoun in Chicago about a Burns song manuscript that spurred Patrick Scott's first research into Craik and Burns. We also appreciate the interest and help shown by Craig Lamont, Gerard Carruthers, Kirsteen McCue, Rhona Brown, and others in the Centre for Robert Burns Studies, University of Glasgow. While the edition has been a collaboration, with us both being involved in all stages of the work, Rachel Mann's preliminary transcription work on the manuscript was funded in part by the *Studies in Scottish Literature* Endowment, University of South Carolina Foundations. Our final thanks must be to Ian Brown, Duncan Jones, and others involved with the Association for Scottish Literature's publications programme, for their confidence and patience.

R. J. M.
P. G. S.

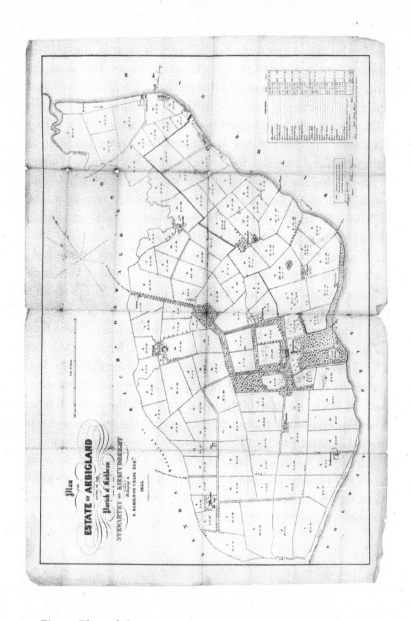

Fig. 1: Plan of the Estate of Arbigland lying in the parish of
Kirkbean and the Stewartry of Kirkcudbright, 1835.
Reproduced courtesy of Mr Jamie Blackett through the
Dumfries Archival Mapping Project.

INTRODUCTION

HELEN CRAIK'S MANUSCRIPT volume *Poems by a Lady* (1790) has never previously been published, and the manuscript itself does not seem to have attracted previous scholarly notice, at least in the past hundred years. Craik herself has been known, first as the acquaintance and correspondent of Robert Burns, and more recently in her own right as a novelist. Indeed, since Adriana Craciun's 2001 essay on Craik's novel *Adelaide de Narbonne* (1800), there has been a fair amount of critical interest in Craik's five Gothic novels, published by the Minerva Press between 1796 and 1805.[1] There has, of course, been a parallel interest, over a longer period, in the rediscovery and critical reassessment of the poetry written by eighteenth-century Scottish women, and the recuperation of poetry by women has played a significant role over the past thirty or more years in resetting the teaching canon and research agenda for British Romanticism and the long eighteenth century.[2]

However, none of this recent scholarship, on Craik, on Scottish women writers, or on Romantic-period poetry, could give significant attention to Helen Craik as a poet, because she never published her poetry and the three privately owned Craik notebooks that had been reported in the 1920s had all vanished. The only poem of Craik's that is at all widely known is her short verse-tribute to Burns inscribed on the title-page of his Glenriddell Manuscript. The Craik entry in the *Oxford Dictionary of National Biography* is representative of responsible recent scholarly comment when it concludes, regretfully, that 'Most of her poetry is now lost'.[3]

Craik is not unique among Scottish women writers of her period in not seeing her poetry into print. Juliet Shields has recently commented:

> In eighteenth-century Scotland, as in much of provincial Britain, authorship was much less closely tied to print than it was in London's commercialised literary marketplace, and the relationship between manuscript and print publication seems to have been fluid rather than oppositional.[4]

Shields adds that this was 'particularly true of poetry'. Many seventeenth- and eighteenth-century Scottish women who were identified by their contemporaries as poets, and who produced a significant body of poetry, never themselves saw their work published. Recognisable examples from the eighteenth century might include Elizabeth, Lady Wardlaw (1677–1727), author of 'Hardyknute'; Elizabeth Rutherford Scot (1729–1789), from Wauchope, who exchanged verse-epistles with Burns; the ballad collector and writer Anna Gordon Brown (1747–1810), whose work is only now being disentangled from its use in Scott's *Minstrelsy of the Scottish Border*; Anne Lindsay (Lady Anne Barnard, 1750–1825), who wrote 'Auld Robin Gray'; and the Jacobite songwriter Carolina Oliphant (Lady Nairne, 1766–1845), author of 'The Laird of Cockpen'. Other examples might include Anne Bannerman (1765–1829) and two of Burns's correspondents, Frances Dunlop and Agnes McLehose.

In earlier periods, commentators have treated this phenomenon as coterie poetry, but the term is in some ways misleading when applied to these Scottish women poets. Even in their own time, their work, and particularly their work with songs and ballads, was not hidden away or held closely for circulation only among friends. Through performance at social gatherings, unattributed inclusion in published song and ballad collections, and as engraved sheet music, works by several of these writers achieved significant if largely anonymous recognition in their lifetime and would later be anthologised and collected under their names. Such social performance and circulation was mostly genre-specific, and Craik's poems, dramatic monologues rather than song or ballad, were not in the relevant genres, but her notebooks, and evidence about a contemporary transcript of her poem on the Queen of Denmark, show she circulated her poems in manuscript, beyond her immediate family circle at Arbigland.

Craik's poems also show that poetry written for private circulation is not insulated from public events. Dorothy McMillan commented that Scottish women's writing had 'a balance of interest between the public and private spheres that is peculiarly female', and that 'Women almost always take an interest, even if not a part, in public life and they write about that interest'.[5] Stephen Behrendt expanded on McMillan's comment to argue that it was '*because* of the gendered roles historically assigned them', that 'the works of women writers exhibit a particular sensitivity to the relationship between the public and the private'.[6] A number of Craik's poems deal with current or recent events, based on newspaper or magazine reports, and in every case she presents the story, not through impersonal narration, but through the voice and perspective of one of the participants.

Juliet Shields has suggested that there was a social or class element in manuscript publication. In addition to the differences she notes between writers in local and regional settings and those living in Edinburgh or London, she also argues that 'authorship had different connotations for elite women, who tended to circulate their poetry in manuscript, and working-class women who tended to publish their poetry by subscription', contrasting the manuscript poetry of Elizabeth Rae Keir and Lady Frances Scott with that of Christian Milne and Anne Ross, household servants whose work, like that of Janet Little, reached print through subscription arranged by their employers and patrons.[7]

Each of these factors may have played a part in Craik's decision to keep her poetry in manuscript form, even after she had left Arbigland when she started publishing regularly as a novelist. Craik's poetry differs in some ways from that of her better-known contemporaries. She does not, for instance, write descriptive poems about Scottish landscape, love poetry, or national or Jacobite song. She does not write explicitly religious poems. Her work certainly includes poems written for her social circle, and it includes longer poems that draw on or rework ballad narratives. Some of the stories she reworks have Scottish sources or Scottish settings. Though alert readers will recognise that her own spoken language was Scots, she does not draw, as some of the women songwriters do, on an obviously vernacular tradition, even in a gentrified form.

The strand in Scottish literature to which she relates is an inward, psychological one, and one looking as much to later developments as to older traditions. Adriana Craciun has argued, in an influential essay on Anne Bannerman and 'Romantic spinstrelsy', that in reworking elements of the ballad tradition eighteenth-century Scottish women poets fashioned a distinctively Scottish version of the Gothic imagination.[8] Almost all Craik's longer poems are narrative and psychological, rather than local or social. They show a distinctive dramatic imagination, voicing the inner turmoil of a single character trapped in a story that is both nightmarish and violent. Even when they are based on an historical event or incident, they are not focused on the outward events. This dominant psychological strain in Craik's manuscript poetry provides a clear path from her poetry in the 1780s to her later achievements as Gothic novelist. The rediscovery of Craik's poetry adds a compelling new voice to the prehistory of Romantic Gothic.

Helen Craik, William Craik, and Arbigland

Helen Craik (1751–1825) was born into a well-established Scottish landowning family on her family's estate, Arbigland, in Kirkcudbrightshire. Her father, William Craik of Arbigland (1703–1798), had taken up farming in 1726, after studying law at Edinburgh. He had started out with a small farm Maxwellfield, part of the larger estate, and he inherited the Arbigland estate itself in 1736, following his own father's death. In 1733, he had married Elizabeth Stewart, the daughter of another local family, the Stewarts of Shambellie, in the next parish, New Abbey. Before marriage, William had had an illegitimate son, James Craik (1727–1814), who studied medicine at Edinburgh University, became an army surgeon in Jamaica, settled in Virginia, served as a surgeon with the Continental Army, was later appointed Physician-General, and was George Washington's personal physician.[9] Of William and Elizabeth's six legitimate children, the first son died young. Helen was brought up with two much older siblings, a sister Ann, born in 1737, and a brother Adam, born in 1740, and with a younger sister Elizabeth. Ann married another local landowner, John Hamilton of Ellershaw, but neither Helen nor Elizabeth married, and Adam was still unmarried when he drowned in 1782, so by the 1780s there was no immediate male heir living at Arbigland. However, because William's father, another Adam Craik (1655–1736), had married twice, with six children from the first marriage to Marion Campbell (whose mother was a Maxwell), and nine from the second, to Margery Aglionby from Nunnery in Cumberland, cousins and second cousins were spread through southwest Scotland and across the Solway.

The Arbigland estate, where Craik would spend the first forty-one years of her life, lay in the parish of Kirkbean, on the western shore of the Nith estuary, some thirteen miles south of Dumfries, as the Nith opened out into the Solway Firth.[10] Long after Craik left Arbigland, an unsigned but widely reprinted article from the *Dumfries Courier* gave this lyrical account of the Arbigland peninsula:

> we know of few places in this part of the country that are better worth visiting than the point of Arbigland, stretching us it does into the clear waters of the Solway, and rising almost like an Oasis amidst the sandy wastes of the Carse [. . .]. Independently of its own fairy scenery, which in a manner divides it from all the world beside, the mansion-house of Arbigland commands a delightful and most extensive prospect. On the right the bold and precipitous shore of Colvend [. . .] stretches till it dips

into the dark and swollen Urr; on the left, the venerable towers of Newabbey and Carlaverock Castle, the well-wooded heights of Maybie, the infant harbours of the Quay and Carse, with a number of other striking objects, are seen receding in gay and pleasing perspective; in the rear, the sailor's land-mark, and the farmer's weather-gauge, the dark and lowering Criffel rears his misty head, as if willing, like eastern sovereigns, to derive importance from his partial invisibility; while in the front, the far-famed Cumberland mountains terminate the prospect, and lend a pleasing contrast to the whole intervening distance of clear blue water, thriving sea-ports, scattered villages, fertile plains, and fleecy uplands.[11]

The original Arbigland house, a stone peel tower, was close to the shore, but in the early 1750s when Helen Craik was born, the Craiks were living at Maxwellfield Cottage, while William Craik designed and built a new Arbigland House, in the classical style associated with Robert Adam, at a final cost of some four thousand pounds.[12] The new house was about a third of a mile inland, nearer the centre of the estate and carefully aligned on an axis giving vistas to the north-east, south-east down a broad walk to the Nith estuary, and south-west across the Solway towards the Lake District and Skiddaw. The house, built of dressed stone, had two main floors, with basement offices below and attic rooms above. The substantial stable block to the west of the house completed the design. The family moved in in 1755, with the public rooms of the house not yet fully finished, and some additions were made by later generations, but in most respects the house remains as it was when Helen Craik lived there. Also remaining is the extensive plantation on each side of the broad walk, with the walled garden on the south side towards the shore end. The setting will have been more open in the eighteenth century, till the trees matured, and it is not now possible to identify the site or probable design of the summer-house about which Craik writes in several poems. The gardens surrounding the house, including the rose garden on the north side of the walk, were later developments, as was the dower house or House by the Shore, which was built in the 1930s. There was quite good access to Arbigland for coastal shipping, at Carsethorn to the north, and Southerness at the south end of the peninsula, but the estate was well off the main eighteenth-century road network, and even in the nineteenth century it was never served by any nearby railway line. That relative isolation, three centuries of sustained agricultural land use, rather than more mixed development, and multigenerational continuity in ownership mean it is still possible to imagine at least something of the home and setting that Helen Craik experienced.[13]

The Arbigland estate had been bought by William Craik, Helen's great-grandfather, and provost of Dumfries, in 1679 from Lord Southesk. While Craik's father was not the biggest landowner in the area, the estate was still substantial: in 1760, following a formal division between family members, the family's combined holdings in the parish were valued at an annual rental of £1161, Scots; the largest portion of the estate was held by Helen's father, almost as much in the name of her brother, and a smaller portion was owned by her brother-in-law Lieut. John Hamilton.[14] Their holdings would be overshadowed in time by those of their richer neighbour and Craik's near contemporary, the Glasgow merchant, Richard Oswald; by the early nineteenth century Oswald's grandson owned land in the parish valued at over three thousand pounds.[15] The contrast between the Arbigland estate, inherited land that had been improved over many years by a resident owner, and the Oswald estate, acquired and improved later in the century, with capital brought from outside Scotland (including for the Oswalds, the profits of slavery), highlights both the growing attractiveness of agricultural land as an investment, and a sharp difference between Craik's achievement at Arbigland and that of many later improvers.[16]

William Craik brought new agricultural methods to an area that was reluctant to change.[17] As a Board of Agriculture report later put it, Craik was 'a man of great originality and uncommon powers of mind', who 'by his own unassisted exertions [. . .] devised and carried into effect a system of the best husbandry, [. . .] when nothing similar was to be seen in the neighbouring country'.[18] The agricultural changes involved quite draconian social upheaval, with the enclosure and consolidation of common fields and small holdings, which in the years immediately before Craik took on Maxwellfield had led to popular resistance in Kirkcudbrightshire that was put down by the military.[19] At Arbigland, Craik enclosed and fenced and drained and limed his lands, using cartloads of seashells from further down the shore.[20] He planted over forty acres of timber. In the 1730s, he and James Maxwell, heir to the nearby estate of Kirkconnell, hunted for coal seams that might provide capital for further improvement.[21] Craik built new stone houses and steadings on the smaller tenant farms into which the estate was subdivided. He experimented with crop rotations and root crops, and he required his tenants to plant according to the rotations he mandated. At least in his earlier years, he started work early in the mornings and worked in the fields alongside his men. He decided that farm workers, often idle in the winter months, could be usefully employed winnowing grain, and on at least one occasion, when they resisted such new tasks, he used his status as a magistrate to threaten them with jail. He adopted one new plough and invented another, for which in 1771 the Society of Arts awarded him a Gold Medal.[22] He spread his ideas both through the agricultural society he founded in Dumfries and by taking 'gentlemen apprentices' who learned how to farm the estates they would inherit.

William Craik had been early in recognising the agricultural potential of southwest Scotland, and by the time Helen reached adulthood he had transformed both the local economy and the local landscape. One of the major contemporary surveys of Scottish agriculture paid tribute to this pioneering role:

> He possesses the unrivalled honour even of beginning, not to mention of carrying on, a most successful reforma- tion in the agriculture of this country. [. . .] he served a

severe apprenticeship, as his farm in its natural state was
not inviting, wild, and ill cultivated when he undertook
it. [. . .] The surest test of improvement is the rent that
can be afforded. [. . .] one farm, which, before Mr Craik
began his improvements, paid of rent L. 35 for 130 acres.
The whole being well inclosed, every wet spot made dry
by under or upper drains, not a stone left to interrupt
the plough, mostly in grass and full of manure, excellent
houses, &c. it is now leased at L. 100 Sterling [. . .].[23]

These results did not come easily. How much labour, as well as
hard-earned expertise, was involved in 'improving' uncultivated
land on the estate, and the patience needed before the investment
paid off, can gathered from the same writer's tribute to Helen
Craik's brother Adam:

There is a large track of flat land near the coast, covered
with heath, which appearing to be irreclaimable, let at no
higher rent, than one shilling per acre. This was a proper
subject for the young gentleman to exercise his skill on. He
began with drawing ditches for carrying off the superfluous
moisture; and, upon the side of the ditches, thorns were
planted for inclosing. The next step was to lay lime on one
field and fleech on another, at the expence of fifty shillings
per acre, and the manure ploughed in before winter. Two
crops of oats successively: Next a dressing for turnip with
dung, which prepares the soil for barley and grass-feeds,
eight pounds red clover, as much white, two bushels rye-
grass: one crop of hay, after which the land is let to tenants
at fifteen shillings per acre for pasture only. If rushes come
up, which is likely from the clay bottom holding water,
Mr Craik thinks of allowing the tenants to break up the
ground, and to repeat the rotation of crops as before.[24]

Before this account reached print, Adam Craik was dead, leaving
William Craik, then in his seventies, to take back management of

the estate and its tenants. Thirty years on, Helen Craik wrote dryly about her father's work on the estate, that 'the female part of his family were never permitted to interfere, in the smallest degree, with those occupations and pursuits, [. . .] we were kept in total ignorance of every transaction'.[25] But this comment may be something of a smoke screen, because she followed it up by saying she felt 'competent to answer' questions her correspondent had posed about her father's work, and he commented that she 'may well be allowed to possess a full share of her father's abilities'. Throughout the 1780s, with her mother and sister both invalids, she will have managed the household, at a time when almost all food and much clothing was home-produced, so intersecting with the estate management, and, together with the farm overseer Samuel Johnstone, she will also have been her father's chief day-to-day recourse to talk about estate issues.[26]

Beyond Arbigland, William Craik was also active in the public and political life of the wider region. His grandfather and uncle had both been provost of Dumfries, the grandfather during the Revolution of 1688–89, and the uncle active in the defence of the burgh against the Jacobite army in 1715. William himself, though he had friends and relatives with Jacobite sympathies, had backed the Hanoverian settlement consistently. In 1741 or 1742, he was sounded out about standing for parliament for the Stewartry of Kirkcudbright.[27] In 1745, he was among several members of the family who made forced loans to the burgh to meet the tribute required by the Jacobite government, but this does not imply support for the Stuarts.[28] In 1750, his influence with Scottish authorities allowed him to help his Jacobite neighbour James Maxwell of Kirkconnell return from exile and regain use, if not full title, of his estates.[29] He was a justice of the peace in both Kirkcudbrightshire and Dumfriesshire, and Craik tells a story of him leaping down from the bench to tackle an accused murderer who had drawn a knife on the constables. He was also a Commissioner of Excise 'from Foot of Nith to Foot of Urr', and from the late 1740s onwards he was Surveyor-General of Excise for Dumfries, a salaried though part-time government appointment, and so was involved in the government's efforts to suppress the smuggling of wine, spirits, tobacco, and later tea, on to the Solway coast from the Isle of Man (then a distinct legal jurisdiction separate from mainland Britain).[30] As Commissioner, he participated with excise officers and the military in stake-outs for smugglers coming ashore and in raids on their storage places, and when the raids were successful, he profited from a one-third share of any captured goods.[31] He went to London in 1764 to advise on how to control the Isle of Man smugglers, when he was offered a better-paid position on the Board of Customs, which he declined to avoid long periods away from Arbigland.

While Arbigland might seem isolated, the Craiks were part of a network of local landed families, drawn both from Kirkcudbrightshire and Dumfriesshire. Their connection with a wider world was centred in Dumfries, about sixteen miles north, little more than half the distance of Kirkcudbright. With a population nearing seven thousand inhabitants, Dumfries was modernising itself, with a new infirmary, assembly rooms, a library, and a theatre, and initiatives in street paving and policing.[32] It was where William Craik and the other Justices of the Peace met for their quarter sessions, and where judges from Edinburgh, including his old friend Lord Kames, a fellow enthusiast for improvement, came on circuit each spring and autumn. For intellectual contact, Dumfries was on the mail routes, bringing recent books and newspapers from Edinburgh and London, and the town had its own weekly newspaper the *Dumfries Weekly Journal* (founded in 1771). In 1792, Robert Heron described it as 'a sort of metropolis' to the two counties, and a social as well as economic centre:

> Dumfries is perhaps a place of higher gaiety and eleg-
> ance, than any other town in Scotland, of the same size.
> The proportion of the inhabitants, who are descended of
> respectable families, and have received a liberal education,
> is greater here, than in any other town in this part of

the island. [. . .] The amusements of this city, its advantages for education, its convenient and healthy situation allure many of the inferior gentry from the neighbouring counties, to spend half, or perhaps the whole year here.[33]

Helen Craik had friends in Dumfries, notably Miss Staig, the daughter of David Staig, provost of Dumfries, whose wife was related to Craik's mother's family, the Stewarts of Shambellie. Craik was an acute observer of fashionable Dumfries society when she went there. During the twice-yearly Dumfries and Galloway Hunt weeks, and during the Dumfries meetings of the Edinburgh-based Caledonian Hunt, visitors came from all over the south of Scotland to join the local gentry for races and lavish balls, a boon to local tradesmen, but, as William Craik came to think, a financial drain for all but the wealthiest.

Craik also had the opportunity to develop intellectually through her father's library at Arbigland and through social interaction. Her father's early education and friendships in Edinburgh and his wide later contacts brought ideas and visitors to Arbigland, giving her access to the crosscurrents of mid- to late eighteenth-century Scottish intellectual and political life. Though there is little evidence of her getting much formal education, her poems draw on a wide range of reading, both from the traditional canon, and more current publications. Andrea Thomson has commented on the importance for upper-class women of such informal self-education:

An emphasis on the ability to converse fluently with one's culturally-engaged peers ensured that the elite eighteenth-century Scotswoman's social skills were often very finely honed. Whilst the education given to upper-class young Scotswomen frequently lacked the intellectual underpinning and academic rigour of that experienced by their male contemporaries, access to a range of print material nevertheless facilitated political, literary and critical engagement. Avid reading and enthusiastic engagement with both literary and contemporary commentary, in turn, frequently fostered a sense of personal fulfilment, increased familiarity with intellectual shorthand and gave rise to the sort of self-confidence that further eased the elite Scotswoman's wider social interaction.[34]

As Kathleen Keown has recently discussed, poetry writing, like drawing, musical performance, embroidery, and French, was often seen as a suitable feminine accomplishment, evidence of a woman's social status, and consequently often also patronised or dismissed. Craik's poetry, however, seems to have given her a means of self-education and self-exploration, more along the lines suggested by Thomson.[35]

Helen Craik at Friar's Carse: Riddell, Burns, and the Origins of the Beinecke Manuscript

The manuscript evidence shows that Craik had been writing poetry since her early twenties, if not earlier. Nearly all the poetry in the Beinecke manuscript was written before she first met Robert Burns, and its interest is independent of him. However, it was Burns's neighbour and friend Robert Riddell who encouraged her to make a fair copy of her collected poems; it was through Riddell that she met Burns; and the clue to rediscovering the manuscript poetry came from her connection to Burns. The links between Burns, Helen Craik, and the Craik family provide almost the only known contemporary documents about her as a writer, outside the poems themselves.

Capt. Robert Riddell (1755–1794), from an old Dumfriesshire family, had lived with his wife Elizabeth at Friar's Carse, an ancient castellated house nine miles north of Dumfries, since 1784. Though he was much younger than William Craik, they were both justices of the peace. Riddell had been educated at Edinburgh and St Andrews before service as an army officer, and the two men had shared interests in Scottish history, antiquities, and music, as well as agriculture, though Riddell was the more serious antiquarian.

In May 1790, Helen Craik and her father made an extended
visit to the Riddells, and one of the attractions of the visit
was the opportunity to meet Burns, then farming at Ellisland,
adjacent to Friar's Carse, and also working as an excise officer.[36]
An additional attraction for her father may have been the presence at Friar's Carse of Captain Francis Grose, the antiquarian,
though the dates he was there in 1790 are not fully known.[37]
Helen Craik already knew and admired Burns's poetry, for her
short verse tribute to Burns first occurs inscribed in a copy of the
1787 Edinburgh Burns edition, where it is dated October 1789:

—*Here* native Genius gay, unique, and strong
Shines through each page, and marks the tuneful song,—
Rapt Admiration her warm tribute pays,
And Scotia proudly echoes all she says;—

Bold Independence too, illumes the theme,
And claims a manly privilege to Fame.—
—Vainly O Burns! wou'd rank and riches shine
Compar'd with inborn merit great as thine,—
These *Chance* may take,—as Chance has often giv'n,
But pow'rs like thine can only come from Heav'n.— [38]

It is likely that Craik had also previously met Riddell and discussed her poems with him. It was Riddell who had suggested
to her writing on the locally based story 'The Maid of Enterkin',
and her prefatory verses to Riddell show she made the fair-copy
Beinecke manuscript for him because he had asked her to do so.
    Burns might well have eyed a social acquaintance with William
Craik, Surveyor-General of Customs, as helping his new career,
and as tenant of Ellisland Burns would also want to meet William
Craik, the pioneer of agricultural improvement, yet the meeting
in May 1790 started a relationship between Burns and the Craiks
that was literary, not just social or professional, and that involved
both the father and the daughter. Soon afterwards, Burns wrote
a lengthy letter to Helen Craik, enclosing two of his unpublished

poems in thanks for the 'pleasure' he had received in reading 'a certain manuscript volume of poems in the possession of Captain Riddel'.[39] Over the next months and years, Burns sent further poems to the Craiks, he visited Arbigland, and he exchanged letters with both father and daughter.[40]

The Craiks' visit to Friar's Carse is linked to the creation of not just one, but two, closely related volumes of manuscript poetry, both written for Robert Riddell: Helen Craik's *Poems by a Lady*, now the Beinecke manuscript, and the first volume of Burns's collection, the Glenriddell Manuscript, now in the National Library of Scotland.[41] Arguably Craik's collection could be called 'The Other Glenriddell Manuscript'. Riddell had both manuscripts bound in the same style, and the title-pages both appear to be in the same hand, which was used throughout the Craik volume and is almost certainly that of Craik herself. Both also include a verse from the other poet: Craik inscribed her earlier tribute to Burns on the title-page she produced for his collection, and Burns inscribed a verse on a preliminary leaf in her collection:

> Envy not the hidden treasure
> > Finer feelings can bestow;
> Chords that vibrate sweetest pleasure,
> > Thrill the deepest notes of woe—

The placement of Burns's inscription in the Craik manuscript, on the verso of Robert Riddell's prefatory verse, suggests it was an impromptu addition, perhaps made while he had borrowed the manuscript from Riddell. It is worth noting that these lines were first addressed to Helen Craik, though Burns would twice repurpose them for other women correspondents. When he wrote to Frances Dunlop on 9 July 1790, he introduced the same lines with the comment that he was 'just finishing the following Stanza', and by the end of July it had become the concluding verse of his song, 'Sensibility how charming', which he promised to dedicate to Mrs Dunlop, though an autograph manuscript of the full song was also found among Craik's papers. A year later, he sent the song to Nancy McLehose ('Clarinda'), again as 'just [...] composed', and a few months later, before it was published, amended the second line to mention 'Dearest Nancy' by name.[42]

However, Burns's four-line inscription meant the notebook could be traced. Though Craik's manuscripts were neglected, and long believed lost, almost any scrap of Burns's handwriting has been treasured by collectors. Because it had the Burns inscription, what is now the Beinecke manuscript has been briefly referenced by Burnsians repeatedly over the years, but often in ways that focused on Burns, rather than Craik. After Riddell's death in 1794, Burns got his Glenriddell manuscript back from Friar's Carse, and Craik's seems to have been returned to her family, perhaps to her father. Its later ownership can be traced through brief small-print glimpses in Burns bibliographies, reference works or the small-print textual notes of Burns editions. Such mentions run from a last-minute addendum in James Gibson's 1881 bibliography, through Henley and Henderson in 1896–97, on to Kinsley's notes, the entry for the song in the *Index of English Literary Manuscripts* in 1986, and the relevant volumes in the new *Oxford Edition of Robert Burns* in 2018 and 2021.[43] Craik's collection was exhibited as a Burns treasure in Glasgow for the Burns centenary in 1896, and again in the Scottish National Exhibition in 1911.[44] Both times it had been lent by a Troon coal magnate and Burns collector Adam Wood, but Wood had died before Neilson wrote up a description of his own Craik manuscript in 1919, and Neilson's article gives remarkably little information about what he called 'the Wood Notebook'. In the 1940s, it was owned by the Oxford scholar E. W. H. Meyerstein, but when he died and the manuscript sold, the Sotheby's catalogue entry was headed Burns, rather than Craik. Since then, the manuscript has been in the James Marshall and Marie-Louise Osborn Collection, overshadowed by other treasures.[45] But once the Osborn Collection was in the Beinecke Library at Yale, it was properly catalogued under Craik's name, and so now, in the twenty-first century, it is discoverable through

WorldCat. Before online searching, Craik scholars could surely not be faulted for not trawling older Burns scholarship or old Burns auction records for inevitably outdated clues.

The Beinecke online catalogue provides a detailed description of the physical manuscript, fully confirming that it is indeed Neilson's 'Wood notebook', the manuscript Craik presented to Robert Riddell. It is a bound notebook, measuring 25 x 19 cms, of 171 numbered pages, preceded by two unnumbered leaves, and followed by a three-page contents list, all in the same neat handwriting.[46] Like the Burns Glenriddell Manuscript, *Poems by a Lady* is a fair copy from earlier manuscripts, with a few (very few) errors in copying, but where there are insertions these are still in the same hand as the original text, confirming that Craik herself made the copy. Some of the Glenriddell Burns, including the distinctive title-page with Craik's own tribute to Burns, seem to be in the same hand, and Nigel Leask has suggested that Craik may even have been among Burns's amanuenses as his volume got under way.[47] Like the Glenriddell Burns, the Beinecke Craik is bound in full calf, with marbled endpapers, stamped in gilt with Robert Riddell's crest and motto ('Hab Shar' 'Virtus Maturit'), with Riddell's armorial bookplate pasted inside the front cover. The entry for Craik's manuscript from the 1898 Burns *Memorial Catalogue* has been clipped and pasted on to the front free end-paper, and Meyerstein's pencilled note from 1947 about the Burns inscription is on the verso of that leaf, facing the title-page. Given the timing for when Burns undertook his first volume, Craik's manuscript notebook, completed in 1790, may well have provided the model for Burns's own project, which was not completed till 1792.

The Beinecke Craik manuscript can be dated with reasonable confidence as written and completed in the late summer of 1790, and includes poems written much earlier. This is one of the differences from the other two manuscripts Neilson reported in the 1920s: the Neilson manuscript begins with a poem, 'The Maid of Enterkin', based on a story published in the *Scots Magazine* and elsewhere in 1781, to which Riddell had directed Craik's attention, so the manuscript is most likely to date from 1788 or later, and it also includes poems evidently written later than 1792. The third Craik manuscript, the Henderson notebook, catalogued in 1908 as '1788–1813', also therefore contains later poems.[48] The 1790 end date for the Beinecke manuscript seems firm; as noted above, the four lines Burns inscribed, or sent for insertion, in the Beinecke manuscript, are a stanza he told Mrs Dunlop he was 'just finishing' in July 1790, and the final poem in Craik's volume satirises James Bruce for his mammoth *Travels to Discover the Source of the Nile*, published early in 1790. However, only a few of the individual poems carry dates, and the volume collects both recent material and poems written years earlier. Craik's elegy to her brother Adam must follow his drowning in 1782. Her poem 'At Werter's Grave' carries the date 1779, suggesting Craik read the first English translation soon after it was published. Her poem 'To Mr D: from Goat's Whey Quarters' must date from 1778 or 1779 when her father's correspondence with Dr William Cullen shows her sister Elizabeth was being treated with goat's whey.[49] Her two epistolary poems 'To a Gentleman' are both dated 1782, with the second specifically dated 18 June. Only one poem in the Beinecke manuscript, 'The Ghost of Queen Mary', might seem to be dated later than 1790, because Craik wrote to Burns on 26 March 1792 promising to send him a poem about Mary Queen of Scots. However, 'The Ghost', a short tribute to Burns's 'Lament' spoken by Mary from beyond the grave, cannot be the same poem: the March 1792 letter said Craik, by then in Carlisle where Mary had been imprisoned, was writing a new poem on 'Q. Mary in her confinement', and so must refer to a second, different, poem.[50]

For other poems, internal references set a date bracket. Because 'To Miss D—' refers to the bursting of the Solway moss, it must be written after 1771. 'To a Lady' references Samuel Johnson's *Journey to the Western Islands of Scotland*, first published in 1775. Her poem 'The Indian Maid' references Hector Macneill's *The Harp*, first published in 1789.

Some of the newsworthy topics on which she was writing confirm this longer timeline. The poem Craik placed first after the dedication, about Queen Caroline Matilda of Denmark, probably dates from 1771, the year the queen was exiled, when the story of her ouster and exile was featured regularly in Scottish newspapers and magazines. 'Under sentence of Death', her soliloquy for the Rev. James Hackman, who had murdered his ex-mistress in a fit of jealousy, filled the newspapers in April 1779. A more recent poem was 'The R^t Honble: the Earl of Caithness to Miss D:', the earl's imaginary suicide letter to his fiancée, whose father had intervened when he discovered the earl's shaky finances; the Earl shot himself in April 1789. In the Beinecke manuscript, completed in the summer of 1790, Craik was collecting poems she had written over a period of twenty years.

Sudden Displacement: Leaving Arbigland

The mystery in Craik's life has been quite why, two years later, in February 1792, at age forty, Craik left her father and sister and the only home she had ever known, to spend the rest of her life with cousins at Flimby Hall, across the Solway Firth in Cumberland.

There is solid contemporary evidence for the abruptness of the move. It certainly came as a complete surprise to Burns. Over the eighteen months since the Craiks visited Friar's Carse in 1790, and Burns inscribed the verse in her manuscript, he had cultivated the relationship with both Craiks. He sent them several further unpublished manuscript poems, and in the autumn of 1791 he asked his Edinburgh publisher James Johnson to send William Craik a copy of Robert Riddell's Strathspeys.[51] In November that year, just three months before Helen Craik left Arbigland, William Craik, now nearly ninety, was pressing Burns to visit them again.[52] As late as January 1792, Helen Craik wrote to Burns from Arbigland, and Burns, who had just moved into Dumfries from Ellisland, replied that he planned to 'intrude' on her 'often'.[53]

When she next wrote, however, on 26 March 1792, she was staying in Carlisle, apparently on her own, and had been writing a new poem about Mary, Queen of Scots, who had been confined in Carlisle before she was moved south.[54] As with many of the letters other people wrote to Burns, only James Currie's précis of her letter survives, in a badly damaged manuscript, but the correspondence with Burns documents not just the timing, but the unexpectedness of her departure.

The most wide-spread explanation for her sudden move is also the most sensational, though no recent Craik scholar has found any contemporary evidence to support it. This is Samuel Arnott's theory that a cross-class romance and the murder of Craik's lover by an outraged relative drove her away. Arnott's article, reprinted in Appendix II, was first published along with George Neilson's more scholarly description of his Craik manuscript, but it is important to note that the theory was promoted by Arnott, not Neilson, and that Neilson had died before Arnott published. In Arnott's theory, Craik had fallen in love, possibly with a groom on the estate, named Dunn, and her father disapproved. The groom, sent to Dumfries on an errand, was found shot dead by the roadside. The authorities, under William Craik's thumb, ruled it suicide, but local rumour said he had been murdered. Craik's family treated her apparently innocent romance or friendship as shameful, and Craik felt betrayed and traduced. No one has yet found a contemporary account of Mr Dunn's murder, or even suicide. Arnott was not the first to circulate the story. It is told more circumstantially in Peter Gray's *Dumfriesshire Illustrated* (1894), where John Dunn is no longer a groom, but 'employed in some capacity by the family', and Craik's brother is said to have returned to Arbigland 'with his gun over his arm' shortly after a shot was heard.[55] Gray even adds that when a passer-by saw a white figure at night near the cross-roads where Dunn died, it turned out to be a distraught Helen Craik.

Craik certainly wrote at least one earlier poem 'To Mr D.', though that was in the late 1770s, and the Mr D. in question remains unidentified. The poem that Arnott uses to clinch his argument, 'Written in the Summerhouse at Arbigland', occurs only in the Neilson and Henderson notebooks, where it is dated 15 February 1792.[56] It articulates Craik's distress at leaving her family home and her outrage at accusations made by other family members. But the extract he gives leaves it unclear just when her 'happier prospects' had been blighted, and whether the blight came from faults wrongly imputed to her or whether her life had been blighted by the behavior of other family members. While it is certainly a poem marking her emotions on leaving Arbigland, it is even unclear from the poem itself whether her lonely weeping in the summer house was recent, or earlier, perhaps many years earlier.

Most Craik scholars rightly treat Arnott's story with caution, though few can resist recycling it, and the recyclings have proved more compelling than the cautions.[57] In the absence of other evidence, the strongest support for Arnott's story would seem to be its similarity to some of her poems about thwarted love, the murder or suicide of one lover, and the guilt or anguish felt by the survivor. Arnott, following a comment by Neilson, saw a marked contrast in Craik's poems between her earlier verses, which were 'as a rule, cheerful, almost sprightly', and 'those of her later years' which were 'of a melancholy kind, dealing largely with such subjects as murder and suicides'.[58] Linking this change to the death of the mysterious Mr Dunn, and Craik's sudden departure from Arbigland, Arnott argued that Dunn's death probably occurred in early 1792.[59]

However, the dates of the poems in the Beinecke manuscript do not match up with this contrast. The Beinecke manuscript seems to have been completed by the fall of 1790, and the poems seem to have been copied into it in the order of their composition. Peter Gray says that Craik only left Arbigland '[s]ome time after Dunn's death', leaving time for her not only to haunt the cross-roads but to arrange for Dunn's body to be retrieved from a suicide's grave for proper burial, which rather prolongs the abruptness.[60] Gray's accusation that Dunn was murdered by Craik's brother, who drowned in 1782, puts such a murder at least ten years before her departure; Arnott had to explain this away by saying the murderer was not her brother, but another near relative whose name he withheld out of respect for living family members. Yet another poem undercuts Arnott's rescue attempt: if, indeed, Helen Craik had been attracted to a Mr Dunn, and he was the unnamed Mr D. of 'from Goat Whey Quarters', written in 1778 or 1779, the romance was still over ten years earlier, and in that poem, as in her charade to Mr D., he seems to be addressed as a social equal. But even allowing the shorter, vaguer, leeway implied by Gray, the poems themselves contradict Arnott's narrative. Some of the violent narrative poems in it were written much earlier, in the 1770s, and there are genial and lightheartedly satiric poems among those written later. The recurrence of this Gothic strain in Craik's poetry, and its re-emergence later in her novels, might suggest she was drawing on personal emotion, refiguring the psychological strains of her life at Arbigland, but it hardly supports taking her writings as direct biographical evidence.

There is a more probable reason for Craik leaving Arbigland in February 1792. This was the imminent marriage of her nephew, William Craik's thirty-year-old grandson, Captain Douglas Hamilton Craik (1762–1844), to Elizabeth Beckwith (1772–1821), a twenty-year-old from Ripon, Yorkshire. It seems likely that William Craik had decided Douglas Hamilton would be his heir years before, soon after the death of his son Adam Craik in 1782. The grandson was using the surname Hamilton Craik in 1783 and 1784, when he was still in the army.[61] Entails such as those on Arbigland and on other Craik landholdings could be complicated by subsequent marriage settlements, and William Craik may also have remembered a lengthy dispute following the death of his own father, between a cousin and an aunt over conflicting entails and bequests made by his grandfather and father, involving the right of unmarried daughters to a responsible allocation of the inheritance, with lawsuits and counterclaims in the court of session, and appeals and cross-appeals to the House of Lords, litigation that stretched on for more than twenty years.[62]

Shortly before the marriage, which was on 8 March 1792, at Ripon, Craik's father decided, instead of bequeathing Arbigland on his death, to hand over the estate and house and almost all his own income to the grandson immediately. Newspaper reports of the wedding already list the groom as 'Douglas Hamilton Craik, Esq., of Arbigland'. [63]

For Helen Craik, the handover cannot have been welcome or smooth. As she later recounts in her memoir of her father (Appendix I), her nephew started out by dismissing William Craik's long-time estate factor and then had to climb down and rehire him. The Craik family were not turned out of the house (her father and her sister Betty seem to have stayed on till they died, in 1798 and 1796 respectively), but Hamilton Craik and his new wife were intruders, inevitably taking over the space and rooms that for many years had belonged to his grandfather and aunts. After the death of her mother, Helen had been the *de facto* mistress of Arbigland, a complex and demanding role for which, even if Helen had been willing to yield her own position, Hamilton Craik's young bride might not have seemed ready or suitable. Elizabeth Beckwith was not Scottish, and town-bred, not country-bred. It is likely there were class differences also: her father and grandfather were not landed gentry, but townsfolk, both serving as mayor of Ripon. If Helen's family had objected to her friendship with Mr Dunn on class grounds, Helen might have seen a double standard. She might also have noticed another, darker, double standard if she had been suspected or accused of more than inappropriate flirtation: she knew her father had had at least one son before his marriage, and she may also have heard that soon after her nephew returned from America he had sought treatment for syphilis. [64] At root, also, will have been what seem to have been negotiations, right up to the marriage, between her father and Hamilton Craik over money; one of her later poems, to her cousin Miss Young, refers to these discussions as 'the committee of ways and means'. In these negotiations her father seems to have made no independent financial provision for Helen Craik or her invalid sister. Craik faced the loss, not just of status but of security for the future. After William Craik died, she would be dependent for life on the good will, the charity, of Hamilton Craik. She chose instead to leave Arbigland and join her uncle and aunts across the Solway. Most recent writers on Craik have noted that the story Arnott spun lacked external evidence. What evidence there is, including the fuller complement of her poems now available, and their probable dating, makes his melodramatic account of Craik's poems as barely disguised autobiography very unlikely. There were multiple reasons why she would take the wrenching decision to leave Arbigland and make a new life elsewhere.

Craik's Poetry in the Beinecke Manuscript

The Beinecke manuscript shows Craik's poetry to be much more varied, more substantial, and ultimately more interesting, than earlier reports indicated. Neilson and Arnott largely dealt in extracts from her poems, and the Beinecke manuscript, with a much-expanded corpus of her poetry, and texts of the complete poems, make it possible to see both the variety of voices Craik could articulate and the subtlety with which she deployed the verse genres and poetic language of her time.

As with other eighteenth-century women poets, it is important not to take her conventional self-deprecation at face value. In her prefatory poem to Robert Riddell, Craik describes walking on the shore near Arbigland, writing poetry:

> On Solway's Banks a humble Muse
> Let Fancy's pow'r prevail,
> And oft along the winding Beach
> Compos'd some artless tale.—
>
> —Oft wou'd she by the gliding Wave,
> Her idle thoughts rehearse
> But merit ne'er presum'd to claim,
> Nor dreamt they rose to verse.—

—As sad or cheerful prospects shone
Unbidden came the rhyme,
No flatt'ring hopes of Fame in view
But just to *pass the time*.—

—Tho partial Friends wou'd sometimes smile
And think the page might do,
Yet much she fears the judging eye
Of Coila's Bard and you.—

'To Captain Riddell', ll. 1–16

When she writes that she 'never dreamt' her poetry would 'rise to verse', and claims she put her 'idle thoughts' into verse 'just to pass the time', and quotes other people's judgement that her verses 'would do', the tone is surely not subservience but her more characteristic playfulness and irony.

While the Burns connection long drew all the attention, the substance of the Beinecke manuscript is thirty-nine poems by Craik herself, with two short prose introductions. Only four of the thirty-nine have any link to Burns: her two poems to Riddell, her poem in response to Burns's 'Lament of Mary Queen of Scots', and her short poem about Burns. The larger significance of the Beinecke manuscript, and this edition, is not in Craik's relation to Burns, but in showcasing the range of Craik's work and giving some sense of the voice behind the poems. Some of her poems are semi-satiric, social or occasional, based on gentry life in Dumfriesshire, writing in an Austen-ish way to men and women friends, deflecting the attentions of army officers in Dumfries, and reading James Bruce's new book of African travels. Neilson and Arnott both assert that Craik's work grew consistently darker and more tragic over time, but the manuscript evidence suggests otherwise. The Beinecke manuscript shows that throughout the 1770s and 1780s Craik was writing dark Gothic narratives as well as satirical, social, newsy poems, and Neilson's report on his manuscript shows she continued to write satirical and occasional verse after the last of her Gothic tales. The evidence for dating is given in the notes to the edited text, but to demonstrate the broad range of Craik's work, the poems are discussed here by category or genre, rather than chronology.

It might seem that Craik's poetry circulated in manuscript, rather than print, because she was disconnected from any contemporary readership. Perhaps keeping it in manuscript form was one reason that so much of it was neglected or lost. Certainly, the meaning of some of her satirical poems has been obscured by the passage of time, and at least one of her poems, 'Lines Written at Sea', was misattributed to someone else because a Victorian editor found it in an unsigned manuscript. Family members in subsequent generations, normally the custodians of literary papers and reputation, may have assumed non-publication meant her poetry was of little value. However, as Margaret Ezell, Harold Love, Carol Barash, Michelle Levy and many others note, lack of publication does not mean lack of a public.[65] Such scholarship on coterie verse, which was passed among members for comments, edits, alterations, praise, and often to curry or repay favours, has brought to light the significance of manuscript poetry. Manuscript verse was a mode by which to exchange texts as well as other forms of 'mutual sociability'.[66] Quite simply put, work written for manuscript circulation was intended to do just that: circulate. Although Craik's work is not necessarily the product of a tight-knit coterie of the kind typical in the seventeenth century, we know she received and exchanged poems with both Burns and Riddell and that she also wrote for and sent verses to others.[67] Furthermore, like the coterie poets of the late seventeenth century, Craik turned her poetry toward social ends. Craik's manuscript offers a glimpse into the social contexts in which she composed it along with a sense of whom it was composed for. The entirety of the Beinecke manuscript serves in itself as an example of Craik's coterie-like activities – curated and prepared as it was for Captain Robert

Riddell, but the poems discussed in this section in particular exhibit the hallmarks of coterie production: they are variously addressed to figures known to Craik, emphasise the importance of friendship, are written on request, are often self-referential, and contain false claims to modesty common to female authors of the period whose circle often included males, such as Robert Burns. The poems discussed in this section have been loosely categorised under the following headings: requested topics, friendship poems and verse-epistles, and charades. These categories are not meant to be comprehensive and there is overlap between them.

Poems Written on Request

'To Miss M: M:' (pp. 99–103), 'Written after riding' (pp. 53–56), and 'To a Lady' (pp. 35–37) are among Craik's verses written upon request: centred on, respectively, loss, writing, and a stick. The first immediately announces its subject matter: '*You* who request *this* mournful Lay / And wou'd the pow'rs of Grief display'. Craik obliges, despite her misgivings: 'Of course the wish'd for strain I'll try, / In spite of Nature's struggling sigh.' Sombre in tone, Craik's elegiac poem details the cumulative effect of successive losses on the Craik family and on Craik herself, describing the deaths of her brother Adam, the subsequent death of her mother, Elizabeth Craik, and that of an unidentified friend or perhaps cousin, J. H. Craik, and makes it abundantly clear that their deaths were unnatural, describing both the 'early urn' and 'th' untimely tomb', leading her to the conclusion that 'Man was doom'd to mourn' – a not-so-subtle echo of Burns's more famous dirge. Throughout the verse Craik's pain comes through and concludes with her longing for 'solitude', having grown 'indiff'rent' 'to the World'. She is, therefore, 'most content when *most* retir'd'. It is worth noting, though, that Craik's emphasis here on resignation and acceptance must, because it is in the Beinecke manuscript, antedate her move from Arbigland to Flimby Hall by at least two years, and probably more.

The Stoic emphasis in 'To Miss M: M:' reads differently if the poem is set alongside another Craik poem, explicitly titled 'To Indifference':

> But come Indiff'rence! Peaceful, blest,—
> Henceforth be my *only* guest,—
> Thou ne'er hearfelt sorrows gave,
> Nor wounds that fester to the Grave—
>
> Pure thy state, serene and free,
> Tears nor anguish follow thee:—
> Come blest *Apathy* divine
> I for ever *now* am thine—.

In this two-stanza verse, indifference is not just accepted, but celebrated and sought. Rather than a symptom of resignation, indifference brings about peace, serenity, and freedom.

'Written after riding' was likewise written on request, for the unidentified Dr M.: 'You turn,—and with mischievous spite / Mid Scotia's mountains bid me write'. Of the three poems, 'Written after riding' is the most explicitly self-referential and also the most explicitly self-deprecating, perhaps because, unlike the other two, this poem was written for a man. The verse turns on claims to modesty, humorously recounting Craik's plea to the various muses to assist her in her task, though, one after another, the muses refuse. Melpomene, muse of tragedy, 'from such dread precipices flies'; Calliope and Clio, muses of poetry and history, find 'all sense of harmony confound'; Thalia, muse of comedy, 'shrinks back with comic fear', and so forth. Craik is left with nothing but 'the Will [to] supply the *deed*' since 'The Muse and *genius* absent too'. Despite her protestations to the contrary, Craik's deft handling and clever rhymes belie her assertion that 'tho some idle lines I trace / The humble rhyme ne'er rose to verse'. This same ironic use disclaiming her poetic pretensions and reliance on her will alone is turned to in 'To Captain Riddell' (pp. 7–8).

The oddest of these poems on demand is 'To a Lady', which states its assigned topic from the start: 'The whim was strange your fancy hit / To ask for lines upon a Stick'. Craik obliges, intent to 'shew in proper time' that the subject, 'as some may cry', is not 'barren'. What follows is a disquieting five-stanza poem detailing the various uses of a stick, with an emphasis on its use in enforcing religion, manners, and marriage, if also enabling resistance. The way Craik develops the poem shows a rather surprising focus on violence; Craik portrays sticks as instruments of control rather than as aids or support. Craik deals with her difficult and violent subject matter through wordplay (e.g. raising cane, l. 29), double entendre (e.g. 'ev'ry *feeling* suff'rer says / It has the *most convincing* ways', ll. 39–40), as well as through literary and periodical allusions. For instance, to describe the stick's use in religion, 'For converts in the Highlands made', Craik succinctly recounts an anecdote from Samuel Johnson's *Journey to the Western Islands of Scotland*, and to depict its power in marriage, Craik notes that in Russia 'Sticks are to the Bridegroom sent'. In so doing, she not only contrasts marriage practices in Russia and Britain, 'For shou'dst thou *hither* find thy way, / Our British Dames might raise the Cane', but also points to contemporary fascination with Russia, evidenced in contemporary newspapers.

Friendship Poems and Verse-Epistles

A second group constitutes verse-epistles or poems about friendship. Friendship poems, a mainstay of coterie productions, are often associated with Katherine Philips who, in the seventeenth century, adopted the form in order to contest traditional beliefs that friendship between men was purer than any other relationship and that women, who were deemed intellectually and emotionally inferior, were incapable of it. Under Philips's careful hands, friendships were depicted as ungendered, as the souls have no sex, and the form took off, gaining popularity especially among women. As such, friendship poetry was frequently written by women for women, although the platonic ideal extended to male-female friendships as well, and served as a capacious form in which women could and did assert their poetic identities. Friendship poetry tends to be occasional, vernacular, and self-conscious. Paula Backscheider has commented that 'in no other poetry do we find so many playful representations of writing'.[68] Earlier forms of friendship poetry emphasised the relationship between writer and addressee and the harmony between souls of idealised friends. Backscheider argues that later eighteenth-century friendship poetry tends to make public judgements on value systems, by challenging, ignoring, or satirising the expectations placed upon women. Despite the seemingly private nature of friendship poetry, these verses frequently comment on the public sphere and the impact of politics on private life.

Craik's friendship poems serve as examples of both the earlier and later varieties. For instance, in her four-stanza poem addressed to a 'gentleman' and intended to have been sent with a neckpin, Craik contrasts her gift with that of the golden apple given by Paris of Troy to Venus. In so doing, she compares love and friendship, placing far more value in the latter: '*One* ball for Love was only giv'n, / For Friendship I give *three.*—'. Friendship and 'Esteem' are cast as superior to love, which 'made Nation's groan'. While it is likely that Craik's poem is meant to allay any misconception of her gift as more than platonic in nature, her emphasis on friendship and its 'unrival'd pow'r' places the verse firmly within the genre. In another such poem, 'To a Lady Sent with a few Flowers', Craik contrasts the brevity of nature to that of art, providing a meditation not only on the natural and artificial flowers that were exchanged but on the poem itself as well as the permanence of their friendship: '*Mine* bloom 'tis true but quickly fade, / While *yours* to latest Time shall show / What I to *Taste* and Friendship owe'. While Craik returns the gift of artificial flowers which were 'form'd *by you*' with carnations and bog myrtle, which 'soon neglected, wither'd lie', her poem that accompanies them serves as more than 'a trifling offering from a friend' that, unlike the flowers, will last.

A similar cultivation of friendship and poetry can be seen in 'To Lady W: M: Constable'. Written in the voice of the exotic bird which was gifted along with the verse, the poem dramatises the bird's removal from 'Ceylon's spicey Isle' to 'cold inclement skies / Where Caledonia's hills arise.' Lamenting its fate, the bird 'lonely wander'd round the shore' until Helen, i.e. Craik, bids it fly to Lady Winifred Maxwell, whose very 'presence chear'd the scene'. Although the Maxwells would move to live within visiting distance of Arbigland, that Helen sent the bird having only 'heard' Lady Maxwell's 'approbation' suggests that the two were not well known to one another at this time; possibly they were loosely acquainted through Burns, with whom Lady Maxwell was a correspondent. It is possible then, to read Craik's poem as an overture of friendship and an attempt to expand her coterie connections. As discussed below, Craik is not averse to name-dropping, announcing in one of her charades a high-ranking member of her coterie, Lady Elizabeth Dalzell. Craik's verse-epistle 'To Mr D: from Goat Whey Quarters' is similar to 'To Lady W: M:' in that her bleak and dreary surroundings would only be improved only by her addressee's presence: 'The same dull scene appears to view / Unless dispel'd by friends like you'. Her depiction of such surroundings, however, is comical and the tone of the poem thus lighter. Treatment for her sister's illness, for which the doctors had prescribed goats' whey, meant that Craik was staying with her in New Abbey, and Craik satirises the isolation and tedium she experienced, where, conversation ran only to 'Barley, Oats, and Hay'.

The importance to Craik of friendship and visitors is seen in her pair of verse-epistles 'To a Gentleman', dated 1782, and written in response to the unnamed gentleman leaving his visiting card while she was at church. Craik's teasing tone suggests the visitor was a previous admirer or even a rejected suitor, who had now called to repair the friendship, leaving a note on his card that 'the Heart shou'd never change'. Craik opens her response by briefly summarising the crux of the day's sermon. Turning to a favoured trope, she mockingly 'wish[es] too in such a cause /

T' explain how orthodox [she] was'. She contradicts him, arguing that hearts should change. Not yet having received a response to her first epistle, Craik eschews 'decorum' and writes again:

> Too long has *Hope* on *Patience* lean'd,
> And Expectation ling'ring seem'd,—
> One week run o'er,—no answer came,
> Another gone—'twas still the same!

She reminds him of his pledge that 'the *heart* shou'd act no changeful scene' and 'with deep regret,—but no surprise', laments the end of their friendship. The second poem is interrupted when Craik receives a response from him, and in the final stanzas she playfully reverses what came before. Because the pair of poems is dated in the Beinecke manuscript as written in 1782, it confirms the need to question Arnott's dramatic account in 'The Romance of Helen Craik' that of a sudden reversal in Craik's marital hopes happened only in 1792.

Other verse-epistles provide glimpses of Craik's social life outside of Arbigland, with comments on courtship and marriage, the societal roles imposed on women, and the social circuit. In 'To Sir W. G.: Baronet' and 'Lines occasioned by a reperusal', which was written as a follow-up to the preceding verse, Craik repeatedly privileges friendship over marriage, variously refusing 'Hymen's fetters', whose 'chain is heavy, at best', and humorously recounting the unhappily married 'old Dragoon', who 'by Fate misled, / At Hymen's shrine a victim bled', but who by dying 'pleas'd *for once* his wife'. In her discussion of Craik's novels, Adriana Craciun argues that, following Mary Wollstonecraft, Craik 'consistently liken[s] marriage to slavery and sees it as 'an institution in urgent need of reform'.[69] In these poems we see the seeds of Craik's philosophical and political resistance to marriage. In contrast to marriage, and as in Craik's poem sent with a neckpin, friendship or 'Esteem', which is 'secure from malice, chance or blame', is deemed 'superior far to Love'. At the same time that this set of poems celebrates Craik's friendship with W. G. (possibly William Gordon (1736–1804), 7th Baronet, of Embo, in Sutherland), it draws upon their shared connections and memories, ranging from the 'old Dragoon' and 'B*** with all his Corps', to 'gay ********' and the 'C*******l, whimsically nice'. Craik's tongue-in-cheek use of disemvowelled names further cements their friendship and connection; after all, Gordon knows as well as Craik the identities of the people about whom she is writing.[70]

Craik also cloaks the identities of those she is discussing in 'To Lady—' and 'To Miss D—'. One could argue that she does so because the subject matter was potentially sensitive. Craik represents courtship and the social circuit as a battle of the sexes and points to her titled friend's potential suitors. Given the descriptions that follow the unidentified names, however, it would not have been difficult for her contemporaries to decipher who she meant. It is far more likely that Craik is engaging in a literary game as she does with Gordon. In 'To Lady—', Craik responds to a letter from a friend who has just lost or quarrelled with a male acquaintance. As Craik's list of contents makes clear, the friend is Lady E. D., most probably Elizabeth Dalzell, née Johnston, referenced also in one of her charades. Craik opens the poem by ironically adopting the voice of the clergy only to reject it as soon as her 'orthodox knowledge' has been 'made known', offering in what unfolds 'a word of her own'. In what follows, Craik reveals the rich social world of late eighteenth-century Dumfries and transfigures the common trope of the inconstant male lover into a positive attribute when enacted by women:

> May Providence send you a far better Corps;—
> And then you can do, like most Nymphs in your case,
> Let a *new* one fill up in the *departed* one's place;
> And *Variety*, all your philosophers tell us,
> Is the surest receipt for forgetting the Fellows.—

Her ironic use of military metaphor, 'you shou'd keep, as all good Gen'rals do / *One* Corps-de-reserve, if you cannot have *two*', advises strategy in navigating the complex societal structure of upper-class Dumfries as well as showing the impact the military had on the Town, not least by ensuring a steady supply of officers at social events: 'then *on* the *floor* when the *foe* shall appear / You'll still have a ****** to guard you from fear—'. Given that Dalzell only took the title of Lady after her marriage in 1775 to Richard, styled Lord Dalzell, it seems improbable that Craik was really advising her to scope out multiple suitors.

'To Miss D—' is centred on the social life of Dumfries and the entertainment on offer during the biannual visit of judges from Edinburgh, which regularly overlapped with the social calendar. In this poem, however, Craik bemoans her absence as she is stuck at home, missing the 'Cards, Assemblies, [and] Balls'. The social season in Dumfries was expensive, and her father had vetoed the visit, saying money was needed for improvements on the estate. Craik suspected that 'Caution in grey Wisdom's guise' had 'whisper'd in [her] Father's ear, / That Women ne'er abroad shou'd roam, / That all their bus'ness lay at home'. She begs Miss D. to report the season's gossip, asking 'was the Laird's dear Hundred pounds / Laid out on trifling caps and gowns!', 'And tell how *****'s gracious Bride / Attention paid the Voter tribe', 'Of smart bon mots who said the brightest', 'did *******'s dame appear / Or was the Knight of ****** there?—', etc. Among such pleas for news, she intersperses pointed commentary about the plight of women. For example, she writes that she 'gladly wou'd renounce the merit / Of striving to *subdue* the spirit' and mockingly compares her curiosity to a 'plague' that from 'Eve to each succeeding Daughter' 'ruin'd' 'Our sex'. Whether the poem shows deep bitterness or detached amusement, or some mixture, depends in part on when Craik wrote it. She refers in the poem to visiting the Solway Moss, the poem must be later than 1771, when the Moss erupted; if the 'Miss D' of this poem is Dalzell, it must be before she married, so Craik would be writing in her early or mid-twenties, when bitterness at social exclusion is understandable, as also William Craik's financial anxiety after the failure of Douglas, Heron, and the Ayr Bank.

Charades

That much of Craik's work was written for an audience and served as a form of mutual sociability is nowhere more apparent than in her literary charades. Although verse-riddles can be found starting in the medieval period, charades didn't become a literary genre unto themselves until the eighteenth century, published in English magazines, newspapers, and on fans as early as the 1740s. Characterised by hints first given for each syllable of the word in question followed by hints for the completed word, charades were adopted from French *charrado*, meaning conversation. And indeed, charades did serve as a form of conversation between the writer and reader. As Elizabeth Bruss notes in her discussion of literary games, charades are a type of rendezvous in which 'the player's objective is to make contact with the other player through some imaginative process of introspection, of search for shared clues'.[71] Although Neilson describes Craik's charades as 'mainly quite undistinguished', they do point to her social network and are grounded in the happenings of her time. The Neilson manuscript contains charades on Fortune, Adam, and Woman, along with a charade on Elizabeth Dalzell:

> My *First* with some help is to Valley allied
> My *Second* the place where Queen Caroline died
> My *Whole* is a compound of wit sense and whim,
> No changeable Proteus more various can seem.

Craik's charade on Dalzell introduces and flatters a high-ranking member of her coterie, Lady Elizabeth Dalzell (see above), thereby making their friendship known, and it also reveals current preoccupations. For example, Queen Caroline's exile in 1772 and subsequent death in 1775 was widely covered in British newspapers and periodicals and served as the subject matter for one of Craik's dramatic monologues. Craik also capitalises on popular interests and tropes in the two charades contained in the Beinecke MS: 'A Charade—To Mr D:' and 'A Charade'. The former, which is a charade on 'nothing', explicitly announces itself as social in nature, 'beg[ging]' Mr D. for 'an answer soon in verse' and thus for the continuation of their game. Craik's references to soldiers and 'ev'ry red-coat quarter'd *here*' provide today's readers with a glimpse of eighteenth-century Dumfries. Moreover, her association of nothing with 'ev'ry Coxcomb's face; / And many a gallant Soldiers skull', 'honour, fame, and reputation', and '—The Courtier's promise' provides a satirical social commentary on the inconstancy of men, their empty promises, and their vapidness (all common tropes) and serves as a contrast to her faithful friend, Mr D. The second of the two charades included in the manuscript is on 'fortune'. Craik depicts fortune as fickle yet desired by all, and her reference to the way in which fortune 'Lays waste the hapless Indian earth' places the charade firmly in its time, implying, perhaps, a critique of the East India Company.

As should be made clear, Craik's charades were not private literary endeavours. They were social games akin to those she played in her disemvowelled verse-epistles. That is, they were cooperative activities that provided a figurative meeting space operated through shared memories, experiences, and acquaintances. Such poems, along with her friendship poems and verses on requested topics, contradict Neilson's assertion that Craik's later poetry evidences grief and sadness and Arnott's attribution of that to the loss of Craik's rumoured love interest. If anything, Craik seemed to have had a thriving social network that she maintained through her verse throughout her life.

Satirical Poems

As numerous critics have noted, the variety of eighteenth-century satire makes definition difficult. Despite its different subjects and aims, Paddy Bullard suggests several traits common in satirical humour: typically it is set among scenes of associational life; it engendered a large body of criticism around its practice; and it is often connected with constructions of nationhood.[72] While much of Craik's verse contains satirical elements, the three poems discussed in this section – 'To R: O: Esq᷑', 'The Soldier's

Joy—A Song', and 'A Humourous Court Martial' – appear to be more straightforwardly so: all focus on one's status in society, a common characteristic of associational life, and the latter two fit neatly into the period's preoccupation with satirising military officers stationed in the Dumfries area.

Described by Neilson as 'very odd', 'To R: O: Esqr' is a petition from Margaret (unidentified) and Helen (presumably Craik) to a wealthy neighbour, for 'Twenty Thousand' pounds. In addition to their estate at Auchentruive, the Oswalds owned Cavens House, adjacent to Arbigland. If the poem dates from the 1760s or '70s when Craik and her friend would have been in their teens or twenties (see headnote), the R. O. in question is likely the older Richard Oswald (1705–1784), who accrued his wealth through the tobacco and slave trades and who had estates near Arbigland; if after 1784, it would refer to his great-nephew, Richard Alexander Oswald (1771–1841), unmarried till 1793, but twenty years younger than Craik. In the poem, Craik teasingly capitalises on the allure of money and its necessity for women on the marriage market:

> Consider Sir, but as the times now go,
> Sans money we must also be sans Beau,—
> And surely you'll allow it wou'd be hard
> From cash and flatt'ry both alike debarr'd,— (ll. 6–9).

As such, the pair 'humbly' request 'A poor ten Thousand of [his] wealth to share' but, believing such a 'pittance' would be beneath Owens, quickly alter their request to 'Twenty', taking care to note that their petition stems not from 'self-int'rest' but rather from a desire for Owens's 'Good *alone*'. In addition to revealing Craik's good humour and precociousness, the poem likewise points to the critical role wealth plays if one wants to attract eligible suitors.

From the poems published in the *Gentleman's Magazine* to sermons and drama, the military garrisons and encampments spread across Britain captured the late eighteenth-century imagination. As Jane Austen's novels indicate, the arrival of a regiment or company in a town such as Dumfries introduced both a new pool of potential suitors and a new kind of social risk, shaking the kaleidoscope of long-settled county families. Contemporary depictions of well-dressed army officers, parading in highly coloured uniforms or lounging in luxurious tents, followed by an entourage of admiring high-society women, point to the anxiety these encampments caused. Robert W. Jones notes that during the 1770s 'the site and spectacle of the camps provided society ladies with an opportunity for brazen affectation while presenting men with a space for foppish dalliance'.[73] Burns describes the officers in Dumfries who paid court to Maria Riddell as 'lobster-coated puppies' and 'a string of coxcombs'.[74] Craik's poems 'The Soldier's Joy' and 'A Humourous Court Martial' explicitly pick up on that theme. For instance, in 'The Soldier's Joy' the gods, summoned by Jove, determine that a soldier's joy lies in '*War, Love,* and *Wine*'. Although the final line of the poem presents war as the soldier's principal concern, Venus and Bacchus stake their claims first, with Mars joining in only at the behest of Bacchus: 'come Mars come along / The case in dispute must to we three belong'. Venus's reference to the '*Doctor's commons*' (the legal forum dealing with matrimonial and divorce law), speaks to the concern that these encampments are disruptive to the proper social order.

'A Humourous Court Martial' also deals with soldiers who, daring to write poetry, have overstepped the bounds of their profession. Consequently, they angered Apollo/Phoebus who 'Complain'd that the Army so witty was grown / The wreaths from his forehead by Soldiers were torn'. Mars's response, that 'no Goose quill shou'd take place of a sword, / Then moments of leisure wou'd grant them no more', points to a particularly popular concern regarding military encampments: that they engendered effeminacy among the armed forces, hence the existence of the professional soldier was effete. As the poem proceeds, Bacchus steps in, distracting the soldiers from their military endeavours – 'marching, and drumming, and fifing'. With

1

bumper in hand, they once again sit down to write, this time a satire. As punishment for their transgression, Apollo condemns them to 'oblivion', for should 'one syllable' of their satire be 'known' they would be 'set [. . .] at variance with half of the Town'. As a result, they are doomed to spend their leisure time fearing and dreading 'the *revealing* / Of *what you confided* to ****** and Helen.—'. While Craik's poem is a teasing rejoinder to two officers whom she and a friend rebuffed, it also speaks to the fear of army officers stepping outside their recognised role. In the final lines the soldiers' fate is tied to the two women. While the final line empowers Helen and her unnamed friend, leaving the soldiers' fate in their hands, it also lends credence to those who were concerned that the intermingling of sexes at the camps, made possible because of an excess of leisure time, would lead to brazen women and effeminate men, an outcome Craik appears to celebrate in this particular poem.

Poems of Real-Life Crime and Intrigue

Real-life scandals covered in newspapers and magazines frequently served as inspiration for seventeenth- and eighteenth-century writers. For example, Aphra Behn's *Love-Letters Between a Nobleman and His Sister*, published between 1684 and 1687, are loosely based on Lord Grey's elopement with his sister-in-law Lady Henrietta Berkeley. While Berkeley's disappearance was initially kept secret, lampoons speculating on her absence began appearing in 1681 and the ensuing trial against Lord Grey attracted a massive amount of publicity. Alexander Pope's *The Rape of the Lock* (1712) is based on the feud between Lord Petre and Arabella Fermor; George Lillo's *Fatal Curiosity*, first performed in 1736, is based on the story of a Cornish murder; Henry Fielding's *The Life and Death of Jonathan Wild, the Great* (1743) is based on the exploits of its titular character, who was executed in 1725; the list could go on. Like broadsides and ballads, this type of literature served up what people then as well as today crave – shocking stories, typically of crimes that had either been recently committed or had resurfaced in the public imagination. To satisfy the public's demands for both sensationalism and realism, such work usually includes lurid descriptions following the declining arc from honest youth to sin, crime and, inevitably, to the gallows.

Craik, too, turned to the papers or monthly magazines for the seeds of some of her dramatic monologues, most specifically 'Lines Written at Sea', 'under sentence of Death', and 'The Earl of Caithness'. Neilson describes the latter two poems as evidence of Craik's 'painful taste' and 'preference for suicidal and murderous subjects' (Appendix II, p. 205). They might equally be taken as evidence that Craik was reflecting or responding to contemporary events. There is, however, something more personal in her poems' recurrent emphasis on survivor-guilt and frenzied emotion, told from a first-person perspective. As Richard Ward and others have argued, crime literature resists closure due to the 'instability and multiplicity of voices' that 'open up space for a range of ideological positions and interpretations'.[75] Craik's tales of murder, suicide, and execution provide a genre through which she could explore extreme and unfettered emotions, vulnerability, violence, and madness, in a way that other genres did not, and that points to the Gothic plots of her later novels.

'Lines Written at Sea', the first full item in the Beinecke manuscript was probably written in or soon after 1771. It is the first non-prefatory item in the Beinecke manuscript, and it appears to be the earliest of Craik's dramatic monologues treating survivor-guilt. In it, Craik recounts the tragic history of Caroline Matilda, King George III's sister, who, through her marriage at age fifteen to King Christian VII, became Queen of Denmark in 1766. Given Christian's mental instability, alcoholism, promiscuity, and violence, the marriage was tenuous from the start, though Caroline had two children, Frederick (1768–1839, later King Frederick V), and Louise Augusta (1771–1843). Following a coup on 17 January 1772, led by Queen Julia, the Queen Dowager, Caroline was accused of being the lover of Christian's

German-born physician and chief minister Johann Friedrich Struensee (1737–1772). Caroline's infant daughter Louise, though she had been baptised as legitimate, was rumoured to be Struensee's child, and Struensee and his political ally Brandt were interrogated, tortured, and brutally executed – publicly beheaded, drawn, and quartered. British political pressure and negotiation allowed Caroline to leave Denmark for exile at Celle (or Zelle), in the small German state of Lower Saxony. She had to leave her children behind, and she died in 1775 from scarlet fever, aged only twenty-four. The fate of Queen Caroline was widely covered in British newspapers and periodicals, usually in favour of Caroline, both at the time of the coup and exile, and after her death.

Craik's monologue begins as Queen Caroline is on a British warship, sailing away from 'Crongsborg's Prison, and from Denmark's Throne' and, through Caroline's voice, Craik recounts her descent from beloved to the object of 'ill-omen'd hate'. Imagining Caroline's thoughts, Craik describes the fall of her fortunes as an '*Injustice*' and attributes it to 'Fate' and 'Julia'. The Queen Dowager is shown as a schemer whose 'ready smile conceal'd a treach'rous heart' and who in 'Friendship's garb' and 'mean self-int'rest play'd her partial game'. By highlighting Julia's betrayal, Craik's poem works to absolve Caroline from guilt. So too does Craik's depiction of Brandt and Struensee; as 'victims doom'd to state and me [Caroline]', Brandt was 'fell[ed]' and Struensee 'murder'd'. Craik never mentions Caroline's alleged affair with Struensee, though her emphasis on Caroline's 'guiltless mind' and Julia's 'deep dissembling art' serves to defend Caroline's reputation.

While the poem deals with betrayal, banishment, and exile in general, the emotional crux centres on Caroline's grief at being separated from her children:

> What black revenge e'er keener pangs imprest
> Then *thus* to tear my Infant from my breast!

Here fainting Nature owns thy pow'rful reign,
And all the Mother throbs thro' ev'ry vein.—

Resolved to bear 'The smiles of Pleasure, or the frowns of Care',
Caroline's 'steady soul' is shaken by 'Love maternal' which 'rends
[her] bursting heart'. Her only plea is that Keith, the British
government's envoy to Denmark, 'protect their helpless state, /
And save [her] Infants from impending fate'. In *Letters Written
during a Short Residence in Sweden, Norway, and Denmark*
(1796), Mary Wollstonecraft picked up on the same theme,
emphasising Caroline's maternal character:

> She [Caroline] was censured, with the most cruel insin-
> uation, for her management of her son, though, from
> what I could gather, she gave proofs of good sense as well
> as tenderness in her attention to him. She used to bathe
> him herself every morning; insisted on his being loosely
> clad; and would not permit his attendants to injure his
> digestion by humouring his appetite. She was equally
> careful to prevent his acquiring haughty airs, and playing
> the tyrant in leading-strings. The Queen Dowager would
> not permit her to suckle him; but the next child being a
> daughter, and not the Heir-Apparent of the Crown, less
> opposition was made to her discharging the duty of a
> mother. (Letter XVIII)

Whereas Wollstonecraft gives some credence to Caroline's alleged
affair, Caroline's final words in Craik's poem emphatically cast
her as an innocent victim of 'Censure's busy tongue': 'those
who *now* with philosophic eye / . . . / May wish in time my
wrongs had been redresst / And blame th' oppressor, as they
blam'd th' opprest.—'. With its emphasis on Julia's treachery and
Caroline's pain, Craik's poem does exactly that. By focusing on
Caroline's thoughts and feelings regarding her children instead
of the political situation that led to her exile Craik humanises
the queen, making her a more relatable and sympathetic figure

while also illustrating how public affairs deeply affect the private lives of women.

Craik bases another of her dramatic monologues, 'under sentence of Death', on one of the most sensational murders of her young adulthood. On the evening of 7 April 1779 James Hackman (1752–1779) shot Martha Ray or Reay (c. 1742–1779), the long-time mistress of the Earl of Sandwich. Although Hackman and Ray's relationship is somewhat uncertain, they were thought to have become lovers after meeting at Sandwich's home at Hinchingbrooke in 1775, where Ray was living. Their relationship broke down when Hackman's regiment (68th Foot) was posted to Ireland. In 1776 Hackman resigned his commission and returned to England where he entered the church, although he remained infatuated with Ray. On 7 April 1779, believing that Ray had taken on a new lover, Hackman followed her to Covent Garden Theatre where he saw her speaking with Lord Coleraine. He then lay in wait for the pair in the nearby Bedford Coffee house where he shot Ray by putting a pistol to her head, and then unsuccessfully attempted to kill himself. Hackman was tried, convicted, and sentenced on 16 April, and hanged three days later on 19 April. The murder and ensuing trial were widely covered in the *Caledonian Mercury* as well as in London papers, and there were also several contemporary separately published accounts. In 1780 attention on the case was renewed when Sir Herbert Croft published his influential epistolary novel sympathetic to Hackman, *Love and Madness: A Story Too True*.

Craik's poem, written in the voice of Hackman, takes place 'a few short hours' before he 'shall breathe no more'. In it she presents a conflicted Hackman with 'warring thoughts at strife', who simultaneously rails at 'headstrong passion's ruling force' and uses it to justify his actions. Hackman's last thoughts, of shame at leaving 'A Murd'rer's name,—the bane of all my race', are notably devoid of guilt. At one point, he even celebrates Ray's death, because in the grave 'Sandwich is no *more* belov'd than me'. Hackman casts himself as passion's 'slave', mitigating his own guilt and agency, and deriding those who condemn his actions:

> Ye Souls that cool philosophy contain,
> Whose blood ne'er riots wild thro' passion's vein,
> Who calmly yield to Reason's boasted light
> By constitution negatively right,
> Say,—whence derive ye approbation's voice?
> Is *merit* yours who merely act from *choice*!—

and

> —O ye unfeeling!—your rash thoughts restrain,
> Ye know not, *cannot know*, what I sustain;
> All other ills calm patience might endure,
> But *this* extends beyond the reach of cure.—

Guided by emotional temperance, the 'reas'ning tribe' is incapable of understanding that Hackman is not a criminal but a victim of the 'venom'd dart' of 'hopeless Love'; his actions constitute 'sacrifice' rather than murder. Consequently, his biggest regret is not the death of his beloved but his own survival, because it is only in death that he can find 'respite from pain' and freedom from passion. By emphasising Hackman's overwrought emotional state and his pain, Craik puts readers in the uncomfortable position of sympathising with him while also questioning the dangers of feeling too much, recalling her poem 'To Indifference' which celebrates the very apathy Hackman describes as 'unfeeling' and 'dull'.

Another tale of love and passion gone awry, 'The Earl of Caithness' recounts the final words of John Sinclair, eleventh Earl of Caithness (1756–1789). Caithness's suicide in April 1789 aroused a lot of interest in the contemporary press, with reports attributing it discreetly to 'disappointment in a matrimonial adventure'.[76] More detailed accounts explained that the Earl's proposed marriage to Miss Dehenney, daughter of an eminent

West-India Planter, had been blocked by her father when he learned that Caithness had deceived him about numerous debts. As she does with Hackman, Craik portrays Caithness in a sympathetic light and casts death as the only solution; it is 'the privilege of humankind', 'The certain cure of a distemper'd mind', and 'but trifling when compar'd' with lack of 'mental ease'. Before killing himself, Caithness resolves to 'soothe those evils' Miss Dehenney is 'doom'd to fill', directing his last words toward her. He assures her that in death he will no longer sorrow, no longer fear 'the pangs of stern *repulse*', and be free from 'Disappointment'. As a 'guiltless wretch' whose only fault was 'Love', Caithness places the blame squarely on 'Passion's force' and 'stern parental duty'. That he must 'steal' 'From icy death this fleeting hour' suggests his death is beyond his control. Caithness's actions, from his courtship and proposal to his suicide were not 'selfish', 'No knee [he] bent at Fortune's fickle shrine'; instead, they were the inevitable product of Love's 'deadly strain'.

Gothic Poems

Like Craik's dramatic monologues based on crime and scandal covered in the press, several of her Gothic poems have their antecedents in printed sources. 'Written by Charlotte at Werter's Grave', for instance, is based on Johann Wolfgang von Goethe's wildly popular but scandalous novel *The Sorrows of Young Werther*, published in German in 1774, with a widely reviewed English translation in 1779. A tragic tale of illicit love, Goethe's novel centres on the love triangle between Charlotte, her husband, Albert, and the romantic hero, Werther, who, tormented by feelings that Charlotte cannot reciprocate, commits suicide at the novel's end. Rather than poeticising the already-told tale however, Craik's poem takes up the story after Werther's death. Suffering from 'madness [which] almost rends the tortur'd brains', Charlotte visits Werter's grave and resolves to join him because 'Woes great as [theirs] alone find comfort there'. Through Charlotte's impassioned soliloquy at the gravesite, Craik presents her in a sympathetic light, which, by the 1780s other writers, such as Charlotte Smith, had begun to do. Charlotte is a victim of 'fate' who 'fill'd [her] lot with complicated woes'. The description of Charlotte's 'mangled' reputation, which 'by busy Censure [was] torn', and the accusation of 'deeds' which 'even in thought [she would] scorn' echoes Craik's 'Lines Written at Sea'. As Craik does with Queen Caroline, she thereby represents Charlotte as an innocent victim beset upon by societal expectations. Craik likewise absolves Werter of any sin:

> —Society 'tis true may blame the deed
> But Heav'n with pity sees the wretched bleed:
> And when our woes o'er Nature's verges rise,
> Marks the poor Victim with indulgent eyes;
> Softens the mandate 'gainst self-slaughter *here*,
> And bids the wretch no *future* vengeance fear.—

As with Charlotte, Werter's crime is to love too much, the inevitable result of which can only be death: 'Death *only* cures thy Victim'. In addition to representing death as a respite from pain, Craik imbues it with agency, calling it a 'blest Pow'r'. In the grave, Charlotte is free of 'Stern Albert' and marital oppression; 'No Albert *there* forbids [her] to be thine'. As in much of Craik's work and more explicitly in her later novels, marriage is represented as a tyrannical institution that denies women agency and subjectivity. Written in the voice of Charlotte, Craik's poem does the opposite.

Through Charlotte's soliloquy Craik offers readers insight into Charlotte's grief by providing an extended moment of psychological introspection. Craik's fascination with extreme emotional states and the repeated conflict between feeling and thinking that marks much of her poetry points to an early interest in the Gothic, which she later embraced and developed in her novels. As Francis Russell Hart has argued, the Gothic represents 'an express fascination with the violent and grotesque subjectivity of emotional states'.[77] What separates the poems discussed in this section from those directly above (which also deal heavily with emotional and mental imbalance), however, is Craik's inclusion of supernatural elements and horror. According to Carol Margaret Davison and Monica Germanà, the Scottish Gothic, which finds its origins in the ballad tradition, is marked by a 'distinctive symbiosis of psychological introspection and supernatural subversion'.[78] Charlotte, for example, imagines seeing Werter 'when through the gloom of some ill-omen'd night / Delusive fancy gives [him] to [her] sight'. From rapturous recollection she quickly moves to 'fancied horror', envisioning the 'Cold streams of gore' that 'surround' her 'wretched frame'. The scene is so dark that even 'Each guardian angel shudd'ring turn'd from blood' and 'resign'd their station here'. In this and five other poems ('under sentence of Death', 'Earl of Caithness', 'The Ghost of Queen Mary', 'Helen', and 'The Monk'), Craik's attention to the physicality of death is noticeably different than in many of her other poems on loss, such as 'To Miss M: M:'. In the former, she takes time to note the messiness and violence of death, depicting, for instance, pools of blood and 'gore'. Although the poem tells the story from Charlotte's perspective, given the context and backdrop of the wider story, Craik is playing with the 'polyphony of clashing voices' that the Gothic allows, thereby challenging the existence of a singular truth.[79]

Craik's two-part poem 'The Indian Maid' likewise constructs a seemingly singular narrative out of a multiplicity of texts. The poem, which is based on the story of Yorick and Inkle, recounts a legend set in the Caribbean in which Inkle, a seventeenth-century English merchant, seduces Yarico, an indigenous woman, after she rescues him from drowning, and then betrays her by selling her into slavery. The tale was first recorded in Richard Ligon's *A True and Exact History of the Island of Barbadoes* (1657, 1673, 1680, etc.), and became well enough known to be frequently recycled for children during the eighteenth century and to be made into an opera by George Colman Jr for the Haymarket Theatre, London, in 1789. The most influential retelling was by Richard Steele, the first to give the names of the two protagonists, in *The Spectator*, no. 11 (1711). Additionally, Craik notes that the poem is 'intended for a companion to *The Harp*'. Hector MacNeill's *The Harp*, set in Scotland, tells a story with some parallels to Craik's poem, about a minstrel and his wife who are caught in a storm. To save his wife's life, the minstrel burns his prized harp, only for her to leave him the following morning for another man. In Craik's poem, Yarico burns her possessions to save Inkle.

By overtly weaving in multiple texts and telling the story from the perspective of Yarico, Craik illustrates the way in which different voices trouble the dominant narrative. In the poem, Craik focuses on Yarico's emotional anguish at the 'treach'rous art' and 'Av'rice' of Inkle, who, in keeping with earlier versions of the story, sells her and his unborn child into slavery. Inkle and, in his role as 'Albion's faithless Son', Britain are cast as dishonorable: 'sad remembrance keeps, / and mourns Britannia's lasting shame'. Conversely, Yarico is 'form'd with passions mild, / A feeling heart, and generous soul'. Through the stark contrast between the two, Craik makes it abundantly clear where her sympathies lie and, as the Gothic frequently does, pits innocence against evil.

Craik's emphasis on Yarico's communion with nature and Inkle's sophistication likewise pits pre-modern sublimity against modernity. For example, Yarico is described as a peaceful 'Indian Queen' whose 'palace' is a 'humble Grot' 'deck'd from ocean's wat'rey bound'. Her 'bow and arrow guiltless hung, / 'Twas there for state,—no wound it gave'; instead, 'Kind Nature healthy food supply'd.' Upon the arrival of Inkle, beneficiary of the 'crimes of polish'd Life', 'so pure a scene [is] destroy'd / For all the empty wealth below'. By depicting the fall of Yarico's Eden, Craik is following an especially Scottish Gothic tradition. As Ian Duncan has argued, the literary romanticisation and objectification of the Scottish Highlands (in Craik's poem, the Caribbean) illustrated two attitudes toward British history and modernisation. In the first, Scotland, which is reimagined as immune to the passage of time and modernisation, is a state from which Britain had fallen. In the second, Scotland is a state from which Britain had emerged.[80] Craik's poem, and its unusual ending, fit neatly into the former paradigm. Unlike previous versions of the tale, Craik makes clear the fate of Yarico and her unborn child after being sold into slavery: 'she plunges in the Deep, / No more alas!—to rise again—'. Craik refuses to 'in oblivion wrap the scene', driving home the tragic affects of the slave trade and attempting to move 'each gen'rous heart' who 'peruses[s] the mournful theme'. At a time when many of the Kirkcudbrightshire gentry, including her neighbours the Oswalds, had built their wealth from slavery, Craik applies a critical lens to Scotland's part in the development of the British empire. The palimpsestic nature of Craik's poem allows her to challenge what Davison describes as 'the foundations of hegemonic authority'. Her sympathies might well have set her at odds with others in her circle.

In 'The Ghost of Queen Mary', Craik promotes a different interpretation of the historical record and thus of the historical truth. Forced in 1567 to abdicate her throne to her infant son, Queen Mary fled Scotland in 1568 for exile in England, hoping for the support and protection of the English queen, Elizabeth I. As a potential Catholic replacement and therefore threat to Elizabeth I, however, Mary was instead held in captivity for nineteen years before being executed on 8 February 1587. Mary's reputation, traditionally depicted by Presbyterian historians as villainous, had been rehabilitated by historians with Jacobite sympathies, most notably William Fraser Tytler, a friend both of Robert Riddell and Burns. Craik's subtitle, 'occasioned by a beautiful Poem written and sent me by Mr Burns', references his poem 'The Lament of Mary, Queen of Scots', which he only completed at the beginning of June 1790. Craik's poem is written in the voice of Queen Mary returning from the dead to praise Burns for reclaiming her name and correcting history.[81] Mary condemns Elizabeth, calling her a 'False Woman!', noting that 'Since Burns was destin'd to record the theme', Elizabeth's crime is subject to 'loud reproach'. By emphasising the impact of Burns's words on public perception of Queen Mary, Craik flatters her friend and gives voice to the people. She thereby disrupts narratives of the past put forth by those in power, or those who, in Angela Wright's words, are 'self-appointed narrators of the nation'.[82] Focused on justice, Queen Mary is now in a position to 'pardon since my native Land', predicting it 'At length unanimously right shall stand'. Queen Mary thus represents a new kind of heroine and female subject, a kind later featured in Craik's Gothic novels. As Craciun explains, Craik's novels imagine heroines who desire justice rather than love, and who publicly participate in politics and philosophy.[83]

In 'The Maid of Enterkin' Craik presents another heroine who falls victim to political machinations. One of two Craik dramatic monologues set explicitly in Scotland, 'The Maid of Enterkin' tells the tale of a Jacobite fugitive and his daughter in the years following the defeat of Prince Charles Edward Stuart and the Jacobite army at the Battle of Culloden in April 1746. Using her father's status as a fugitive against her, the maid's unwanted suitor threatens to expose her father unless she yields to his attentions. The poem centres on the female speaker's distress and grief after her father flees into the hills to protect his daughter and dies from exposure. The maid resolves to mourn her father one hour for every year of his life and hopes then to join him in the grave. In her dedicatory address, Craik credits her subject matter to Captain Riddell, who had an interest in post-Culloden Jacobite-related songs and stories and whose home at Friar's Carse was a few miles south of Enterkin. Riddell had probably seen a story published in the *London Chronicle* in October 1781, but subsequently reprinted in *Scots Magazine*. Though Craik's poem closely follows that source, she changes the narrator of the tale, from the male traveller of the published story, an outsider recounting events many years after they happened, to a female speaker, deeply involved with what has happened, and mourning her fugitive-father's death. Craik was sufficiently proud of this poem to include it, without any substantive revision, in her first novel, *Julia St. Pierre: A Tale of the French Revolution* (1796), where Julia and her friend Miss Rutland are reduced to tears on hearing it read aloud.

In this poem, as with much of her work, Craik explores the tension between reason and emotion and imbues her central character with a full range of subjectivity. The maid, with 'ev'ry woe opprest', is 'From *Reason* torn'. Her 'filial duty' 'to *Frenzy* gives the rein'. Consequently, the maid is beset upon by 'Ideal Phantoms' and a 'burning Madness' 'Till mental suff'ring close the weary scene'. To that, however, Craik adds an exploration of familial and political duties and, through the father figure, provides an alternative model that does not rest upon parental and political tyranny. The maid's love for her father and his for his daughter is placed in contrast to her suitor's supposed love. Whereas the former is 'blest' from the heavens 'with calm *Content*', and through '*Patience* and *Virtue* [had] ev'ry want supplied', the latter is in 'enmity with Heav'n' and is 'from Hell's black centre driv'n'. Whereas the maid's father flees so as not to force his daughter's hand, her assailant attempts to preclude any agency she has. Craik sharpens the contrast between the two male figures through her pointed depiction of the assailant as a 'legal Villain'. Though an outlaw, her father is an honourable man. Coupled with the maid's assertion that 'Treach'ry comes disguis'd like smiling Love', Craik's depiction of the 'legal Villain' is an additional reminder that state-sanctioned narratives are often used to advance hegemonic projects. Craik's representation of an ideal father, who, because of the political tenor of the poem, cannot be separated from an ideal ruler, is at odds with some of her other work. As Adriana Craciun writes, 'the connection between parental and political tyranny was a recurring theme in Craik's novels' and is also front and centre in the poem which closes her manuscript, 'The Monk'.[84] Nevertheless, in 'The Maid of Enterkin' Craik suggests that such a connection is not inevitable.

In 'Helen', Craik engages with the Scottish ballad tradition, reworking the well-known ballad, 'Fair Helen' or 'Helen of Kirkconnell Lea', set in the Borders in the early sixteenth century. The ballad tells the tragic story of Helen of Kirkconnel, daughter of a wealthy local landowner, who was courted by two suitors but expressly preferred one. Walking beside the Kirtle river with her beloved, Adam Fleming, Helen saw the rival suitor, sensed danger, threw herself in front of Adam, and was shot to death. Adam responded by killing Helen's assailant with his sword. Craik's poem is set several years later, when Adam returns from exile, inconsolable, visits Helen's grave and dies upon it from guilt and grief. Craik's poem is voiced by Helen herself, observing Adam's return and distress, and although Craik follows the ballad story, her dramatic monologue allows more explicit emotional expression and more attention to Helen's physical fate. Fleming is 'from all enjoyment,—ev'ry comfort torn' and suffers 'deep affliction' from 'the pangs of an ill-omen'd Love.—'. Helen returns from the afterlife as a 'Form etherial', the blood from her wound a 'crimson flood' 'bursting forth' and 'Her floating garments drench'd appear'd in gore'. She foretells Fleming's death, promising 'to guide [him] to divine repose' and assuring him 'An *early* Passport to serener scenes'. By giving Helen a voice, Craik transforms her into an agent in the poem rather than, as in the ballad, secondary to Fleming's grief. Though Helen was a victim in life, the intrinsic malleability of the ballad tradition lets Craik make her a heroine in death. John Niles and Eleanor Long have commented about this process that

> the life story of a song is not one of slow change or gradual deterioration. On the contrary, the song's long frozen periods of stable memorization are interrupted by periods of thaw during which its constituent elements of formulas, motifs, plot, and tune become partially fluid as a new person learns the song and shapes it to his or her own dialect, experience and aesthetic values.[85]

Here, as in 'The Monk' and her later novels, Craik is very much interested in exploring alternative versions of female agency. 'Helen', perhaps, offers us a glimpse of the direction she later takes. (92)

'The Monk of la Trappe', which is the last, and lengthiest, of the dramatic monologues contained in the Beinecke manuscript, picks up and furthers many of the themes Craik explored in her previous work, including marriage, parental and political tyranny, grotesque emotional imbalance, oppression, survivor-guilt, and betrayal; it is also arguably the most patently Gothic of her poems in its settings and violence and clearly foreshadows the five Gothic novels Craik would publish after leaving Arbigland; and, in it, Craik overtly asserts ownership over her creativity. Gone are the humble assertions of artless and accidental authorship that she made in 'To Captain Riddell'. Instead, Craik boldly declares in her preface that her story is original and she later recycles the poem into a prose retelling, as a rediscovered manuscript or suicide letter, in what is now her best-known novel, *Adelaide de Narbonne* (1800). In the poem, Craik recounts the tale of star-crossed lovers, St Julian, the narrator, and Laura, a highborn maid he met while she was fleeing a promised marriage to Count Albert. St Julian saves Laura from a band of ruffians and they subsequently fall in love and elope. The setting at their secret union is entirely Gothic in its description and portends the horror to come:

—But while the Priest devoted victims join,
Prophetic nature shudder'd at the shrine;
Recording Angels heav'd a mournful sigh,
And sculptur'd Saints had anguish in their eye.—
—The lengthen'd Isle a hollow murmur sends,
A deep'ning horror oer the scene extends.—
A sudden crash of thunder bursts around,
And gleaming Lightening flashes on the ground;—
While shrouded Ghosts, who from their Graves were
thrown,
Had to the altar for protection flown.

The dying wish of Laura's father is to exact vengeance on the pair for their disobedience. To fulfil that wish, her brother Medina and a band of masked men kidnap St Julian, bringing him to Florence where he is commanded to kill Laura, after which he would be set free. St Julian refuses, but to save his life Laura kills herself. Guilt-ridden, St Julian lives out his remaining days as a monk at the abbey of La Trappe, leaving a record of the story to be found after his death.

That Craik would include a prose retelling of 'The Monk' in her novel should come as no surprise. Craciun writes that 'Beginning with its first sentence and through all four volumes, *Adelaide de Narbonne* exacts an unrelenting attack on marriage as a form of political and economic tyranny'.[86] A central theme running throughout the poem is marital oppression; even the plot turns on Laura's refusal to wed Count Albert. While Craik attacks marriage on several fronts, her most pointed critique is conducted through Laura. For instance, when first rescued by St Julien, Laura 'talks of marriage, mis'ry and the Grave—', linguistically putting the three on the same plane and equating marriage with death. When Laura later thanks St Julien for saving her, Craik goes further, suggesting that marriage is a fate much worse than death: 'I owe you *more* than Life' (emphasis added), because he had saved her when she was 'For e'er condemn'd to be proud Albert's wife'. And no wonder. Whereas marriage is oppressive, time and time again the 'healing hand' of 'friendly Death' offers Craik's various protagonists an escape, perhaps their only escape, from societal mores and parental tyranny: 'I go *where* Parents can oppress no more'. Craik emphasises the lack of agency women have in matrimonial decisions and the violence of them by describing Laura's betrothment in war-like terms; her hand is variously 'threaten'd' and, 'sanction'd by a Father's stern command', 'seized' by Count Albert. Craik is especially critical of marrying for money. Whereas she rules it out in other poems, her distaste is amplified in 'The Monk'.[87] For the critical role wealth played in marital arrangements, one need only refer back to 'the Earl of Caithness' or 'To R: O: Esq'' As the two women playfully remind R: O:, 'Sans money we must also be sans Beau'. Noting that Count Albert's 'chief merit was in fortune plac'd', Craik makes clear that Laura's father is motivated by 'sordid av'rice', rather than his daughter's wishes. In that same stanza she contrasts Count Albert's wealth with 'an accomplish'd mind', casting the latter as 'Superior'. Laura's 'filial duty,—and Count Albert's Love;—' precludes her from any kind of agency. For Craik, it seems from this poem, marriage is simply swapping filial fetters for what she elsewhere calls 'Hymen's fetters'.

It is tempting to cast Craik as staunchly opposed to marriage and to emphasise that, as Craciun argues, she sees it as especially oppressive, a form of tyranny that reduces women to property. However, Craik's view of marriage can be far more nuanced, at least in 'The Monk'. Through her description of Laura and St Julian's relationship Craik puts forward a model of matrimony that allows for female agency, subjectivity, and desire:

> —Brief let me be,—my name, my rank she knew,
> And in our hearts a mutual passion grew;—
> Her charms, her merit, more conspicuous shown
> As op'ning time made worth unequal'd known;
> And oft from Life's insipid round I stole
> 'To feast on Reason and the flow of soul.'—
> —At length she deign'd our union to approve,
> And with her hand repaid my ardent Love—

St Julian's courtship is markedly different from that of Count Albert. For one, it is 'mutual' and 'approve[d]' by Laura. She has 'deign'd' it so and as such repays St Julian's love with her hand. That is to say, her hand is neither 'seized' nor 'threatened'; instead, she freely offers it. Craik further emphasises the importance of mutuality when she notes that '[Laura's] Parent', the obvious villain in the tale, 'View'd *mutual* duties and her fate with scorn'. In such a set up, women are willing and active participants in their destiny rather than objects of exchange. Craik is thus able to offer an alternative that resists masculine power without throwing out marriage in its entirety.

Craik resists male authority by reconfiguring notions of masculine honour, as seen through the figures of St Julian and Medina, Laura's brother. 'Tho not of Princely rank', St Julian is known to be 'Brave,—learn'd,—aspiring,—eager for renown' and in possession of 'a polish'd mind' (something Craik has deemed superior to wealth). As such he is a 'manly model' who rescues maidens and gentlemen alike: his 'valour once preserv'd [Medina's] threaten'd Life.' He refuses to kill Laura in exchange for his life, 'spurn[ing] *such* mercy from [his] inmost soul', and offers himself instead. Though not born to nobility, in Craik's hands St Julian is emphatically noble. By contrast, Medina, who is honour-bound to fulfil his filial duty, becomes an agent of Laura's death: 'Her father *thus* his dying will explain'd, / And by the hand she lov'd, her death ordain'd—'. Consequently, Medina, whose heart is filled with 'vengeance', is one of 'Four Ruffians mask'd'. And when defied, he, 'with threat'ning eye' 'retract[s] the word [he] gave', dooming both Laura and St Julian. In going back on his word, Medina clearly marks himself, and by extrapolation all the despotic and patriarchal interests he stands for, as dishonourable.

There is much more that can be said about 'The Monk'. One issue deserving further discussion is Laura's suicide, important as suggesting some of the ways in which Craik's Gothic heroines both are and are not self-portraits. Like fair Helen of Kirkconnell, but unlike Helen Craik, Laura sacrifices herself in order to save her beloved. And like fair Helen, Laura later returns from the dead 'drenched in vital gore' and 'calls [St Julian] hence' to the after-life 'where Parents curse not, nor rash judgements wound'. The setting in which Laura turns the sword upon herself, and its distinctly Gothic atmosphere, is defined by the pictures that line the wall: portraits of Portia and Monimia, two Roman women who also committed suicide over disrupted or forbidden love. The scene, then, illustrates three women (Portia, Monimia, and Laura) who exercise agency and defy patriarchal power through their acts of violence, even though aimed at themselves. As such, they represent what Craciun argues is a 'new kind of (proto)feminist female subject, one who actively participates in the traditionally male realms of political debates and political assassination'.[88] Rather than hiding in a convent, 'A willing Vot'ry ever to remain', thereby cloistering herself in a gendered private sphere, Laura secretly defies her father's wishes by marrying a man of her own choice and rejects the only option usually made available to fleeing literary heroines.[89] By becoming the dispenser of justice at the poem's climax, actively yielding the sword that kills her, Laura openly defies her brother and ultimately wrests power from her male persecutors. Laura's suicide is not an act of self-abnegation but an exertion of physical agency and an act of defiance. Helen Craik did not kill herself, and she had written Laura's story well before she left Arbigland, but arguably Laura's story prefigures and rehearses the agency she then exercised, even if its Gothicism and melodrama differ from Craik's crisper, and more controlled, if no less outraged, tone when she comes later to write about her own resistance.

While 'The Monk of la Trappe' is the last long poem in the Beinecke manuscript, it is not the note on which Craik ends the collection. While the very last item, Craik's squib on Bruce's travels, was presumably written and added in just as she was finishing up, the immediately preceding poem, 'Lines Written upon hearing that a circle of Mr E***'s *intimate friends* had received the accounts of his Death with the utmost indifference', gives an intriguing sense of Craik's own developed perspective on her abilities. We don't know who Mr E. was, but his abilities and wit had alienated his friends, leaving him isolated and ultimately unmourned. Craik's comment is not unfeeling about Mr E.'s tormented regrets, but she contrasts self-absorbed deathbed melodrama, and 'the thoughts of what we might have been' with 'True Worth', 'Virtue', and the 'consolation of a mind at ease'.

Helen Craik at Flimby: An Independent Life

The Beinecke manuscript collects Craik's poetry up to the summer of 1790 as she wanted it to be seen. It was a careful fair copy prepared for two readers, Robert Riddell and Robert Burns, whom she respected, and who respected her. It includes almost all her known poetry from the previous fifteen or twenty years, and it provides the only full text and first-hand source for any of her longer poems. It is clear, however, from her letters to Burns and from Neilson's and Arnott's accounts of the other two Craik notebooks, that she went on writing poetry after 1790, that she was still actively engaged in her poetry in February 1792, when she took the decision to leave Arbigland, and that she was still entering material, her own and other people's, in at least one of these notebooks well after she moved to Flimby. Those notebooks are still unlocated, leaving Neilson's and Arnott's articles as the only available source for Craik's later poems. Their articles are given in full as Appendix II of this edition, and only brief extracts from the poems have been quoted in the discussion here.

Both the other notebooks have a very clear provenance back to Craik herself. What Neilson called the Henderson notebook, then owned by Robert Henderson of Penicuik, had been given by Craik to her friend Anne Staig of Dumfries, then by Miss Staig to General Goldie of Goldielea, handed down to his daughter, and then owned by his son-in-law, James Starke, of Troqueer Holm, near Dumfries, till 1908, when it was auctioned in Edinburgh.[90] Neilson gives little information about it, but the 1908 cataloguer dated the contents '1788–1813'. Based on Neilson's notes, Arnott indicated that most of its contents matched poems in the notebook owned by Neilson himself. These included Craik's 'Lines Addressed to Miss Staig with the foregoing Poems':

> You who *through chance* and *change* have *prov'd the same,*
> Whose bosom glows with *Friendship*'s *purest* flame,
> Whose tongue ne'er stab'd *where* Fate *too heavy* prest,
> Nor unreprov'd let pass th' unfeeling jest; . . .
> If *wrapt* in *gloom* the pensive strain appears,
> The *pen* that trac'd it *oft was steep'd* in *tears.*
> With *tears* the page was often deluged o'er,

Forc'd from the bleeding HEART'S *half* broken *core*, . . .
Then ANNA!—*still* let *Friendship's pow'r* prevail,
And o'er *each error* throw *Indulgence'* veil.

Neilson offered a much fuller description of the notebook he owned himself. Although he had family links to the Craiks, he had acquired the notebook relatively recently. It had been Craik's own notebook, not for working drafts, but into which at various dates from the late 1780s to the early 1810s she copied completed poems. She had bequeathed the notebook along with Burns's letters and manuscript poems to Gilbert Young of Youngerfield, her executor and residual legatee, and it seems to have stayed in that family for at least seventy years, till Gilbert's son Major Thomas Young of Lincluden died in 1896, and perhaps till the sale of Craik's Burns manuscripts in 1913. George S. Neilson (1858–1923) was a practicing lawyer in Glasgow but also a well-regarded historian of Scottish law and an expert on medieval Scottish charters.[91] His *Glasgow Herald* articles in 1919 give a responsible summary of his Craik notebook, at some points going page-by-page, providing confirmation that many of the poems in Neilson and Henderson notebooks were ones that were also included in the Beinecke manuscript. Perhaps because of the original newspaper readership, some of his comments about Craik's poems now seem rather defensive or even patronising, and he seldom quotes more than short passages, while of course the Beinecke manuscript preserves the complete poems. The final third of his article focuses on two poems by Burns that (presumably) Craik herself had transcribed.[92] One of these, 'Written in a Window in Stirling', is certainly authentic, but had been published in 1788, before Craik met Burns, so might well have come from a printed source. The second, longer poem, titled 'A Monody on the Fatal 29th Decr., 1789', has parallels in Burns's diction and style, but Neilson is rightly oblique about claiming Burns as the author; there is no other mention of it in Burns's own papers or letters, and it has never been accepted into the Burns canon.[93]

However, the Neilson notebook contained several other poems, or extracts from poems by Craik herself, of more direct biographical interest, that like the poem to Miss Staig were clearly written after the Beinecke manuscript was finished. Neilson himself printed Craik's verse invitation, 'A Card from J. M. Esq.', announcing a party given by John Maxwell of Kirkconnell. The poem provides a wonderful, sharp-eyed picture of social networking among the landed families of the Dumfries area and east Kirkcudbrightshire. Neilson gives good annotations of Craik's affectionate allusions; guests would include Maxwell of Carruchan, Colonel de Peyster, and 'Captain Craik', who for Craik still means her father, not her nephew. Neilson suggests the phrase 'Goldie-lee's beauteous inmate' refers to Burns's new confidante Maria Riddell; Maria's husband Walter only purchased Goldielea early in 1792, and he renamed it soon afterwards.[94] If Neilson's identification is right, Craik was still enmeshed in local society up to the month of her departure, and, judging by her very un-Gothic self-portrait, she anticipated enjoying it:

> . . . on Helen he'll gladly bestow his sweet wine
> To prevent her from scribbling nonsensical rhyme.—

A second significant poem from the Neilson notebook comes in Arnott's article, rather than in Neilson's. This was 'Lines Written in the Summerhouse at Arbigland in 1792', which Arnott reports as also present in the Henderson notebook. In the Beinecke manuscript, there are different, earlier, and happier, poems referring to the summerhouse, but this poem, dated 25 February 1792, the day she left Arbigland, voices both sadness and anger at leaving home and leaving Scotland.

> Deprived of peace—to calumny a prey,
> HERE Helen wept her lonely hours away;

> Though guiltless, forc'd *imputed* guilt to bear,
> No justice destin'd—and no pity near. . . .
>
> *Scotia!* from thee my streaming eyes I turn,
> Now doom'd to rest in SOME far distant urn!
> Exil'd from all I valu'd!—country, home!
> Near Solway's banks, no more, alas! to roam;
> O'er youthful scenes where pleasure led the way,
> Where fond *remembrance* oft shall ling'ring stray. . . .
>
> Scotia, farewell! Long cherish'd Land, adieu!
> Soon, soon on *thee* shall close my aching view!
> No more; but ah! let anguish speak the rest,
> For *deep'ning* anguish rends my hapless breast,
> I go!—sad Nature's *final* pang is o'er.
> Scotia, farewell! *now fate can* wound *no more!*

Arnott used 'these despairing words, so full of deep feeling', as confirming local tradition and as indicating 'the period at which the tragic event of the murder or suicide took place', but, as noted above, while it is clear the poem was written about Craik's emotions on leaving her home, nothing in it says the weeping or the dispute with her family happened then rather than being among her memories of the summerhouse in earlier years, and while there is much about anguish nothing hints at murder or suicide. The importance of the poem lies rather in showing Craik using for her own experience the kind of first-person voice she had used earlier in depicting the Queen of Denmark or Goethe's Charlotte.

A third late poem, also given by Arnott rather than Neilson, provides a perspective leaving Arbigland that seems much closer to her own voice. A friend's well-intentioned mother had sent her a tartan handkerchief to remind her of her love for Scotland, and Craik's reply scarifies the recent experience she was glad to leave behind. Robert Riddell had 'expostulated' with Douglas Hamilton Craik about Helen Craik's impending departure, and

Hamilton Craik commented tactlessly "Tis all for the best'. Craik's broadside is worth quoting at length:

> MY LOVE FOR MY COUNTRY!!! from *whence must* it flow?
> From falsehood—injustice—each species of woe?
> From *cunning's deep* fountain too *winding* to sound,
> From Avarice grasping at *all* seen around;
> From the *envy* of *some* who with malice pursued me,
> From the *coolness* of *Those* who mistakenly view'd me;
> From inhuman connections—from Nephews and Nieces
> *Who all for the best* tore my conduct to pieces;
> *Being* formed by *self-int'rest* with morals *so* civil
> As for sixpence to sell *half* their *kin* to the Devil;
> Yet that *once* they spoke truth must I think be confest
> Since THEIR WORDS I can echo "twas all for the best!!"[95]

As well as supporting the case made earlier for why Craik moved to Flimby so abruptly, this poem is surely one of her best poems and one of her most personal.

The Neilson and Henderson notebooks show that Craik did not wholly abandon poetry after leaving Arbigland in 1792, but she would soon make what might seem a surprising change of direction in her writing. Where her poetry had been shared only in manuscript, among friends, she now redirected her narrative abilities to prose fiction, and she sent her work to a prolific London publisher, William Lane. From 1790 through to about 1820, Lane's Minerva Press imprint became shorthand for Gothic and sentimental fiction, multivolume novels produced chiefly for younger women readers and marketed to the circulating libraries.[96] Long disparaged by critics, as they had been by Jane Austen in *Northanger Abbey* (1817), the Minerva Press novels have been substantially reassessed in more recent Romantic-era criticism.[97] Over a period of ten years, Craik published five novels, all anonymous, with the Minerva Press: *Julia de St. Pierre* (1796), *Adelaide de Narbonne* (1800), *Henry of Northumberland* (1800), *Stella of the North* (1802), and *The Nun and her Daughter* (1805). It was Adriana Craciun's essay on the first of these novels that initiated the current reappraisal of her work. As suggested in the discussion of the Beinecke manuscript poems, the new direction in Craik's writing had been foreshadowed in some of her longer narrative poems.

After the novels, Craik's traceable writings are few: the most notable are the memoirs of her father printed in Appendix 1. She may be a plausible source, if not actual author, for the unsigned newspaper article about Arbigland from 1821 quoted earlier in the introduction.[98] There is even, in 1815, a possible exception to her lifelong avoidance of publishing poetry. This is a ten-line newspaper poem signed 'Helen' that was 'suggested by' the fund drive for a memorial to Burns in Dumfries. When Burns died, in July 1796, his grave in St Michael's kirkyard was marked with a simple flat slab. Visitors were often disparaging, and by 1813 Burns's local admirers launched a subscription to build a mausoleum 'resembling a temple'.[99] Peter Turnerelli was commissioned to produce as its centrepiece his well-known marble sculpture of Burns at the plough visited by his muse. The foundation stone was laid in June 1815; the building itself, by a local architect, was finished in September; and Burns's remains were transferred to the new site on 19 September, though the sculpture only arrived four years later.[100]

VERSES
Suggested by the Subscription for the Mausoleum of Burns.

Light sorrows speak, great grief suspends the tongue,
Else here had Scotia's Bards a tribute hung;
Mute Eloquence thus long survey'd the ground,
And Sadness yet no classic numbers found.
Shall then, O BURNS!, a Sister humbly dare
Approach the hallow'd spot, and triumph there?
Shall the pure incense of your favour'd Fair
Attend this instance of thy Country's care,

That bids, at length, a sad Mausoleum rise,
In proud magnificence, where Genius lies?

Dumfries.   HELEN.[101]

There is no external evidence confirming the attribution to
Craik, but the topic and the neoclassic couplets seem to fit Craik,
as does the pretence that 'Helen' is only writing about the
mausoleum because Scotia's (male) Bards have failed to do
so. Two Dumfries friends, Dr William Maxwell and Provost
David Staig, were on the mausoleum fundraising committee;
moreover, if the attribution holds, it confirms that Craik had
maintained or renewed ties in the Dumfries community.

When Craik left Arbigland in 1792, she had moved first briefly
to Carlisle, before moving in with her uncle and aunts from the
other branch of the Craik family, at Flimby, the Cumberland
estate her grandfather had bought for the children of his second
marriage, on the south side of the Solway Firth, between Maryport
and Workington. Flimby, with well under a hundred households,
and a population of less than three hundred, was smaller than
Kirkbean, though it would grow a little in Craik's last years.[102]
The Craiks' home, Flimby Lodge, was a substantial two-storey
stone Georgian house, with a slate roof, and a Doric portico.[103]
While the Flimby Craiks were a little younger than her father,
they were still well on in years, and Helen Craik took on the role
at Flimby that she had been playing at Arbigland for her elderly
father and her invalid sister. They were a long-lived family, with
the oldest, her uncle John, living till 1803; as she later wrote,
'on me has devolved the severe and melancholy duty of laying
their aged heads in the grave; where the remains of the last of its
regretted members (my aunt Barbara) were deposited, in May
1809, in her ninety-second year'.[104]

Helen Craik inherited money from several of them, and she
also inherited a half-share in a section of the Craiks' Flimby
estate that was sold in 1807 for £16,504, split equally between
her and, ironically, Douglas Hamilton Craik.[105] Her sister

had died in 1796, and her father in 1799, aged ninety-four, still at Arbigland. She continued to live in Flimby Lodge, and there is a record of her continuing active management of her remaining holdings.[106] As she wrote in 1810, when she was soon to turn sixty:

> With this money, and the handsome increase to it made by my late ever respected relatives here, I am now, thank God and them, in rather more than easy circumstances; and can say, what many richer people cannot say, that I am healthy, happy, and contented.[107]

Ten years later, staying in an inn in Maryport, the itinerant actor and memoirist Samuel Ryley received an unexpected invitation to dinner at Flimby Lodge, 'written in a neat and lady-like hand'. The writer, he recounted, had read his books and wanted to meet their author. He asked where the lodge was and who lived there:

> 'Sir', said the landlord innkeeper, 'Miss Craik, the owner of it, is a lady highly respected in the neighbourhood; she is said to be very high learned; reads and writes a good deal, although I believe in her seventieth year.'[108]

Ryley had never met a woman author before and seems to have been slightly over-awed. Despite her age, she

> preserved the remains of fascinating features, and her easy address and suavity of manners were quite free from that distance and hauteur that her rank and riches might have produced [. . .] excellence of language, and elegance of deportment, rivetted my attention, and increased my respect.[109]

It was, he wrote, 'an honour [. . .] seeing and conversing with this truly amiable and most accomplished of the sex'.[110] Ryley's is the only first-hand description we have found of Craik at

Flimby, and his complimentary language is conventional enough, but the incident still conveys something of Craik's character and personality. In possession of an independent income and head of her own household, Craik was free to live her life as she saw fit. She remained unmarried, and she became well known in the area for her charitable work.

When she died, still at Flimby, on 11 June 1825, aged seventy-three, rather than selecting a single heir, she left a revealing variety of smaller bequests and annuities to relatives, friends, and former employees, including some she had known in Kirkbean, though none seem to be linked to the Hamilton Craiks of Arbigland.[111] Among the beneficiaries were two old Dumfries friends, Miss Ann Staig and Dr William Maxwell, both getting one hundred pounds, and several relatives of the next generation, including Stewarts and Christians and Curwens. Isabella Neilson Hamilton, 'daughter of my late aunt Hamilton', would get two hundred pounds when she turned twenty-one, and another relative, Mrs Blamires of Workington, was left five hundred pounds. Other bequests included one hundred pounds each to Mary Stewart in Edinburgh, and the sisters Jane and Euphemia Stewart, a guinea apiece to 'five poor women of the parish of Flimby', and twenty pounds a piece to two well-off male friends to buy 'a ring or some other token' to remember her by. To some of the household staff she left lifetime annuities of twenty or forty pounds, together with continued use of their housing. Her executor, and residuary legatee, was her cousin Gilbert Young of Youngerfield, Lincluden, near Dumfries.

When she came to be memorialised locally, it was as a prominent figure in the community but not as a poet or novelist. The memorial plaque in St Nicholas's Church, where she was buried, praises her as 'to the afflicted a kind and consoling friend and to the poor an indulgent and liberal benefactress', but is silent about her writing, as also about her parentage and any connection to her Kirkcudbrightshire home and relatives.[112] Some of the newspaper death notices from the other side of the Solway were a little more forthcoming. The notice in the *Dumfries Weekly Journal* read:

> On Saturday last, at Flimby Lodge, near Mayport, Miss Helen Craik, in the 74th year of her age. She was a lady of very considerable literary talents; and, we understand was the authoress of several works both in French and English, which were published anonymously. The benevolence of her disposition was unbounded; she was the protector of the orphan, the friend of the friendless. The poor in her neighbourhood will long lament her loss, for she had a heart 'open as day to melting charity,' and a hand ever ready to succour them in all their wants. Miss Craik was the youngest daughter of the late Wm. Craik, Esq. of Arbigland.[113]

It remains to be seen what today's scholars will make of this newly rediscovered manuscript and the new availability of a substantial corpus of Craik's poetry. As previously noted, in our own commentary we have made no attempt to offer comprehensive explication, aiming only to provide the general contexts and possible composition dates for Craik's verse. Additionally we have tried to show some of the varied literary themes, genres, and movements Craik engaged in, pointing out where, and how, Craik's work fits into, furthers, or subverts late eighteenth-century literary traditions and cultural expectations.

In working on the Beinecke manuscript, it has become clear to us that the Craik who emerges from the poems does not match well with Arnott's melodramatic account in 'The Romance of Helen Craik'. Craik was not Arnott's embittered woman, grieving the alleged murder of an unidentifiable lover. Craik's poetry has a continuing tragic strain, especially in her dramatic monologues, but this draws on her reading, not her life. In the late 1700s stories based on true crime and the Gothic dominated the popular presses. Well versed in Radcliffe and Walpole, Craik was no stranger to Gothic fiction, and both novels and magazines fed her literary imagination. Such reading encouraged her to voice, through her characters, extreme and unfettered emotions, vulnerability, violence, madness, and oppression. She had been exploring such emotions years before the sudden departure from Arbigland on which the Arnott story hinges. Alongside this, however, Craik was also a social poet who used verse to foster and cement friendships with neighbours and to engage with the ideas of others through their writing. Craik's poetry allowed her some imaginative space in which to explore alternative models of femininity, masculinity, filial duty, friendship, marriage, subjectivity, and agency. Many of her protagonists were sad, woeful souls doomed to linger in exile and unrelenting grief, but that was not Craik's own story, and certainly not her whole story.

Endnotes

1   Adriana Craciun, 'The new Cordays: Helen Craik and British representations of Charlotte Corday, 1793–1800', in Adriana Craciun and Karl E. Lokke (eds), *Rebellious Hearts: British Women Writers and the French Revolution*, (Albany, NY: State University of New York Press, 2001), pp. 193–232.

2   See, e.g., Nancy Kushigian and Stephen Behrendt (eds), *Scottish Women Poets of the Romantic Period: An Electronic Archive* (Alexandria, VA: Alexander Street Press/ProQuest, 2001–07, and updates), which provides texts and short critical introductions to some sixty poets. The growth of interest can be traced through, e.g., Catherine Kerrigan (ed.), *An Anthology of Scottish Women Poets* (Edinburgh: Edinburgh University Press, 1991); Douglas Gifford and Dorothy McMillan (eds), *A History of Scottish Women's Writing* (Edinburgh: Edinburgh University Press, 2007); Glenda Norquay (ed.), *The Edinburgh Companion to Scottish Women's Writing* (Edinburgh: Edinburgh University Press, 2012); and chapters by Leith Davis and Kaur Janjua, Juliet Shields, David Radcliffe, Kate Louis Mathis, and JoEllen DeLucia, in Leith Davis and Janet Sorensen (eds), *The International Companion to Scottish Literature of the Long Eighteenth Century* (Glasgow: Scottish Literature International, 2021).

3   Adriana Craciun, 'Craik, Helen (1751–1825)', in *Oxford Dictionary of National Biography* (2004, revd. 2011); cf. 'Helen Craik' ['Poetry: Lost Poems'], in Susan Brown, Patricia Clements, and Isobel Grundy (eds), *Orlando: Women's Writing in the British Isles from the Beginnings to the Present* (1995–2022): orlando.cambridge.org (accessed 26 October 2020).

4   Juliet Shields, 'How to Become an "Authoress" in Provincial Scotland: Women's Poetry in Manuscript and Print', in Davis and Sorensen, pp. 132–48 (p. 132).

5   Dorothy McMillan, 'Introduction', in *The Scotswoman at Home and Abroad* (Glasgow: Association for Scottish Literary Studies, 1999), p. xiv.

6   Stephen C. Behrendt, 'Scottish Women Writers', in his *British Women Poets and the Romantic Writing Community* (Baltimore, MD: The Johns Hopkins University Press, 2009), p. 211.

7   Shields, p. 132. As Shields notes, by the end of the century, this distinction blurs, particularly for middle- and upper-class Scottish women poets, such as Anne Grant or Maria Riddell, who published their poems after they were thrown financially on their own resources; cf. also Behrendt's discussion of Joanna Baillie and Anne Bannerman (Behrendt, pp. 228–42), and the examples discussed in Patrick Scott, 'Burns and the mysterious "Authoress"', *Eighteenth-Century Intelligencer*, 37.1 (March 2023), 7–13.

8   See, e.g., Adriana Craciun, 'Romantic spinstrelsy: Anne Bannerman
    and the sexual politics of the ballad', in Leith Davis, Ian Duncan,
    and Janet Sorensen (eds), *Scotland and the Borders of Romanticism*
    (Cambridge: Cambridge University Press, 2004), pp. 204–24; Ruth
    Perry, '"The Finest Ballads": Women's Oral Traditions in Eighteenth-
    Century Scotland', *Eighteenth-Century Life*, 32.2 (Spring, 2008),
    81–98; Ruth Perry, 'The Printed Record of an Oral Tradition: Anna
    Gordon Brown's Ballads', *Studies in Scottish Literature*, 38.1 (2012),
    71–91.

9   For Craik's rebuttal of rumours that the American naval hero John
    Paul Jones (1747–1792), who was raised in the gardener's cottage on
    the Arbigland estate, was also William Craik's illegitimate son, see
    Monthly Magazine, 52 (December 1821), 418 (in Appendix II).

10 For a detailed contemporary account of the parish and its changes
    during the eighteenth century, see Edward Neilson, 'Parish of Kirk-
    bean', in Sir John Sinclair (ed.), *The Statistical Account of Scotland*,
    15, pt 7 (1795), pp. 119–33.

11 'The Old Stag of Arbigland', reprinted from the *Dumfries Courier*,
    in e.g., *Morning Chronicle*, 23 November 1821, p. 4; *Cumberland
    Pacquet, and Ware's Whitehaven Advertiser*, 3 December 1821, p. 4;
    Westmoreland Gazette, 8 December 1821, p. 1. It is tempting to
    attribute this article to Craik herself, and the main part of it, an anec-
    dote about an old gander (Scots, 'stag') crossing the Solway to mate
    involves Willam Craik, but the tone does not match her other known
    non-fictional prose.

12 On Arbigland House, see John Gifford, *Dumfries and Galloway:
    The Buildings of Scotland* (London: Penguin, 1996; New Haven:
    Yale University Press, 2002), pp. 104–06; on building costs, see
    James Blackett, 'Arbigland Estate Records', *Kirkbean Parish Heri-
    tage Society—Arbigland Estate* (2004): www.kirkbean.org/history/
    arbigland-estate-records (accessed 19 April 2023).

13 Arbigland was owned and farmed by successive Craiks from 1679–
    1852, and then following its purchase by General Stewart, by successive
    Blacketts, from 1852 till the present day. For a valuable perspective,
    see Jamie Blackett, *Red Rag to a Bull: Rural Life in an Urban Age*
    (Wykey, Shrewsbury: Quiller, 2018).

14 *Valuation Roll, Antient and Modern, of the Stewartry of Kirkcud-
    bright* (Dumfries: at the Courier Office, 1820), Appendix, p. xi. The
    1760 valuation followed a Deed of Division in June 1760, presum-
    ably when lands were assigned to Adam Craik and John Hamilton;
    the same valuation was entered in 1780, in 1799, following William
    Craik's death, and in 1819.

15 Ibid., p. 31. For Craik's poem to Richard Oswald, see 'To R: O:
    Esqʳ.'. A similar contrast is seen in the next parish, New Abbey, where
    Oswald held land valued at £1045 while William Craik's brother-in-
    law William Stewart of Shambelly totalled £724; Ibid., p. 75.

16 On the Oswald slave-ownership, over several generations, see the remarkable *Legacies of British Slavery* database (University College London), based on the post-emancipation Slave Compensation records, at www.ucl.ac.uk/lbs/search/. No Craik or Hamilton relatives, from either Kirkcudbrightshire or Dumfriesshire, or Cumberland, are listed among known slave-holders in the database, though note the caveats given by Nicholas Draper, 'Scotland and Colonial Slave Ownership: the Evidence of the Slave Compensation Records', in T. M. Devine, (ed.), *Recovering Scotland's Slavery Past: the Caribbean Connection* (Edinburgh: Edinburgh University Press, 2015), pp. 166–86; and cf. Eric J. Graham, *Burns & the Sugar Plantocracy of Ayrshire* (Edinburgh: MPDB, 2014), pp. 49–60. For Helen Craik's poem about a young woman trapped into slavery, see 'The Indian Maid'.

17 On Craik as an agriculturalist, see, e.g., James Webster, *General View of the Agriculture of Galloway* (Edinburgh: James Paterson, 1794), pp. 13–14; Edward Neilson, in *Statistical Account*, pp. 122–26; Samuel Smith, *A General Survey of the Agriculture of Galloway* (London: for Richard Phillips, 1810), pp. 38–54; 'Account of William Craik, Esq. of Arbigland', *Farmer's Magazine*, 12 (June 1811), 145–65 (which includes the letters from Helen Craik, given in Appendix I below); George Chalmers, *Caledonia: or, an Account, historical and topographic, of North Britain*, 3 vols (London: Cadell, 1807–24), I, pp. 286–89; G. W. Shirley, 'Two pioneer Galloway agriculturalists—Robert Maxwell of Arkland and William Craik of Arbigland', *Transactions of Dumfriesshire and Galloway Natural History and Antiquarian Society*, 3rd ser., 13 (1925–26), 129–61; and Jamie Blackett, *Red Rag to a Bull*, pp. 163–64. On the agricultural society, see, e.g., Wight, *Present State of Husbandry in Scotland*, vol. 2 (1778), pp. 443–44; Edward J. Cowan, 'Agricultural Improvement and the formation of early agricultural societies in Dumfries and Galloway', *Transactions of Dumfriesshire and Galloway Natural History and Antiquarian Society*, 3rd ser., 53 (1977–78), 157–167. More generally, see Andrew McCulloch, *Galloway, A Land Apart* (Edinburgh: Birlinn, 2000), pp. 426–32.

18 Smith, *General Survey*, p. 47.

19 On the upheaval caused by enclosure and improvement, and the Galloway resistance in the 1720s, see, e.g., William Ferguson, *Scotland 1689 to the Present* (Edinburgh: Oliver and Boyd, 1968), pp. 166–74; Christopher A. Whatley, *Scottish Society, 1707–1830: Beyond Jacobitism, towards industrialisation* (Manchester: Manchester University Press, 2000), pp. 143–58; Peter Aitchison and Andrew Cassel, *The Lowland Clearances: Scotland's Silent Revolution, 1760–1830* (East Linton: Tuckwell, 2003); Alister Livingston, *The Galloway Levellers: a study of the origins, events, and consequences of their actions* (unpub. M.Phil., University of Glasgow, 2009); T. M. Devine, *The Scottish Clearances: A History of the Dispossessed* (London: Allen Lane, 2018).

20 For some of Craik's expenditure on specific improvements, see
A. E. Truckell, 'Arbigland Accounts 1751–1759', *Transactions of the
Dumfries and Galloway Natural History and Antiquarian Society*,
67 (1992), 81–86; James Blackett, 'Arbigland Estate Records', as
cited above.

21 R. D. Thornton, *William Maxwell to Robert Burns* (Edinburgh: John
Donald, 1979), p. 12.

22 Sir Henry Trueman Wood, *A History of the Royal Society of Arts*
(London: John Murray, 1913), p. 127n.

23 Andrew Wight, *The Present State of Husbandry in Scotland* extracted
from reports made to the Commissioners of the annexed estates, vol.
3, pt 1 (Edinburgh: Willliam Creech, 1784), pp. 68–72; quoted in
Farmer's Magazine (1811), pp. 148–49.

24 Wight, p. 72.

25 *Farmer's Magazine* (1811), p. 156.

26 Allowing for variation across locality and class, eighteenth-century
Scottish women's role in the multitasking of household management
was economically important as well as complex; for contemporary
depictions, see, e.g., John Galt, *Annals of the Parish* (Edinburgh:
Blackwood, 1821; ed. Robert P. Irvine, Edinburgh: Edinburgh University Press, 2020), pp. 28–31, 100–02, 104–05; Anne MacVicar
Grant, in Dorothy McMillan (ed.), *The Scotswoman at Home and
Abroad* (Glasgow: Association for Scottish Literary Studies, 1999),
pp. 70–71.

27 Craik refers to 'the disputed election of 1740', but must mean either
the contested election in 1741, or the byelection held the following year,
when the M.P. died, and his replacement was returned unopposed; see
R. Sedgwick (ed.), *The History of Parliament: the House of Commons
1715–1754* (1970), online. Later, when William Craik held a crown
appointment, he was unable to exercise his vote directly in parliamentary elections, but he remained influential.

28 William M'Dowall, *History of the Burgh of Dumfries, with Notices
of Nithsdale, Annandale, and the Western Border*, 3rd ed. (Dumfries:
Thomas Hunter, 1906), p. 866.

29 Thornton, *William Maxwell*, p. 17. Later, Helen Craik's brother, Adam
Craik, and John Maxwell of Terraughty, had appealed to the Court
of Session to help the next generation of the Maxwells of Kirkconnell
make fair allocation to the younger sons: Thornton, p. 36.

30 M'Dowall, pp. 553–58, 598–99; McCulloch, pp. 418–20; *The Universal Scots Almanac for . . . 1770* (Edinburgh: Ruddiman, n.d.), p. 100;
The Universal Scots Almanack, for . . . 1795 (Edinburgh: Robertson,
1795), p. 39.

31 Between June 1754 and March 1755, Craik's share of seizures
came to £48.02: James Blackett, 'Arbigland Estate Records', where
Mr Blackett also suggests that Craik himself was involved with a
smuggling syndicate.

32 On these developments, see Bob Harris and Charles McKean, *The Scottish Town in the Age of the Enlightenment* (Edinburgh: Edinburgh University Press, 2014); see also K. A. Manley, *Books, Borrowers, and Shareholders: Scottish Circulating and Subscription Libraries before 1825* (Edinburgh: Edinburgh Bibliographical Society, 2012), pp. 158–59. This paragraph draws on the Dumfries chapter in Patrick Scott, *Robert Burns, A Documentary Volume* (Farmington Hills, MI: Gale/Cengage, 2018), esp. pp. 286–91.

33 Robert Heron, *Observations Made in a Journey Through the Western Counies of Scotland in the Autumn of M.DCC.XCII*, 2nd ed. (Perth: Morison: Glasgow: Stewart & Meikle, 1799), pp. 77–80; cf. William Burnside, 'Parish of Dumfries', in Sir John Sinclair (ed.), *The Statistical Account of Scotland* vol. 5, pt 7 (1793), pp. 119–44.

34 Andrea Thomson, review of Katherine Glover, *Elite Women and Polite Society in Eighteenth-Century Scotland*, in *Journal of Scottish Historical Studies*, 35.1 (April 2015), 115–17 (p. 116).

35 Kathleen Keown, 'Eighteenth-Century Women's Poetry and Feminine Accomplishment', *Review of English Studies*, 73 (2021), 78–99.

36 For background on Burns's Ellisland years, see Scott, *Robert Burns, A Documentary Volume* (2018), ch. 4, pp. 230–85.

37 Grose had visited Riddell in May 1789, making Friar's Carse his base as he gathered Ayrshire material for his *Antiquities of Scotland*, and he returned the following summer, when Burns gave him a letter of introduction to Dugald Stewart (see Roy, *Letters*, II: pp. 40–41, undated letter with an assigned date [July 1790]). Bill Dawson has recently argued (without reference to Craik) that 'Tam o' Shanter' was written in late May 1790, that is during the Craiks' visit, not later in the year as generally thought: see Bill Dawson, 'Questions around the Composition of "Tam o' Shanter"', *Burns Chronicle*, 130.1 (Spring 2021), 99–102.

38 Text here from inscription, signed H. C., and dated October 1789, in Burns, *Poems Chiefly in the Scottish Dialect* (Edinburgh: Creech, 1787), Mitchell Library, Glasgow: call no. 311219.

39 Burns to Helen Craik, 9 August, 1790: Roy, *Letters*, II: pp. 46–47.

40 These interactions are detailed in Patrick Scott, 'The Missing Manuscript of "A Red, red rose"', *Editing Burns for the 21st Century* (Centre for Robert Burns Studies, 24 September 2018).

41 NLS MS 86; for transcription and notes, see Nigel Leask (ed.), *Commonplace Books, Tour Journals, and Miscellaneous Prose* [*Oxford Edition of Robert Burns*, vol. 1] (Oxford: Oxford University Press, 2014).

42 Burns to Mrs Dunlop, 9 July 1790, and 30 July 1790; Burns to Mrs McLehose, July 1791, and 15 December 1791: *Letters*, II: pp. 35, 43, 99–100, 123–24. Burns published the song in Johnson's *Scots Musical Museum*, IV (1792), as song 329, and later it was also included in Thomson's *Select Collection*, III (1802), song 32.

43 James Gibson, *A Bibliography of Robert Burns* (Kilmarnock: James M'Kie, 1881), p. 339 (Addendum); W. E. Henley and T. F. Henderson (eds), *The Poetry of Robert Burns*, 4 vols (Edinburgh: T. C. and E. C. Jack, 1896–98), III: p. 373; Kinsley, II: p. 546 (Kinsley 317), III: p. 1343; Pittock, *OERB*, III: pp. 111–12; McCue, *OERB*, IIV: pp. 496–97.

44 *Memorial Catalogue of the Burns Exhibition . . .* (Glasgow: William Hodge, 1898), p. 392, item 1198; *Scottish Exhibition of National History, Art & Industry Glasgow (1911): Palace of History Catalogue of Exhibits* (Glasgow, Dalross, 1911), p. 180, item 139. A clipping with the 1898 catalogue entry is pasted on the front endpaper of the manuscript.

45 The Craik manuscript goes unmentioned in, e.g., Laurence Witten, 'Contemporary Collectors, XXII: James Marshall Osborn', *The Book Collector*, 8.4 (Winter 1959), 383–96, or Stephen Parks, 'The Osborn Collection: A Fifth Biennial Report', *Yale University Library Gazette*, 52 (January 1978), 101–21.

46 We have not included a transcription of Craik's manuscript contents list in this edition, but variations in the titles between the poems and her contents list are recorded in our notes.

47 See Nigel Leask, in *Oxford Edition of Robert Burns, vol. I: Commonplace Books, Tour Journals, and Miscellaneous Prose* (Oxford: Oxford University Press, 2014), pp. 172–73, and p. 379, n. 8.

48 The catalogue entry when the Henderson manuscript was auctioned at Dowell's in Edinburgh in November 1908 dated it as '1788–1813': see Beinecke provenance file. The contents of these other manuscripts are discussed later in this introduction, and fuller provenance details on them are given under 'Unlocated Manuscripts' in the Bibliography.

49 Letter from William Craik to Cullen, 4 August 1778, *The Cullen Project*, Royal College of Physicians of Edinburgh, doc 1541; and cf. docs 1544 and 4294.

50 Ewing 1938, letter 286.

51 Burns to James Johnson, *Letters*, II: p. 92. In addition to the two known letters from Burns to Craik, and the Beinecke inscription, Burns autograph manuscripts with a Craik provenance through her executor Gilbert Young include 'On Reading, in a Newspaper, the Death of — M'L—' (completed 1787; the Adam-Rosenbach MS); 'Written in Friar's Carse Hermitage' (written June, rewritten December, 1788; not located); a four-stanza version of 'Sensibility, how charming' (written June 1790; possibly that in the Robert Burns Birthplace Museum); 'Lament for Mary Queen of Scots' (completed June 1790; location not identified); and 'Lament for James, Earl of Glencairn' (completed September–October 1791; location not identified). Also from Craik's own papers was a manuscript of 'Fragment: Elegy Intended for Miss Burnet' (written January 1791; now in the Rosenbach Library), inscribed as a gift from 'Miss Craik of Flimby Lodge' in April 1818. See *Index to*

English Literary Manuscripts, 3.1 (1986); R. B. Adam, *Autograph Poems and Letters of Robert Burns* (Buffalo, NY: privately printed, 1922), pp. 5, 9; *Robert Burns 1759–1796, a Collection of Original Manuscripts* . . . (Philadelphia: The Rosenbach Company, 1948), pp. 16, 39–40. The manuscript of 'A red, red rose' (written ca. August 1793, published April 1794; the Bemis MS, now in the Lilly Library), found in 1877 among the Arbigland papers of Douglas Hamilton Craik, may have been given to William Craik, rather than Helen.

52 Ewing (1938), letter 203.

53 Roy, *Letters of Robert Burns*, II: p. 128.

54 Ewing, *Letters Addressed to Robert Burns*, p. 27 (letter 286). Her description of this poem makes clear it is a second poem about Mary, not the poem in the Beinecke manuscript, 'The Ghost of Queen Mary— occasioned by a beautiful Poem written and sent to me by Mr Burns'.

55 Peter Gray, *Dumfriesshire Illustrated, etc.* (Dumfries: Maxwell, 1895), pp. 158–59; see also Alan Temperley, 'The Groom of Arbigland', in his *Tales of Galloway* (London: Skilton and Shaw, 1979), pp. 266–68.

56 Arnott (1924), p. 77: see Appendix II.

57 For such recycling see, e.g., Patrick Scott, 'The Missing Manuscript' (2020).

58 Arnott (1924), p. 77: see Appendix II.

59 Ibid., pp. 80–81.

60 Gray, p. 159.

61 *London Gazette*, 6 March 1784, reported in *Caledonian Mercury*, 15 March 1784, p. 1.

62 Robert Dundas, *Memorial for Mary Craik, eldest daughter of the deceast Adam Craik of Duchrae, and Mrs. Winnifred Maxwell, her Mother and Tutrix, against Mrs. Jean Craik, and Mr. Stewart of Castle-Stewart, for his interest* (Edinburgh; 12 July, 1735); John Rankine, William Harvey, and Robert Berry (eds), *Scots Revised Reports: House of Lords, Series I, 1707–1797* (Edinburgh: William Green, 1898), pp. 310–12 (21 May 1753); pp. 344–45 (25 March 1757). During the intervening period, Mary Craik had died, and the case revived in the Scottish courts on behalf of her younger sister Grizel; Grizel Craik lost on the central issue (whether the entail precluded her father's bequest to her), but was awarded fifteen hundred pounds based on equity, a decision the House of Lords upheld.

63 *Star and Evening Advertiser*, 14 March 1792, p. 8; *Bath Chronicle*, 15 March 1792, p. 3.

64 Letter from Alexander Co[u]pland of King's Grange to Dr William Cullen, Edinburgh, 4 June 1785, regarding Captain Douglas Hamilton Craik (Patient), who has been treated 'with various forms of mercury', because he has 'Symtoms of a true Syphilis': *Cullen Project*, doc. 2646. Hamilton Craik, believing he had syphilis, sought out a doctor twenty miles away, instead of near Arbigland or in Dumfries, who treated him with mercury. Cullen had not actually examined the patient, but

nonetheless rejected Copland's diagnosis: Letter of William Cullen, Edinburgh, to Alexander Copland, King's Grange, 1 July 1785, *Cullen Project*, doc. 5090.

65 See, e.g., Margaret Ezell, *Social Authorship and the Advent of Print*, (Baltimore, MD: Johns Hopkins University Press, 1999) and Ezell, *The Patriarch's Wife*, (Chapel Hill, NC: University of North Carolina Press, 1987); Harold Love, *The Culture and Commerce of Texts*, (Amherst, MA: University of Massachusetts Press, 1993); Carol Barash, *English Women's Poetry, 1649–1714* (Oxford: Clarendon Press, 1990), and Barash, *Women's Writing and the Circulation of Ideas* (Cambridge: Cambridge University Press, 2002); Zeynap Tenger and Paul Trolander, 'Katherine Phillips and Coterie Critical Practices', *Eighteenth-Century Studies*, 37.3 (2004), pp. 367–87; Michelle Levy, *Literary Manuscript Culture in Romantic Britain* (Edinburgh: Edinburgh University Press, 2020).

66 Love, p. 129.

67 See Letters, II, pp. 46–47 and 128 and Ewing 1938, letter 298. On the connection between Burns and Craik, cf. Patrick Scott 'The Missing Manuscript of "A Red, Red, Rose"', *Editing Burns for the 21st Century*, 23 September 2020.

68 Paula Backscheider, *Eighteenth-Century Women Poets and Their Poetry: Inventing Agency, Inventing Genre* (Johns Hopkins University Press, 2005), p. 176.

69 Adriana Craciun, 'Revolution, Romanticism and the Long Nineteenth Century', *19: Interdisciplinary Studies in the Long Nineteenth Century*, 2 (2006), 8.

70 The common eighteenth-century practice of 'disguising' real names with dashes, asterisks, and ellipses, was rarely meant to obscure identities; it could be used playfully, as in Craik, to establish an inner circle of readers in the know. In published political satire, Andrew Benjamin Bricker has argued, the variety of typographical tics was less to prevent identification than as a defence in defamation suits: cf. Andrew Benjamin Bricker, 'Libel and Satire: The Problem with Naming', *ELH*, 81.3 (2014), 889–921.

71 Elizabeth W. Bruss, 'The Game of Literature and Some Literary Games', *New Literary History*, 9.1 (Autumn 1977), 153–72 (p. 159).

72 Paddy Bullard, 'Describing Eighteenth-Century British Satire', in Paddy Bullard (ed.), *The Oxford Handbook of Eighteenth-Century Satire* (Oxford: Oxford University Press, 2019), 1–22 (2).

73 Robert W. Jones, '*Notes on The Camp*: women, effeminacy and the military in late eighteenth-century literature', *Textual Practice*, 11.3 (1997), 463–73 (p. 465).

74 Roy, *Letters*, II: p. 260; Kinsley, *Poems*, II: p. 770.

75 Richard M. Ward, *Print Culture, Crime and Justice in 18th-Century London* (London: Bloomsbury, 2014), p. 10.

76 *Gentleman's Magazine*, 65 (April 1789), 375.

77 Francis Russell Hart, 'Limits of the Gothic: The Scottish Example', *Studies in Eighteenth Century Culture*, 3 (1974), 137–53 (p. 141).

78 Carol Margaret Davison and Monica Germanà, 'Borderlands of Identity and the Aesthetics of Disjuncture', in Davison and Germanà (eds), *Scottish Gothic* (Edinburgh: Edinburgh University Press, 2017), p. 3.

79 Davison and Germanà, p. 5.

80 Ian Duncan et al., 'Introduction', in Leith Davis, Ian Duncan, and Janet Sorensen (eds), *Scotland and the Borders of Romanticism* (Cambridge University Press, 2004), pp. 1–19; Katherine Haldane Grenier, *Tourism and Identity in Scotland, 1770–1914* (Farnham: Ashgate, 2005), pp. 135–36 (both cited by Davison and and Germanà, pp. 1–3).

81 The relation between the two poems is discussed more fully below, in annotations to Craik's text.

82 Angela Wright, 'Scottish Gothic', in Catherine Spooner and Emma McEvoy (eds), *The Routledge Companion to Gothic* (London: Routledge, 2007), pp. 76–86 (p. 76).

83 Adriana Craciun, 'The New Cordays', in Craciun and Lokke (eds), *Rebellious Hearts* (2001), p. 194.

84 Ibid., p. 214.

85 John D. Niles and Eleanor R. Long, 'Context and Loss in Scottish Ballad Tradition', *Western Folklore*, 45.2 (2006), 83–109 (p. 92).

86 Craciun, 'The New Cordays', p. 197.

87 In 'To Sir W. G.: Baronet' (1782), Craik writes: 'No empty rank, nor riches, e'er / Shall make me Hymen's fetters bear.— ' (ll. 43–44); and, in 'To a Gentleman' (1782) she alludes to the scene in Shakespeare's *The Merchant of Venice* in which Bassanio must choose correctly between a gold, silver, and lead casket in order to win Portia's heart and the right to wed. He correctly rejects the gold and silver (ll. 57–58).

88 Craciun, 'The New Cordays', p. 194.

89 For Craik's perspective on convents as sites of seclusion or safety, cf. Craciun, 'The New Cordays', p. 213.

90 *Sale of Books belonged* [sic] *to the late J. G. H. Starke, J. P., Troqueer, Dumfries* (Dowell's Rooms, Edinburgh, Nov. 1908), lot 1110; for Dowell's file copy, see National Library of Scotland, NLS Acc. 7603/173, and cf. E. W. H. Meyerstein's notes in the Beinecke provenance file. We are grateful to Dr Ralph McLean of the National Library of Scotland for checking the Dowell's auction records for us.

91 E. L. G. Stones, 'George Neilson (1858–1923): memoir', *Miscellany One, Stair Society*, 26 (Edinburgh: for the Stair Society, 1971), 1–10; D. B. Smith, revised Hector L. MacQueen, 'Neilson, George (1858–1923)', in *ODNB* (2004).

92 Neilson also notes a short poem identified by J. C. Ewing as in the hand of Robert Riddell.

93 Chris Rollie, in 'A Monody on the Fatal 29th December, 1789: A Rediscovered Poem by Burns', *Burns Chronicle*, 110 (1998), 62–69,

put forward a case (based on Neilson's newspaper article) for Burns's authorship, listing parallels in phrasing with his known poems, and suggesting that the poem commemorated a coach upset after visit to the Dumfries theatre by Provost David Staig and his daughters.

94 Inviting the Walter Riddells may have been a polite but unrealistic response to rumours of their imminent arrival; Maria was still in London in August 1791, when her daughter was born, and even after the couple moved up to Dumfriesshire later in the year, they stayed initially with the Robert Riddells at Friar's Carse, not at Goldielea: see James Mackay, *RB: A Biography of Robert Burns* (Edinburgh: Mainstream, 1992), pp. 493–94.

95 Arnott appends Craik's own explanatory footnote, summarised above: ' "'Tis all for the best," said Mr H—— when the late Captain Riddell of Friars' Carse expostulated with him on certain *existing* circumstances; "'Tis all for the best," re-echoed the *Committee* of *Ways* and *Means*, and *for once* I completely *agree* with them.' Since Craik left Arbigland in February 1792, and Robert Riddell did not die till 1794, two years later, either the footnote, or the poem itself, was written significantly later than the incident it describes.

96 For the scale of Lane's enterprise, see Dorothy Blakey, *The Minerva Press, 1790–1820* (London: Oxford University Press for the Bibliographical Society, 1939).

97 See, e.g., Elizabeth Neiman, *Minerva's Gothic: The Politics and Poetics of Romantic Exchange, 1780–1820* (Cardiff: University of Wales Press, 2019).

98 *Cumberland Pacquet, and Ware's Whitehaven Advertiser*, 3 December 1821, p. 4.

99 Christopher A. Whatley, *Immortal Memory: Burns and the Scottish People* (Edinburgh: John Donald, 2016), pp. 26–27; James A. Mackay, *Burnsiana* (Ayr: Alloway Publishing, 1988), pp. 31–32.

100 James Gibson, *The Bibliography of Robert Burns* (Kilmarnock: James M'Kie, 1881), pp. 322–323.

101 *The Star* (London), 5 September 1815, p. 4; this may not have been the first or only newspaper appearance of the poem.

102 William Parson and William White, *History, Directory and Gazetteer of the Counties of Cumberland and Westmoreland* (Leeds: Edward Baines for William White, 1829), pp. 296, 338.

103 Listed Building, Grade II, 1977 (English Heritage Legacy ID: 71851). After Craik's death, it remained briefly a private residence, for Miss Watson, but then became a girls' school; Flimby Lodge and the remaining estate was sold in 1851 to the Earl of Lonsdale (see *Illustrated London News*, 15 February 1851, p. 131). From the 1880s into the early twentieth century it housed children and a school for the Cockermouth Union Workhouse (see *16th Annual Report of the Local Government Board 1886–1887* [C 5131], London: H.M.S.O.,

1887, p. 310). By 1977 it was derelict, and it is not described in either edition of the Pevsner guides (Pevsner 1967, Hyde 2010).

104 *Farmer's Magazine* 12 (1811), pp. 161–62. The Flimby Craik household when Helen Craik first lived there comprised, in order of their deaths, Ann Elizabeth (Nancy) Craik, b. 1720, who died in January 1803; James Craik, b. 1715, who died in December 1803; Margery Craik Neilson, b. 1723, whose husband Capt. William Neilson had died in 1766, and who herself died in 1807; and Barbara Craik, b. 1717, who died in 1809: see 'Bishop's Transcripts, Flimby Parish, 1713–1812', at: www.waughfamily.ca/Bell/OPR/OPR_Flimby1713-1812.pdf (accessed April 15, 2023). James Craik made new wills in 1793 and 1796, which included a bequest to Craik of four hundred pounds, but the bulk of his estate went to his sisters, and Craik appears to have been the ultimate beneficiary: she was also executrix for her aunt Margery Neilson, and on Margery's death was also added as administrator of James Craik's residuary estate: see transcript of will of James Craik of Flimby, 27 June 1796, as proved 31 January 1804, with addendum dated 19 October 1807 transferring administration to Helen Craik: PROB 11/1403/281.

105 The land sold included 113 acres of mature timber, freehold in the land on which it stood, 'together with all the Minerals contained and under the Land: and Wood Land, which contains Seams of excellent Coal': *Cumberland Pacquet and Ware's Whitehaven Advertiser*, 14 October 1806, p. 1. Craik explained the slightly tortuous legal route by which she was able to inherit an estate initially limited to her grandfather Adam Craik's male line: see *Farmer's Magazine*, p. 162, and Craciun, in *Oxford Dictionary of National Biography* (2004). Douglas Hamilton Craik lived on at Arbigland till 1844; his first son died as an infant, his second son in 1824, and his remaining son and heir, John Hamilton Craik, though living till 1877, was unmarried and sold Arbigland in 1852.

106 See, e.g., *Cumberland Pacquet and Ware's Whitehaven Advertiser*, 12 April 1825, p. 1, when Craik was selling land 'lately staked out by the Enclosure Commissioners' containing 'valuable Seams of Coal'.

107 *Farmer's Magazine*, p. 162.

108 Samuel William Ryley, *The Itinerant in Scotland*, 3 vols (London: Sherwood, 1827), p. 290. Ryley's nine autobiographical volumes are notoriously cavalier with facts; he may have rewritten Craik's invitation letter to be more flattering, but the incident itself seems credible. Cf. Mark Sorrell, 'Ryley [formerly Romney], Samuel William (1759–1837)', in *ODNB* (2004): doi.org/10.1093/ref:odnb/24422. In August 1821, Robert Southey, then poet laureate and visiting friends in Maryport, also visited Flimby Lodge to dine with Miss Craik: see Ian Packer and Lynda Pratt (eds), *The Collected Letters of Robert Southey*, Part 6, letters 3711 and 3718, online at *Romantic Circles*: romantic-circles.org/editions/southey_letters/Part_Six/.

109 Ibid., p. 291.

110 Ibid., pp. 291–92.

111 Last will and testament of Helen Craik of Flimby, 6 May 1825, as proved by her executors, 10 November 1825: transcript in the National Archives, Kew, PROB 11/1705/149.

112 The inscription states that the tablet was 'erected by an affectionate and grateful relative', who remains unidentified, but suggests she kept her earlier literary accomplishments separate from her later extended family contacts.

113 *Dumfries Weekly Journal*, 21 June 1825. A brief notice in *The Star* (London), 20 June 1825, p. 4, omits mention of her writing. While at least two of two of Craik's novels were set in France, with French title-characters, this seems to be the only claim that she wrote books in French.

POEMS BY A LADY

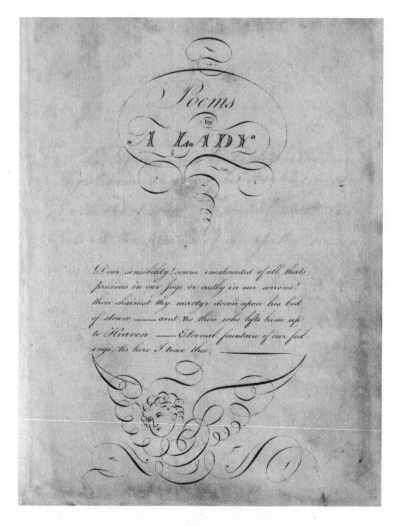

Fig. 2: Frontispiece to Helen Craik, *Poems by a Lady*
Courtesy of the James Marshall and Marie-Louise Osborn
Collection, Beinecke Rare Book and Manuscript Library,
Yale University.

POEMS BY A LADY

Dear sensibility! source inexhausted of all that's precious
in our Joys, or costly in our sorrows! thou chainest thy
martyr down upon his bed of straw—and 'tis thou who
lifts him up to Heaven—Eternal fountain of our feelings,
'tis here I trace thee.—

MS p. [i], unnumbered title-page.

Epigraph: from Laurence Sterne, *A Sentimental Journey through France and Italy*, by Mr Yorick, vol. II, 2nd ed. (London: for T. Becket and P. A. De Hondt, 1768), p. 181.

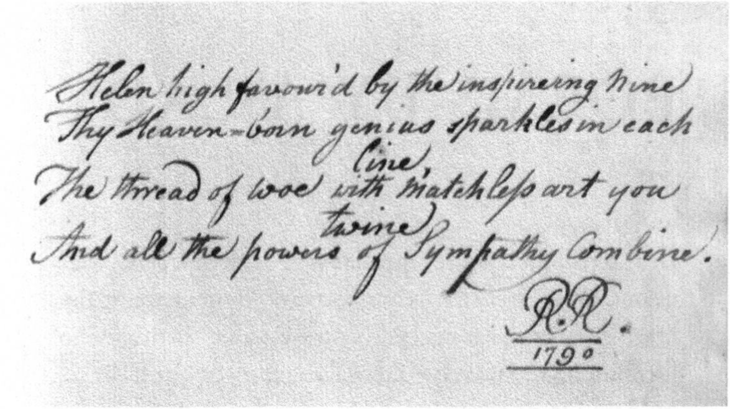

Helen high favour'd by the inspiring Nine
Thy Heaven-born genius sparkles in each
        line,
The thread of woe with matchless art you
            twine,
And all the powers of Sympathy Combine.
                            R.R.
                        1790

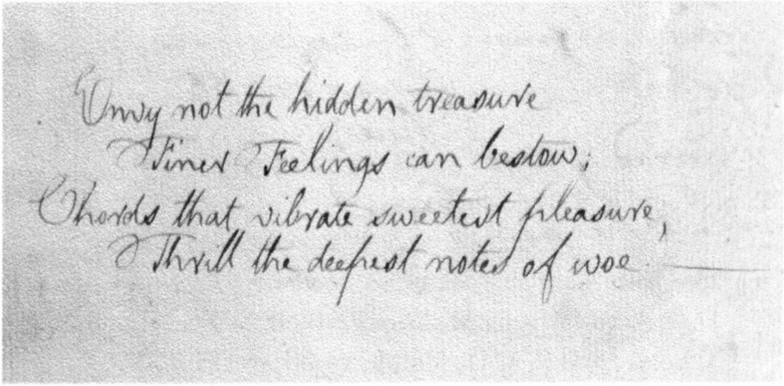

Envy not the hidden treasure
    Finer Feelings can bestow;
Chords that vibrate sweetest pleasure,
    Thrill the deepest notes of woe. ——

Fig. 3: Prefatory Verses in the hands of Robert Riddell
and Robert Burns, from Helen Craik, *Poems by a Lady*
Courtesy of the Beinecke Library, Yale University

Helen high favour'd by the inspiring Nine
Thy Heaven-born genius sparkles in each line,
The thread of woe with matchless art you twine
And all the powers of Sympathy Combine.

R. R.

1790

Envy not the hidden treasure
 Finer Feelings can bestow;
Chords that vibrate sweetest pleasure,
 Thrill the deepest notes of woe—

MS pp. [iii]–[iv]. These two items appear on the recto and verso of an unnumbered preliminary leaf of the Beinecke MS, the recto with lines to Helen Craik by Captain Robert Riddell, for whom the notebook was created and bound, so presumably before binding, and the verso with the lines 'Envy not', unsigned but in the hand of Robert Burns, perhaps added after the book was bound, to the conveniently blank page.

Envy not the hidden treasure: these four lines are in Burns's hand
 and were later used as stanza 4, ll. 9–12, in Burns's song,
 'Sensibility how charming'; the early text here was also sent
 to Mrs Dunlop on 9 July 1790 (*Letters*, II: 33), but revised
 before inclusion in song 329, in *Scots Musical Museum*, IV
 (1792). See also Burns's letter to Clarinda (Agnes McLehose),
 15 December 1791 (*Letters*, II: 123–24), Kinsley, I: 546, and
 Pittock, *OERB*, III: 111–12

TO CAPTAIN RIDDELL

This dedicatory poem addressed to Robert Riddell of Glenriddell (1755–1794) allows Craik to express conventional modesty about her abilities as a poet and to paint a convincing self-portrait of the circumstances and local setting in which she wrote her poetry. It was at Riddell's home at Friar's Carse, on the Nith north of Dumfries, that Craik first met Robert Burns, then living nearby on his farm at Ellisland. The dedication poem makes clear that Craik had written this manuscript fair copy of her poems at Riddell's request (l. 18), and that she expected him to show it to Burns (ll. 15–16), as Burns's letter to Craik on 9 August 1790 (*Letters*, II: 46–47) indicates Riddell had indeed done.

On Solway's Banks a humble Muse
Let Fancy's pow'r prevail,
And oft along the winding Beach
Compos'd some artless tale.—

5   —Oft wou'd she by the gliding Wave,
Her idle thoughts rehearse
But merit ne'er presum'd to claim,
Nor dreamt they rose to verse.—

—As sad or cheerful prospects shone
10   Unbidden came the rhyme,
No flatt'ring hopes of Fame in view
But just to *pass the time.*—

—Tho partial Friends wou'd sometimes smile
And think the page might do,
15   Yet much she fears the judging eye
Of Coila's Bard and you.—

¶

  —Alone from Gratitude you know
  The thoughtless promise came;
  Which may my humble Muse subject
20 To bold presumptuous name.—

  —O! then indulgent view the Lines
  Which trembling I impart
  They reach not to the Critic's head
  Nor rise above the heart.—

MS pp. 1–2.

1–4. **Solway's banks . . . beach:** Craik's home at Arbigland House, fourteen miles south of Dumfries, is about a mile from the shore of the Solway Firth. Craik uses similar lines to open a second set of dedicatory verses to Riddell, introducing her poem 'The Maid of Enterkin' (pp. 74–75 below).

16. **Coila's Bard:** Robert Burns. Coila, the tutelary spirit or muse of central Ayrshire, appears to Burns in his poem 'The Vision'.

18. **thoughtless promise:** Craik's promise to Riddell to make this fair copy manuscript for him.

LINES WRITTEN AT SEA BY THE LATE QUEEN OF DENMARK DURING HER PASSAGE TO STADE—1772

The tragic history of Queen Caroline Matilda of Denmark (1751–1775) seems to be the earliest of Craik's dramatic monologues treating survivor-guilt. Several of these monologues are about a relationship that has been broken by the murder of the survivor's presumed lover. In 1766, Queen Caroline, the youngest sister of the British king, King George III, then aged fifteen, had been married to King Christian VII of Denmark (1749–1808), and on her arrival in Denmark she was welcomed by rapturous crowds. Given Christian's mental instability, alcoholism, promiscuity, and violence, the marriage was tenuous from the start, though Caroline had two children, Frederick (1768–1839, later King Frederick V), and Louise Augusta (1771–1843). Increasingly, Christian's German-born physician Johann Friedrich Struensee (1737–1772), a proponent of Enlightenment ideas advocating the modernisation of Denmark's absolutist government, became the major influence in the marriage as well as in political affairs, and following a coup against his influence on January 1772, led by the Queen Dowager, Caroline and Struensee were accused of being lovers; her infant daughter, though she had been baptised as legitimate, was rumoured to be Struensee's child. Struensee, and his political ally Enevold Brandt, were interrogated, tortured, and brutally executed (publicly beheaded, drawn, and quartered). Only British political pressure and negotiation allowed Caroline herself to leave Denmark for exile at Celle (or Zelle), in the small German state of Lower Saxony. She had to leave her children behind, and she died in 1775, aged only twenty-four. In a short poem in the Neilson manuscript (Appendix II), Craik mentions Matilda when using Zelle for the second word in a charade on Dalzell.

Given its prominence as the first full item in Craik's manuscript, there seems no reason to doubt her authorship, but, bizarrely, the poem was first published as having been written by Queen Caroline herself. A partial copy of this poem (lines 1–39 only) 'written as if copied in haste, in the hand of an imperfectly educated person' was found after his death among the papers of Sir Robert Keith, the British representative in Copenhagen at the time of the Queen's exile, and was included in Mrs Gillespie Smyth (ed.), *Memoirs and Correspondence (Official and Familiar) of Sir Robert Murray Keith, K. B.*, 2 vols (London: Colburn, 1849), I: 299–300. While punctuation differs from Craik's own manuscript, there are few substantive variants (noted below as *Smyth*). After leaving Denmark, Keith became British envoy in Vienna, but he had inherited an estate in Scotland at Murrayshall, Newlands, Peeblesshire (for which he was also M.P.). There seems, however, to be no record of direct contact between Keith and the Craik family. Mrs Smyth commented that, apart from Keith preserving it, 'no other clue to its authenticity can be given' (p. 300). Cf. also Matthew Hall, *The Royal Princesses of England* (London: Routledge, 1858), pp. 203–04; and Sir C. F. Lascelles Wraxall, Bt., *Life and Times of Her Majesty Caroline Matilda, Queen of Denmark*, 3 vols (London: W. H. Allen, 1864), III, pp. 154–55.

Craik does not indicate her source for Caroline's story, but it was widely covered in British newspapers and periodicals, usually with a strongly pro-Caroline perspective, both at the time of the coup and exile, and after Caroline's death: see, e.g. in Scottish papers: *Caledonian Mercury*, 27 January 1772; 5 February 1772; 8 February 1772; 10 February 1772; 12 February 1772; 15 February 1772; 17 February 1772, and many more; *Caledonian Mercury*, 8 June 1772 (reprinting on its front page Christian Rothes's pro-Caroline pamphlet *The Real Views and Political System of the Regency of Denmark*); *Caledonian Mercury*, 24 May 1775; and *Scots Magazine*, 34 (January 1772), 42–45; 'The late Transactions in Denmark Explained', *Scots Magazine*, 34 (February-March 1772), 60–62, 118–120; Ibid., pp. 98–100; *Scots Magazine*, 34 (March 1772), 160–63; 'Affairs in Denmark', *Scots Magazine*, 34 (April 1772), 212–15; *Scots*

Magazine, 34 (May 1772), 257–60, with an account of the executions; *Scots Magazine*, 34 (June 1772), 325–27. Several articles in the *Scots Magazine* also appeared in the *Gentleman's Magazine*, in London, but note also: 'Junius on the Imprisonment of the Queen of Denmark', *Gentleman's Magazine*, 42 (February 1772), 130–33; 'On the barbarous treatment of the Queen of Denmark', *Gentleman's Magazine*, 42 (May 1772), 221; and 'Letter: Character of the late Queen of Denmark', *Gentleman's Magazine*, 45 (July 1775), 320–22.

Craik was not the first to try a poem on the subject: see *The Vindication of Innocence: an Elegiac Poem. Sacred to the memory of Her Majesty Caroline Matilda, late Queen of Denmark* (London: Bew, 1775). For a sympathetic modern summary of the story, see Henry L. Fulton's note in his *Dr. John Moore, 1729–1802* (Newark, DE: University of Delaware Press, 2018), p. 307, n. 55; or, more fully, Hester W. Chapman, *Caroline Matilda, Queen of Denmark* (New York: Coward McCann and Geoghegan, 1971).

———————

—*Le genre humain serait trop malheureux, s'il etait au foi commun de commettre de choses atraces, que de les croire*—

    —At length from Sceptr'd Care and deadly State,
    From galling Censure and ill-omen'd hate,
    From the vain Grandeur where I lately shone
    From Cronsborg's Prison, and from Denmark's
           Throne
5   I go———
    Here fatal Greatness thy delusion ends,
    A humbler lot the closing scene attends.—

    —Denmark farewell!—a long, a last adieu!
    Thy less'ning Prospects *now* recede from view;—

10 No ling'ring look an ill-star'd Crown deplores,
　　Well pleas'd I quit thy sanguinary shores
　　Thy shores where victims doom'd to state and me
　　Fell hapless Brandt and murder'd Struensee!—
　　Thy shores, where ah! in adverse hour I came,
15 To me the Grave of happiness and fame.—
　　—Alas! How diff'rent then my Vessel lay!
　　What crowds of Flatt'rers hasten'd to obey!
　　What numbers flew to hail the rising Sun!
　　'How few now bend to that whose course is
　　　　run'!—
20 —By Fate depriv'd of Fortune's fleeting train,
　　Now 'all th' oblig'd desert, and all the vain.'—
　　—But conscious worth that Censure can controul,
　　Shall, 'gainst her charges arm my steady soul,
　　Shall teach the guiltless mind alike to bear
25 The smiles of Pleasure, or the frowns of Care.—

　　—Denmark farewell!—for thee no sighs depart,
　　But Love maternal rends my bursting heart;—
　　Oh Cronsborg's Tower where my poor Infant lies,
　　Why—why so soon recede you from my eyes!
30 Yet stay!—ah me!—nor hope nor pray'r avails,
　　For ever hence exil'd Matilda sails!—
　　—Keith form'd to smooth the path affliction treads,
　　And dry the tear that friendless sorrow sheds,
　　Oh! gen'rous Keith protect their helpless state,
35 And save my Infants from impending fate,
　　Far, far from deadly pomp each thought remove,
　　And as to me their guardian Angel prove.—

　　—Yes Julia!—*now* superior force prevails,
　　And all my boasted resolution fails,
40 No aid from cold philosophy is near,
　　I feel alas! I am no Stoic *here*.—

What black revenge e'er keener pangs imprest
Then *thus* to tear my Infant from my breast!
Here fainting Nature owns thy pow'rful reign,
45   And all the Mother throbs thro' ev'ry vein.—

——O! dire effect of deep dissembling art,
Whose ready smile conceal'd a treach'rous heart,
Alas! In Friendship's garb destruction came,
And mean self-int'rest play'd her partial game,
50   Robb'd me of Peace,—of Fortune,—Fame and
        Friends,
And pour'd each curse that adverse fate attends.—

—But night's dark shades descend,—while o'er the
        Main
I turn to Elsineur,—but turn in vain!—
Like my lost state no trace remains behind
55   But what from mem'ry's torturing aid I find,—

—Good Heav'ns how dreadful!—from each
        comfort hurl'd,
Exil'd!—forlorn!—abandon'd by the World!—
My name the jest of Censure's busy tongue,
My fate detail'd for future times to shun!
60   While *fancied* errors shall the wise avail
'To point a moral, or adorn a tale.'—

—But tho to me no Pow'r attention pays,
Unmov'd 'tho Europe my sad fate surveys,
'Tho to condemn me, all the World agree,
65   And smiling Pleasure turns her face from me,—
Yet *Time* and *Chance* may clear the clouded scene,
And Censure yield to Pity's gentler theme;
Then those who *now* with philosophic eye
Stand from my falling fortunes cooly by,

70   Perhaps may find each deep imputed crime
     A *venial* error, free from form'd design,
     Too late may own, 'tho plung'd in mis'ry here,
     Injustice doom'd me to the lot severe,
     May wish in time my wrongs had been redresst
75   And blame th' oppressor, as they blam'd
     th' opprest.—

MS pp. 3–7.

Epigraph: 'Le genre humaine . . .': Voltaire, *Histoire du Siècle de Louis XIV*, chap. 26. Not in *Smyth*.

4. Cronsborg's Prison: Variant spelling of Kronborg, a castle located in the town of Helsingør, Denmark, used as a prison from 1739 until the 1900s.

9. Prospects . . . recede: Prospect . . . recedes *Smyth*.

13. hapless Brandt and murder'd Struensee!: Enevold Brandt (1738–1772) was a companion and favourite of King Christian VII as well as friend and political ally of Johann Friedrich Struensee (1737–1772), Queen Caroline's presumed lover and the King's Privy Counsellor. Struensee's orders were declared to have the same effect as if they were signed by the King, who was known to be mad. Both Brandt and Struensee were arrested along with Queen Caroline and both were executed on 28 April 1772.

19. 'How few now bend to that whose course is run': varied from 'Let others hail the rising sun / I bow to that whose course is run', in David Garrick, *Ode on the Death of Mr. Pelham* (1749), ll. 1–2; Garrick's Ode was included in Dodsley's *Collection* and other anthologies. No quotation marks in *Smyth*.

21. 'all th' oblig'd desert . . .': Alexander Pope, *Epistle to Robert, Earl of Oxford* (1721), l. 32.

25. frowns of Care: William Hayley, *The Triumphs of Temper* (1781) 1. 100: 'To turn the frowns of care to smiles of joy'.

27. **Love maternal:** At the time of her exile, Queen Caroline had two young children, Frederick VI (1768–1839) and Louise Augusta (1771–1843), the latter of whom was thought to be Johann Struensee's daughter, although she was officially accepted as the King's daughter. She never saw them again. **bursting:** bleeding *Smyth*.

28. **Cronsborg's Tower where my poor Infant lies:** Louise Augusta, who was still nursing, was imprisoned with her mother.

31. **hence exil'd:** exile'd hence *Smyth*.

32. **Keith:** Sir Robert Murray Keith of Murrayshall (c. 1730–1795), British diplomat and ambassador who was sent to Copenhagen on 24 June 1771. Keith is credited with negotiating Queen Caroline's exile by threatening a British naval bombardment of Copenhagen if she was harmed as well as convincing the Queen that there was no possibility of re-establishing herself in Denmark. Keith escorted her to Germany and then returned to London. As a reward for his efforts, George III knighted Keith and made him envoy-extraordinary and plenipotentiary to the imperial court in Vienna (*ODNB*). In an intercepted letter supposedly written by the Queen to Keith, she writes 'the thought of my reputation being tarnished, and my dear children abandoned to the mercy of a people unjustly prejudiced against the legitimacy of the birth, overwhelms me with the most piercing grief', begging him to continue to do 'all the good offices in [his] power'. ('Account of the late Revolution at Copenhagen', *Gentleman's Magazine*, June 1772, p. 360).

38. **Julia:** Juliana Maria of Brunswick-Wolfenbüttel-Bevern (1729–1796), Queen of Norway and Denmark between 1752 and 1796 and step-mother to King Christian VII of Denmark. On 17 January 1772 Juliana Maria convinced her step-son to sign the arrest order for Queen Caroline, Struensee, and Brandt, thereby bringing about the coup.

43. **tear my Infant from my breast:** while Frederick, then age three, had been taken from Caroline at the time of the coup, her second child, Louise, still remained with her. A favourite game had been for Caroline to put Louise down, pretend

to be leaving her, and then turn back and pick her up to hug. When Caroline was taken away by armed guard, to board a British ship for exile, Louise played this game repeatedly, till Caroline rushed from the room in tears. See Hester Chapman, *Caroline Matilda, Queen of Denmark* (1972), pp. 173–74, and cf. *Memoirs of an Unfortunate Queen* (1776), p. 98, and Wraxall (1864), III, p. 152.

53. **Elsineur**: Kronborg castle, immortalised as Elsinore in William Shakespeare's *Hamlet*.

61. **'To point a moral, or adorn a tale'**: Samuel Johnson, *The Vanity of Human Wishes* (1749), l. 222.

TO R: O: ESQ^R

This teasing application from two young ladies asking a very rich neighbour, visitor, or family friend to give them enough money to attract eligible suitors and husbands reads differently depending on the identity of the potential benefactor. In Craik's contents list, the poem is titled 'The Petition to R: O: Esq'. Margaret is unidentified; 'R. O.' was identified by Neilson (1924) as Richard Alexander Oswald (1771–1841), prospective future heir to the huge fortune and estates built up by his namesake and great-uncle, the tobacco-lord, slave-trader, and diplomat Richard Oswald (1705–1784). It was the elaborate funeral cortege of the elder Richard's widow Mary, Richard Alexander Oswald's aunt, in 1788, that had dislodged Burns from the inn at Sanquhar, provoking his satire on the family's pretensions (Kinsley, *Poems*, I: 446–47). Following the death of the first Richard, his nephew, George Oswald (1735–1819), also a tobacco-trader, had inherited the estates at Auchencruive in Ayrshire, and Cavens House, quite near Arbigland, in Dumfriesshire, so in the 1780s the younger Oswald was still only heir-apparent. In 1795 Robert Burns described him to a friend admiringly:

> did you ever, my dear Syme, meet with a man who owed more to the Divine Giver of all things than Mr Oswald? A fine fortune; a pleasing, engaging exterior; self-evident amiable dispositions, with an ingenious, upright mind, & that too informed much beyond the usual run of the young fellows of his rank and fortune.
>
> (*Letters*, II: 355)

But Richard Alexander Oswald had a long time to wait before he would fully inherit; indeed he would not even reach twenty-one till 1792, the year Helen Craik left Arbigland, and it was the following year before he married. If the verses were written after 1784, they can perhaps be read as two women in their late thirties teasing a teenaged boy about his future or family

wealth. It seems more likely, however, that the poem dates from
earlier in Craik's life, perhaps in the late 1760s or 1770s, when
it would have been quite appropriately addressed by the young
Helen Craik and her friend, then in their teens or early twenties,
to the first Richard Oswald, who died in 1784.

    —The humble petition of Margaret and Helen
    Who wish that their arguments may be
       prevailing.—

    Sheweth,—

    —That shou'd your Honour some surprise express
5   To find the modest cause of this address,
    Consider Sir but, as the times now go
    Sans money we must also be sans Beau,—
    And surely you'll allow it wou'd be hard
    From cash and flatt'ry both alike debarr'd,—
10   For Men, whate'er they proudly may advance,
    After harmonious Gold delight to dance,
    And Women,—so satiric Poets rhyme,
    Have no aversion to its tuneful chime.—
    —Then since both Sex its charms alike admire,
15   The one thing needful since they all desire,
    Wonder not Sir that we prefer this pray'r
    A poor ten Thousand of your wealth to share,
    An year's superfluous cash between us two
    Wou'd ne'er be felt by one so rich as you;—
20   But shou'd *this* pittance your great spirit deem
    Too small for *us* to ask, for *you* too mean.
    Why Sir the fault will rectify with ease;
    We'll take, ev'n,—Twenty Thousand if you please;
    The *largeness* of the gift we'll both excuse,
25   Nor any sum 'tho e'er so *much* refuse.—
    —From whence the wise may logically gather

That want of Prudence can be charg'd to neither.—
And since the World allows *each good* abounds
In the blest sum of twice ten Thousand pounds,
30 All must confess the genius truly great
Who *ev'ry virtue* can *at once create*,
That you this wond'rous character obtain,
We *here* have made the method short and plain,
From more impartial motives we advise,
35 For,—*as you see*,—self-int'rest we despise;
Your Good *alone* has all our study been,
We but the instruments to make it seen.
Then Sir, one smiling *yes* propitious say,
And your Petitioners as bound, shall pray.—

MS pp. 8–10. This poem was also in the Neilson MS (now missing); Neilson quotes only three lines (16–17, 23), with no substantive variants.

15. **one thing needful:** Satiric reuse of Christ's words to Mary and Martha in Luke 10. 42.

TO LADY W: M: CONSTABLE,
WITH A BIRD OF PARADISE

This poem is written in the voice of an exotic bird, forced to leave its homeland for exile in Scotland. The addressee, Lady Winifred Maxwell Constable (1736–1801), was the granddaughter of the 5th Earl of Nithsdale, who after the failed Jacobite rising in 1715 had escaped from the Tower of London to join the Jacobite court in exile in Rome. When Lady Winifred married William Constable (later Maxwell-Constable) they lived at his Yorkshire house, Everingham Hall. Following the death of her grandmother in 1776, she, as the only surviving daughter of the 6th Earl, had inherited the Maxwell ancestral home at Terregles (or Terreagles), in Kirkcudbrightshire, three miles outside Dumfries, so within visiting distance of the Craiks at Arbigland. Subsequently, the Maxwell-Constables rebuilt Terregles House as their main home, demolishing the original tower house. It is mysterious why Craik or the Craik family thought the Maxwell-Constables would want to be given a Bird of Paradise, and equally a matter of speculation how one was available in Kirkcudbrightshire for giving. Though she was fifteen years older than Craik, and, in Walter Scott's phrase, 'a singular old curmudgeon' (Kinsley, III: 1324), Lady Winifred and Craik clearly got on, and perhaps because of her Jacobite connections she was also an acquaintance and correspondent of Robert Burns; for Burns's song, 'Nithsdale's Welcome Home', on the Maxwell-Constables' return and the rebuilding of Terregles, for which Robert Riddell wrote the tune, see *Scots Musical Museum*, IV (1792), song 364; Kinsley, *Poems*, I: 500.

 —In distant Ceylon's spicey Isle
 A gay Inhabitant a while,
 I careless skimm'd the ambient air,
 And sipp'd the dewy fragrance there,

5   No higher scenes of bliss I knew,
For then I ne'er had heard of You.—

—But Lo!—Britannia's Sons appear,
And I must quit my native sphere,—
Borne far to cold inclement skies
10   Where Caledonia's hills arise,
There doom'd to serve a humble Maid,
Beneath yon gloomy mountain's shade,
—No more I sip the fragrant dew,
No more the painted Fly pursue;
15   Nor circling through the ambient air
Skim, on light wing, devoid of care.—

—But far from eastern regions torn
Where spicey sweets enrich the morn,
Where orient beams eternal play
20   Nor seasons feel the Sun's decay,
Condemn'd to shrink from ev'ry blast
My Form defaced, my beauty past,
Unseen,—unpity'd,—and unknown,
Ev'n Hopes last ling'ring prospect flow'n
25   I lonely wander'd round the shore
And trembling heard loud Boreas roar.—

—At length your presence chear'd the scene,
You came!—'twas Ceylon once again,
Gay Fancy rais'd its Fairy view,
30   When honour'd with applause from you,
Your approbation Helen heard,
And long'd to see her Bird prefer'd,
Well pleas'd she bid me take my flight
And lowly at your feet alight;
35   *There* all that was respectful say,
And her best wishes thus convey,—

¶

    —'Calm as our skies still flow your time,
    'Warm be your Friends as Ceylon's clime;
    'Weak prove each Foe that wou'd molest,
40   'The gentle province of your breast;—
    'Exhaustless as Potosi's Mine
    'May wealth and pleasure round you shine.—
    'May merit still your heart befriend;
    'May to your wishes Heav'n attend;
45   'And when,—tho late,—you close your eyes
    'Awake—a Bird of Paradise.'—

MS pp. 11–12, with a passage for insertion written on p. 10. In Craik's contents list, the poem is titled 'The Bird of Paradise to Lady W: C:'. Neilson mentions the poem as being in the Neilson MS, but does not give any extracts.

1. **Ceylon's spicey Isle:** When Craik was writing, Ceylon (Sri Lanka), was still under the colonial control of the Dutch; it passed to the British in 1796. Ceylon was also known as the 'Spicey Isle', because of cinnamon, which was native to the island, along with black pepper, cloves, nutmeg, and mace.

13–26. **No more I sip:** these lines appear in the Beinecke MS on the facing page, with an asterisked note: '*Additional Lines to be inserted at the mark in the Bird of Paradise.—'.

14. **the painted Fly:** i.e. butterfly.

23. **Unseen,—unpity'd,—and unknown:** Cf. William Diaper, 'would have lov'd unpity'd and unknown', in *Nereides* (London: Silver, 1712), p. 25; James Beattie, 'dropped into the grave, unpitied and unknown', in *The Minstrel*, I (London: Dilly, 1771), p. 1; Burns, 'Love's veriest wretch, unseen, unknown', in 'Farewell thou stream' (1793, after Craik: Kinsley, II: 684).

26. **Boreas:** God of the north wind.

41. **Potosi's Mine:** Located in Potosi, South America's most elevated town at four thousand metres above sea level, the mine is the richest silver mine in Bolivia and has been in operation since 1546. Burns references it in 'The Vision', in his *Poems* (1786), l. 270, as does Anna Letitia Barbauld in 'The Groans of the Tankard' in her *Poems* (1773), l. 54.

46. **Bird of Paradise:** Of three species, this is the greater Bird of Paradise, 'with feathers on the sides that are longer than the body, and two long bristly feathers in the tail', which feeds on butterflies and is found in large flocks in the Molucca Islands: see *Encyclopedia Britannica* (Edinburgh, 1771), II, pp. 454–55.

INTENDED TO HAVE BEEN SENT WITH
A NECK PIN WHICH WAS MADE WITH
THREE GOLDEN BALLS

This short poem, even if never actually sent, seems to be skilful self-protection against Craik's gift being misinterpreted by its recipient (specified as 'a Gentleman' in a variant title). Without knowing who the recipient was, there is no way of knowing if this was Craik's gentle let-down for a former suitor, or a pre-emptive strike against future possible embarrassment. Lines 1–6 recount the mythological tale in which, on the orders of Jupiter, Venus (goddess of love), Juno (goddess of marriage), and Minerva (goddess of wisdom) were taken to the top of Mount Ida so Paris of Troy could choose who of the three was the most beautiful, and give her the golden apple. He chose Venus, swayed by her promise to grant him Helen, subsequently leading to the Trojan War. The three golden balls on the pin have, of course, no connection or reference to the common shop sign for pawnbrokers.

   —When Venus on fam'd Ida's top
   The golden prize obtain'd,
   She promis'd Love, the Youth was caught,
   The Apple Venus gain'd.—

5   Tho giv'n for Love, with War and strife
   The gift made Nations groan,
   Mine free from Love as Wars alarms
   For Friendship comes alone.—

   Friendship alone is all I ask
10   The sole request I make,
   Then let this Trifle mem'ry guard
   And wear it for my sake.—

¶

    Hence shall Esteem superior shine,
    Its pow'r unrival'd be;
15 *One* ball for Love was only giv'n,
    For Friendship I give *three*.—

MS pp. 13–14. In Craik's contents list, the poem is titled 'Lines intended to have been sent to a Gentleman with a neck pin'.

1. **fam'd Ida's top**: in Greek mythology, Mount Ida, Crete's highest summit, is the mountain of the goddess Rhea and birthplace of Zeus.

THE FOLLOWING LINES ARE SUPPOSED TO BE WRITTEN BY MR HACKMAN WHEN UNDER SENTENCE OF DEATH FOR THE MURDER OF MISS REAY—1779—

This death-cell monologue is based on one of the most sensational and widely debated murders of Craik's young adulthood. On the evening of 7 April 1779 James Hackman (1752–1779), a lieutenant in the 68th Foot, murdered Martha Ray or Reay (c. 1742–1779), the long-time mistress of the Earl of Sandwich, whom the infatuated Hackman had been stalking. Though the exact relationship is somewhat uncertain, Hackman and Ray were thought to have become lovers after meeting at Sandwich's home at Hinchingbrooke in 1775, where Ray was living, but she repeatedly refused his proposals of marriage. The ODNB entry for Ray, however, dates their introduction earlier, in 1771. Their relationship broke down when Hackman's regiment was posted to Ireland. In 1776, Hackman resigned his commission and returned to England, ostensibly to enter the church, although he remained infatuated with Ray. Early in 1779, Hackman was rapidly ordained deacon on 24 February, ordained priest on 29 February, and then the next day on 1 March presented (appointed) to the vicarage of Wiveton, Norfolk. On 7 April, believing that Ray had taken on a new lover, Hackman followed her to Covent Garden Theatre where he saw her speaking with Lord Coleraine. He then lay in wait for the pair in the nearby Bedford Coffee house where he shot Ray by putting a pistol to her head, and then tried but failed to kill himself (*ODNB, s.v.* Hackman). At first Hackman admitted the crime, but was later persuaded to plead innocent; he was tried, convicted and sentenced on 16 April, and hanged three days later on 19 April.

Hackman's case, and the letters he had written to Ray and to a friend about his planned murder-suicide, got wide newspaper coverage, e.g. in the *Caledonian Mercury* (14 and 17 April 1779), as well as in London papers, and there were also several contemporary separately published accounts. Some contemporaries believed Hackman had been insane at the time of the murder. Others blamed his reading of Goethe's suicide novel, *The Sorrows of Werther* (1774; English translation, 1779).

James Boswell visited Hackman in prison and may have assisted him with the statement Hackman read at his trial. Boswell also wrote at least four articles related to the case which were published during April 1779 in the *St. James Chronicle* and the *Public Advertiser*, including a brief denial that he had himself attended Hackman's execution (Paul Tankard, *Facts and Inventions: Selections from the Journalism of James Boswell*, New Haven: Yale University Press, 2014, pp. 96, 100, 101).

The following year attention was revived when Sir Herbert Croft wrote an influential epistolary novel, sympathetic to Hackman, titled *Love and Madness: A Story Too True* (1780). For discussion of the Hackman case, and Croft's sympathetic treatment, see John Brewer, *A Sentimental Murder: Love and Madness in the Eighteenth Century* (London: HarperCollins, 2004); Maximilian E. Novak, 'Sex, Madness and Suicide in Sir Henry Croft's *Love and Madness*', in *Sex and Death in Eighteenth-Century Literature*, ed. Jolene Zigarovich (London: Routledge, 2013), pp. 165–82.

    —The curtain drops—the tragic scene is o'er
    A few short hours—and I shall breathe no more—
    By headstrong passion's ruling force undone
    Black infamy obscures my setting Sun.—
5   —A Murd'rer's name,—the bane of all my race,
    Reproach,—Contempt,—each species of disgrace
    Attend my steps,—Curse on the erring tube!—
    Wou'd I had died when fixt on death I stood!
    No longer *now* with warring thoughts at strife,
10   I *then* in peace had clos'd a wretch'd Life.—

¶

   —In peace!—who lov'd like me yet lov'd in vain
   In Heav'n nor Earth the Cherub must obtain!—
   Ye Souls that cool philosophy contain,
   Whose blood ne'er riots wild thro' passion's vein,
15   Who calmly yield to Reason's boasted light,
   By constitution negatively right,
   Say,—whence derive ye approbation's voice?
   Is *merit* yours who merely act from *choice!*—
   —Too oft Indiff'rence clad in Wisdom's guise
20   The Stoic's vaunted fortitude supplies,
   Acquires the name of virtues ne'er possest,
   And steels with Apathy th' unfeeling breast.—
   —Had fate ordain'd me passions dull as these,
   Insipid Life perhaps had clos'd in ease;—
25   No fell revenge Humanity disarm'd,
   Nor restless Jealousy my breast alarm'd,—
   Receiv'd alike the good or ill that came,
   Nor knew what *Feeling* meant,—unless by name,—
   Had calmly thought—no stubborn passion's slave,
30   No mental wound that festers to the Grave;
   Unstain'd with crimes,—at length resign'd my
         breath,
   In Life's meridian doom'd no shameful death.—

   —Now change the prospect,—turn where passion
         reigns,
   See my torn bosom Reason's force disdains!—
35   There:—drench'd in blood my more than Angel lies,
   To hopeless Love I made the sacrifice!—
   —No longer *now* absorb'd in proud disdain
   She'll bless her Sandwich, and deride my pain,—
   While Life in streams of gore for ever flies,
40   No jealous fears from icy Death can rise;
   With pleasure in the Grave her charms I see,
   There Sandwich is no *more* belov'd than me.—

¶

—Extatic thought!—this gives a pause to pain!
Revenge at least if nothing more I gain!—
45   Revenge on whom?—myself—already curst,
Of bloody villains most supremely worst!—
—Maria dead!—what—ha!—by Hackman slain!
From the wild conflict of a jarring brain
Defend me Heav'n!—ev'n at her still lov'd name
50   The blood runs cold,—it thrills thro all my frame.
Convulsion blunts a moment's dreadful pain,
Yet soon,—too soon,—reflection comes again.—

—Ye reas'ning tribe from erring passion free
That blame at ease the fatal deed and me,
55   Know ye who thus my conduct disapprove,
'Tis *more* than Death a rivalship in Love?—
A happy Rival!—Heav'ns!—what venom'd dart
Has pow'r *like this* to rend the human heart!—
—O ye unfeeling!—your rash thoughts restrain,
60   Ye know not, *cannot know*, what I sustain;
All other ills calm patience might endure,
But *this* extends beyond the reach of cure.—

—Not guilty plead!—O Death for ever blest
Come,—quickly come, and lay my head at rest,
65   Thy pangs are ease!—mistaken friends forbear,
The Bloody Hackman must not linger *here*.
The plea of Madness vainly ye advise,
From subterfuges mean like these he flies,—
So often wreck'd on Disappointment's coast,
70   All taste for Life the hapless wretch has lost;
And sure 'tis time our woes shou'd finish here,
When crush'd with ills, beyond our strength to bear,
If then his pray'rs can any grace obtain
Not Life he begs,—but *quick* respite from pain.—

MS pp. 15–19. In Craik's contents list, the poem is titled 'Hackman's Lines'. Nielsen notes that the poem is contained in the Beinecke [Wood] manuscript but does not cite any lines.

7. **the erring tube!:** barrel of gun, Alexander Pope uses 'tube' to refer to a gun in *Windsor Forest*, l. 129: 'He lifts the tube, and levels with his eye' (*Poems*, ed. Butt, p. 109), as does Robert Burns in *Ode for General Washington's Birthday*, line 1: 'No Spartan tube, no Attick shell' (Kinsley, II: 771). Craik uses the term again in 'The R^t Honble: the Earl of Caithness to Miss D:', l. 59.

8. **Wou'd I had died:** After shooting Ray in the forehead, Hackman turned a second pistol on himself, but the ball grazed his forehead. He proceeded to beat himself with both pistols until he was restrained (*ODNB, s.v.* Hackman).

32. **Life's meridian:** the sun at midday, high point, as also used by Robert Burns in 'Written In Friars Carse Hermitage, on Nithside' (1788, second version, l. 16; Kinsley, I: p. 416), and in Craik's 'Written by Charlotte at Werter's Grave', l. 61.

38. **She'll bless her Sandwich:** John Montagu (1718–1792), the fourth earl of Sandwich who is also credited with inventing the sandwich to provide convenient food at the gaming table. Montagu had long been separated from his wife, who had been declared insane, and he took Ray as his mistress c. 1761. They lived together for eighteen years and had nine children, five of whom survived into adulthood (*ODNB, s.v.* Ray, Montagu). Upon hearing of Ray's murder Montagu was reported to have 'wept exceedingly' (*Morning Post*, 9 April 1779).

47. **Maria dead:** Martha Ray.

63. **Not guilty:** Craik's manuscript has an asterisked footnote 'Mr Hackman's friends desired him to plead *not* guilty—'. Despite his initial decision to plead guilty, Hackman entered a not guilty plea because he would not be 'accessory to a second peril of my life' and 'the justice of my country ought to be satisfied by suffering my offence to be proved'. At his trial,

Hackman read a letter possibly written by James Boswell, in which he attributes his act to 'a momentary phrensy [which] overcame me, and induced me to commit the deed I now deplore' (*ODNB, s.v.* Hackman).

TO MR D: FROM GOAT WHEY QUARTERS

This verse-letter gives Craik's satirical complaint about the isolation of life at Arbigland and New Abbey ('Goat-Whey Quarters'), five miles from Arbigland, where the chief topic of conversation was agricultural improvement. The poem seems to date from 1778, during the illness of her sister Elizabeth or Betty. Goat's whey was thought to remedy many physical ailments (see, e.g., the *Medical Museum*, 3 (1764), 370). In a letter addressed to Dr William Cullen and dated 4 August 1778, William Craik reports that 'the Goats whey', which he hoped 'would have remedied' his daughter Betty's 'declining state of health' had 'no sensible good effects from her using it' and that she had attended 'the season of the Whey at a place about five miles from this', i.e. at New Abbey (letter from *The Cullen Project*: cullenproject. ac.uk/docs/1541/).

While the addressee of this poem is unidentified, Craik also wrote 'A Charade' addressed to Mr D. and other poems addressed 'To Lady E: D:' and 'To Miss D—'. In the latter poem, Craik also laments her isolation at Arbigland, complaining that she was kept from going into Dumfries for social gatherings because her father preferred to spend money on improving the estate.

     O—Excil'd by Fate's severe decrees
     To barren Sands and boist'rous Seas,
     Where gloomy Criffel bleakly stands,
     And storms descending drench the Lands;
5   Where whistling Boreas stuns the ears,
     With all the musick of the Spheres,
     And choice discourse, each tedious day
     Consists of Barley, Oats, and Hay,—
     —On themes so bright I strove in vain
10   Some sparkling knowledge to obtain,—
     But under adverse planets born,
     No earthly skill have I in Corn;

—Nay,—what you'll say is ten times worse
Scarce know a Farmer from his horse,
15   And therefor seiz'd the first warm weather
To bid them all adieu together.—

—But changing place is not the thing,
Contentment we must likeways bring.—
The same dull scene appears to view,
20   Unless dispel'd by friends like you;—
'Twas long before the secret found,
I sought the smiling Nymph around,—
Surpris'd she came not to my aid,
I all the blame on fancy laid;
25   Till Phœbus whisper'd in my ear
'*Go ask my fav'rite * * * * * here*'.—

—Obedient I the task receive,
And, as he bids, your presence crave.—
—Tho few inducements may appear,
30   Tho small the House, and mean the chear,
Yet, will we use our utmost pow'r
To make you spend a happy hour,
And, if *you'll come*, with thanks profound
Confess *Contentment* beams around.—

MS pp. 20–21. In Craik's contents list, the poem is titled 'To Mr D: from Newabbey'. This may be the poem Neilson mentions as in his manuscript, without quoting, titled 'To a Gentleman—from Newabbey—' (Neilson: 72).

3. **Criffel:** The most prominent hill on the north side of the Solway, in Kirkcudbrightshire, some two-and-a-half miles south of New Abbey.

5. **Boreas:** god of the north wind.
25. **Phœbus:** god of the Sun.
26. Mr D., the unnamed 'fav'rite', must have a name with two syllables, and probably five letters.

TO A LADY

Craik introduces the topic of this unpleasant little poem, alternatively titled 'The Stick', as having been proposed by the addressee, and it might perhaps best be viewed as simply a bravura exercise in verse-making to order. How she develops it, though, with the focus on violence and control, notably in manners, religion, and marriage, must be attributed to Craik, and the fascination with wife-beating in Russia and her certainty that 'our British Dames' would quickly take back control, is notable. Nonetheless, the wordplay is disquieting, and, simply as free association on a given topic, the poem seems curiously lopsided: there are, for instance, no lines on sticks as the support of the elderly or disabled, or as an aid to the shepherd herding sheep, or as the material for a warming fire.

    —The whim was strange your fancy hit
    To ask for lines upon a Stick,—
    —It must be own'd the subject's new
    And first propos'd alone by you,—
5   But tho it's barren, some may cry,
    Yet the assertion I deny,
    As,—ere I now conclude this rhyme,
    I hope to shew in proper time.—

    —Thro' Life good manners to produce
10   A stick has been of sovereign use,—
    The proud to bend,—the rude to tame,
    Have often trembl'd at its name;
    But shou'd its name be found in vain,
    Itself applied will credit gain.—

15   —Ev'n our Religion owns its aid,
    For converts in the Highlands made,
    A Chief applied it to his Clan,

And Protestants made ev'ry man:
Their conscience critically hit,
20   And all *bow'd down* before the Stick.—

—In Russia,—as its Hist'ry shows,
The Fair are emulous of blows,
And think of *Love* the surest test
What—we wou'd call a *serious* jest.—
25   —There Sticks are to the Bridegroom sent
As means of future compliment,—
—All-pow'rful gift in Russia stay,
For shou'dst thou *hither* find thy way,
Our British Dames might raise the Cane,
30   And quickly pay the debt again.—

—Ev'n Heros us'd to warlike arms
Find in the *Staff* a thousand charms.
And, 'tho they scorn the threaten'd Cane,
Adore it by the *other* name.—
35   —Still might this copious subject flow,
But need I more its merits show?—
—Religion, Manners, Marriage o'er,
Are proofs sufficient of its pow'r,
And ev'ry *feeling* suff'rer says
It has the *most convincing* ways.—

MS pp. 22–24. In Craik's contents list, the poem is titled 'The Stick'.

15–20. In *A Journey to the Western Islands of Scotland* (1775) Samuel
Johnson writes of 'the religion of the Yellow Stick'. On the
Island of Rum the inhabitants, comprising fifty-eight families,
remained Catholic despite the laird Maclean's Protestantism.
According to Johnson, 'one Sunday, as they were going to mass

under the conduct of their patroness, Maclean [the Laird] met them on the way, gave one of them a blow on the head with a yellow stick, I suppose a cane, for which the Earse [Irish/ Highlanders] had no name, and drove them to the kirk, from which they have never since departed' (103).

21–27. 'Except at Petersburg and Moscow, married women are seldom to be seen. Instead of a ring, they are married with a whip and a bundle of rods. Hence another obstacle to social commerce': *Scots Magazine*, 34, (January 1772), 17.

TO A GENTLEMAN

This is the first of two linked poems written in 1782 to an unnamed gentleman, who seems to have called at Arbigland and left his card while Craik was out at church. The date comes on the second poem in the pair, written two weeks after the first, and also titled 'To a Gentleman' (see pp. 130–33 below). While the visitor remains unidentified, Craik's teasing tone suggests he was a previous admirer or even a rejected suitor, or a presumed suitor who had been already committed to someone else, and who had now called to repair the friendship, either to renew his attentions, or to explain why he had disappeared. He had left a note on his card that 'the Heart shou'd never change'. The bone of contention between them seems to have been about one or the other objecting to the excessive compliments voiced by the other one. Craik briskly reports that the morning's sermon had been about retaliation, on which see the note to line 9 below.

———————————

    —'Twas Sunday,—long the Bell had rung,
    The Church was full, the pray'r begun,
    Resolv'd instruction to obtain
    I hasten'd too, my seat to gain;
5   And firmly fixt whate'er seem'd good
    To put in practice,—*when* I *cou'd.*—
    —The subject was *retaliation*,
    A fav'rite with the whole creation,
    Peruse Saint Paul,—the text you'll see,
10   *'This do* in *memory of me.'*—

    —Returning Home your Card I find,
    The text came quickly to my mind,—
    —Intent to show the weight I lay
    On *what* our Saints and Parsons say:
15   Nay,—wishing too in such a cause
    T' explain how orthodox I was;

No fitter moment fate supplies,
My good resolves to realise,
And who shall say I am to blame?
20   The mandate from the scriptures came.—

—While you to Heathens have recourse
For aid, to give your flatt'ry force;
While Phœbus and Minerva bend
And on each line well pleas'd attend.—
25   —*Sheer compliments* you surely know,
Can only from *such* Patrons flow,—
Ideal Beings, *like your praise*,
That *fancy's* 'baseless fabricks' raise;
Form'd to delude the hapless mind
30   To syren praise like yours inclin'd.—

—But I who tread on firmer ground
And from Saint Paul assistance found,
To *truth* my claim may boldly lay,
And bid you credit *what* I say;
35   —*Too much* applause can I bestow?
The candid loudly answer *No!*—
Can falsehood from such causes come?
Ev'n unbelievers here are dumb,—
Then hush,—no more due praises shun,
40   Nor flattr'y give me in return;
Else what's sound principle in me,
In *you* will prove rank heresy.—

—But to the substance of your Card,
From whence, digressing, I have stray'd:—
45   —Most men wou'd think your system strange
Which says 'the *Heart shou'd never* change,'—
—*Revers'd* the case wou'd *truer* hold,
Some *few* examples might be told
All tending to demonstrate clear

50   What,—but I'll timely finish *here*,—
      Truths often may be hateful found,
      Man's Heart's too deep for me to sound.—

      —As to '*the tale you must unfold*',
      For pity's sake let it be told,—
55   Dismiss *Reserve*,—I hate the name,—
      From mean Suspicion first it came.—
      A *secret* Portia *we* can show,
      While Midas,—was a man you know.—

      —But—'a fourth page begun indeed!
60   'Heav'ns! *What* am I condemn'd to read'!—
      —The *hint's* in time,—no more I'll say,
      But quickly hasten to *obey*;
      Submission is *you know our* lot,
      And *man* takes care 'tis *not forgot*.
65   Yet ere I close this tedious strain,
      Of which, with truth, you may complain,
      While you confess, sans compliment,
      The Sunday's ev'ning rightly spent,
      Mine like the Parson's text shall be,
70   *This do* in memory of me.—

                      1782

MS pp. 25–29. In Craik's contents list, the poem is titled ''Twas Sunday—long the Bell had rung'. In a second poem also titled 'To a Gentleman' Craik laments not having yet received a response to this verse, see pp. 130–33. She dates the second portion of that poem June 18 [1782], suggesting that this first poem was penned some weeks before.

2. the pray'r: the opening or bidding prayer that began the Presbyterian service. Craik was arriving late.

4. **my seat to gain:** As late as the mid-seventeenth century, most Scottish parish kirks were devoid of seating, with the exception of pews that were set up by private individuals for their own use. Later, it became the obligation of heritors and town councils to provide seating for two-thirds of those who were twelve years and over: G. Hay, 'Scottish Post-Reformation Church Furniture', *Proceedings of the Society of Antiquaries of Scotland*, 88 (November 1954), 53. Until the late twentieth century, parishioners could rent their pews in the church, guaranteeing them a particular seat; rents were typically paid quarterly and the rate varied depending on the location, popularity of the minister, and the general demand for seats (Graeme Morton, *History of Everyday Life in Scotland, 1800–1900*, Edinburgh: Edinburgh University Press, 2010, p. 121).

9. **Peruse Saint Paul:** In Romans 12 Paul speaks against retaliation, exhorting his followers to 'Bless them which persecute you: bless, and curse not' (Romans 12. 14). The retaliation to which Craik refers here is her response to his correspondence.

10. **'*This do* in *memory of me*':** Not St Paul, but Christ's words at the Last Supper (Luke 22. 19), used in the communion service, here used satirically in asking the gentleman to write back.

11. **Card:** small card bearing a person's name, title, and rank that was left or presented on paying a visit (*OED*), inviting a visit in return. Conventionally, a newcomer to a district would leave a card first and would not expect to come back until receiving a card in response. Neilson notes that while '"card of invitation" was in full vogue from about 1770 . . . there are signs of its adaptation as a literary form or medium' (73).

23. **Phœbus:** Apollo, god of the sun, said to ward off evil.
    Minerva: Athena, goddess of wisdom.

28. **'baseless fabricks':** In Shakespeare's *The Tempest*, Prospero remarks on the 'baseless fabric of this vision' (IV.I.151). Craik uses the phrase in 'To Sir W. G.: Baronet', l. 13.

53. **'*the tale you must unfold*':** Craik's addressee has promised to give her some further confidential details from a local

scandal and she urges him not to hold back. The phrase echoes Shakespeare's *Hamlet* IV.5.5: 'Pity me not, but lend thy serious hearing to what I shall unfold'.

57–58. **Portia . . . Midas:** In Shakespeare's *The Merchant of Venice*, Portia's love interest, Bassanio, must choose correctly between a gold, silver, and lead casket in order to win her heart and the right to wed. He rejects the gold casket, stating 'therefore then, thou gaudy gold, / Hard food for Midas, I will none of thee', as well as the silver casket on the basis that silver is the metal of common coin, correctly choosing the lead casket, which contains a portrait and a poem written by Portia (III. ii.103–04).

59. **'a fourth page':** Craik is imagining her addressee's reaction to the length of the verse-letter she is writing.

70. *This do:* i.e. write back.

WRITTEN BY CHARLOTTE
AT WERTER'S GRAVE

Craik's poem is based on Johann Wolfgang von Goethe's wildly popular but controversial novel *The Sorrows of Young Werther* (1774). The novel recounts the love triangle between Charlotte (the speaker of the poem), her husband, Albert, and the romantic hero, the artist Werther. Werther had earlier fallen in love with Charlotte, returns to their home area to find her married, and is tormented by a love that she cannot now reciprocate. Though the novel was already known by reputation, the English translation by Richard Graves, *The Sorrows of Werter: A German Story Founded on Fact,* in two volumes (London: Dodsley, 1779), was widely excerpted and discussed in periodicals from its publication in late April 1779 onwards; see e.g. *Critical Review,* 47 (June 1779), 477; *London Review,* 10 (July 1779), 3–39; *Monthly Review,* 61 (July 1779), 74; *Town and Country Magazine,* 11 (August 1779), 437. The earliest Scottish mention seems to be an advertisement for the second edition in the *Caledonian Mercury,* 17 June 1780, 3.

Craik's poem picks up just as Goethe's novel has ended, after Werther has committed suicide with Albert's pistols, which he had asked to borrow for a journey and which Charlotte had reluctantly sent to him. Goethe pointedly writes 'I will say nothing of Albert's great distress, nor of the situation of Charlotte', and the last sentences of the novel are similarly reticent:

> In the night the body of Werter was buried in the place he had himself chosen. The Steward and his sons followed him to the grave. Albert was not able to do it. Charlotte's life was despaired of. The body was carried by labourers, and no priest attended (1779, II: 171–72).

Craik's poem takes up the story after that, with Charlotte visiting his grave; Craik sympathetically articulates Charlotte's remorse

over the suicide and her feelings about Werther and their affair.
As Maximilian Novak points out, early British commentary
blamed Werther's suicide on Charlotte, but by the 1780s, other
writers, including Charlotte Smith in her *Elegiac Sonnets* (1784),
were sympathetic to her: see Novak, 'Sex, Madness and Suicide
. . .', in Zigarovich (ed.), *Sex and Death in Eighteenth-Century
Literature* (London: Routledge, 2013), pp. 165–82 (p. 176).
Slightly later, another Scottish poet, Anne Bannerman (1765–
1829), would also use Goethe's story for a ten-sonnet sequence
in her *Poems* (Edinburgh: Mundell, 1800), pp. 99–108, but as a
third-person narrative tracking major stages in Goethe's novel,
not a soliloquy from Charlotte after Werter has died.

    —From a vain World to us replete with woe,
    From hopeless Love the bane of peace below,—
    From human laws for dire destruction giv'n,
    From black Despair, and ev'ry curse of Heav'n
5   I come,——
    O'er thy cold Grave a bursting heart I bend,
    And mourn thy premature,—thy fatal end!—
    —Here meditation plung'd in horror reigns,
    'Till madness almost rends the tortur'd brains!—
10   —Around *this* scene,—where e'er I turn my eyes,
    A thousand pangs from *recolection* rise;—
    Here first alas! by adverse fate inspir'd
    Thy hapless breast the deadly secret fir'd;—
    Wou'd dark oblivion had receiv'd the tale,
15   And wrapt my head in Death's eternal veil!
    Wou'd I had died with thee!—from Life's dull yoke
    Had slipt my neck,—and Nature's bondage broke!—
    Releas'd the suff'ring Soul from sordid day,
    And firmly follow'd *where* you led the way.—

20   —Sure the cool wise in vain each pow'r employs
    That poignant mis'ry's last recource destroys!—

In vain they argue,—vainly they arraign,
Alas! If destin'd we shou'd here remain,
Less woe less feeling were of course bestow'd;
25 *More fortitude* at least to bear the load;—
—Society 'tis true may blame the deed,
But Heav'n with pity sees the wretched bleed:
And when our woes o'er Nature's verges rise,
Marks the poor Victim with indulgent eyes;
30 Softens the mandate 'gainst self-slaughter *here*,
And bids the wretch no *future* vengeance fear.—
—When through the gloom of some ill-omen'd
  night
Delusive fancy gives thee to my sight,
No recollection clouds the transient scene,
35 No pangs of deadly horror intervene:—
I hear thee,—view thee,—feel thy circling arms,—
And Werter still my bleeding bosom charms.—
—Once more—ah no!—what dreadful scenes arise,
Low at my feet a murder'd Lover lies!—
40 Cold streams of gore my wretched frame surround,
Gastly and deep appears the self-made wound—
Stern Albert storms,—the vision fleets in air,
And fancied horror wakes to *real* despair.—

—Forget thee Werter!—no!—while breath remains,
45 'Till the last drop desert by ebbing veins
I'll think on thee!—Thy gen'rous Love the theme
Of noon-tide reverie and mid-night dream.—
—Yes,—the poor wretch who *now* lies mould'ring
  here,
Was tender, faithful, gen'rous and sincere;
50 Sad recollection dwells upon the tale
'Till ev'ry trace of cold Indiff'rence fail;—
—I saw thee bend beneath a weight of woe,
I saw thy tears in deepest sorrow flow,
Thy vain request still vibrates on my ear,

55 With horror still thy last resolve I hear,—
    Thy *last* indeed!—for me thy bosom bled,—
    For me the parting Soul in anguish fled!—
    For me the dire explosion rends the skies,—
    For me the self-devoted victim dies!—
60   —Wou'd I had never been!—or being, doom'd
    In Life's meridian too, like thee, entomb'd!—
    —But fate forbade,—its bitterest portion chose,
    And fill'd my lot with complicated woes;—
    —Ev'n Love which makes surrounding mortals
        blest
65 Deprives my bosom of eternal rest:
    Nought in his train to my sad view appears
    But endless horror, suicide and tears.—
    —Accus'd of deeds that ev'n in thought I scorn,
    My mangled fame, by busy Censure torn,—
70 Yet ah!—to thee too ridgidly severe,
    No sound of hope approach'd thy list'ning ear!—
    A bleeding bosom and untimely Grave
    Were *all* the favours wretch'd Charlotte gave.—

    —Alas!—while Prudence steept in anguish stood,
75 Each guardian Angel shudd'ring turn'd from blood,—
    Deplor'd our fate,—beheld thy exit near,
    And with a groan resign'd their station here.—

    —But hush repining,—*Time* that cures each ill
    Shall bid my throbbing heart at length be still,
80 Shall doom the wretch, who now in secret mourns,
    To the cold earth *where* dust to dust returns.—
    —Werter I come!—in happier climes we'll join,
    No Albert *there* forbids me to be thine,
    Be thine!—that thought extatic rapture gave,
85 Yes!—I will meet thee in the clay cold Grave,—
    —Woes great as ours alone find comfort there,

Death *only* cures thy victim, fell Despair!—
—Then come blest Pow'r!—one healing pang
decree,
For Heav'n nor Earth has pity left for *me*.—

MS pp. 30–35. In Craik's contents list, the poem is titled 'Charlotte at Werter's Grave'. In the Neilson manuscript the poem is dated 1779 (68).

6. **A bursting heart I bend:** Goethe's novel ends with the intimation that Charlotte may die of a broken heart.

7. **mourn thy premature,—thy fatal end!:** Werther shoots himself in the head with Albert's pistols, believing suicide to be the only solution to the love triangle between himself, Charlotte, and her husband, Albert, but does not die until twelve hours later.

42. **Stern Albert:** Charlotte's husband.

46. **Love:** Craik inserted 'Love' above the line, indicating that this is a fair copy manuscript, and in copying she had at first skipped the word.

54. **Thy vain request:** Werther wrote to Albert requesting the use of his two pistols for a trip he was supposedly taking. On Albert's orders and with deep misgiving, Charlotte had retrieved the weapons and given them to the waiting servant.

61. **Life's meridian:** the sun at midday, high point, as also used by Robert Burns in 'Written In Friars Carse Hermitage, on Nithside' (1788), l. 16 and in Craik's 'under sentence of Death': p. 28, l. 32.

81. **dust to dust:** Genesis 3. 19; commonly used in the burial service. Cf. 'The Maid of Enterkin', l. 79.

85. **clay cold Grave:** Craik uses the same phrase in 'Helen: an Epistle to A Friend', l. 58.

A CHARADE—TO MR D:

Craik wrote several of these literary charades or puzzles, though she included only two in the Beinecke manuscript, this one on 'Nothing' and the later one on 'Fortune' (p. 69 below). A charade was a literary riddle popularised in eighteenth-century France in which clues or hints are first given separately for each syllable of a word (or phrase) and then clues for the complete word (cf. *OED*). Charades could be purely literary, as here, or, as in Victorian parlour games, with each syllable acted out or mimed. Craik also addresses Mr D. in 'To Mr D: from Goat Whey Quarters', and has two other poems addressed to a Miss and a Lady D.: 'To Lady E: D:' and 'To Miss D—'.

—————————————

—That Life at *best* is but a *jest*
I fear will never stand the test,
Because, when e'er we look around
More *real ill* than *good* is found:—
5   —A serious jest at least it seems,
Made up of many painful dreams;—
But since we cannot change the scene
From *what it is*, and still *has* been,
We'll e'en like others have our jest,
10   And of bad bargains make the best.—

—To you the following I rehearse,
And beg an answer soon in verse,
An answer if you'll deign to send,
And *this way* let your wit extend;
15   Tho Gratitude is reckon'd rare,
The *word that's meant* I'll freely spare,
Then you with Brutus may exclaim
That Thanks, like virtue, is a name.—

48

¶

      —My *First* delights in *contradiction*,
20   And utterly detests conviction;
      Nay,—is with *Yes* so much at odds,
      They constantly take diff'rent roads.—

      —My *Second* is applied to all
      That *Matter* we, or *Spirit* call,
25   And *just* as you *before it* place
      Is *substance*, or is *empty space*.—

      —Philosophers have often own'd
      My *Whole* their deep researches crown'd;—
      But yet so common is the case
30   It dwells in ev'ry Coxcomb's face;
      And many a gallant Soldier's skull
      Of *this*, and *this alone*, is full.—
      This, many, many thousand years
      To all eternity appears;—
35   *This was* before we held our reign,
      And may, when we are gone remain;—
      —With *This* the Villain pays his debts,—
      'Tis *all* that merit often gets—
      This Demi-reps of ev'ry station
40   Hold honour, fame, and reputation,—
      This Brutus, all his trials past,
      Concluded Virtue *was at last*;
      If true, the dying Heathen spoke,
      Than Life is *This*, and but a joke.—
45   —Esteem and Love 'tho' styled our bliss,
      Alas!—too often end in *This*.—
      —*This* ev'ry red-coat quarter'd *here*,
      Presumes to whisper in our ear;
      And 'tho he thinks it not amiss,
50   Yet the sum total ends in *This*.—

—The Courtier's promise *This* attends,
He gives it to his dearest friends;—
But such the favour he bestows
No Gratitude the *getter* owes,—
55   From whence a doubt of course must flow
Whether it is a gift or no.—

—Now tell me *This*, 'tis far from hard,
And it shall be your sole reward.—

MS pp. 36–39. In Craik's contents list, the poem is titled 'A Charade on *Nothing*'. Neilson notes his manuscript as having a quite different charade on the same word (see Appendix II, p. 211).

1. Life at *best* is but a *jest*: John Gay, 'My Own Epitaph' (1720): 'Life is a jest; and all things show it. / I thought so once; but now I know it'.

17–18. Then you with Brutus . . . : According to Cassius Dio's *Roman History*, Brutus's last words were 'O wretched Valour, thou wert but a name, And yet I worshipped thee as real indeed; But now, it seems, thou wert but Fortune's slave' (47.49).

19. My *First*: the first syllable is no.

23. My *Second*: the second syllable is thing.

28. my *Whole*: nothing.

39. Demi-reps: women of doubtful reputation (*OED*).

47. *here*: in the 1770s and '80s army regiments were regularly stationed in Dumfries.

57. *This*: i.e. nothing.

THE SOLDIER'S JOY
—A SONG

British military units were frequently stationed in Dumfries because of its strategic situation on a main route from England into Scotland. Their officers added variety to the pool of eligible bachelors attending social events in the town. Craik's satire on the officers' limitations, in this song and also in her poem 'The Court Martial', suggests she largely avoided entanglement, but some cross-reference on local attitudes to their presence can be gathered from Burns's comments on the officers who hung around Maria Riddell (see e.g. 'lobster-coated puppies', *Letters*, II: 260; 'a string of coxcombs', *Poems*, II: 770). Many of the officers stationed would have been English, hence Craik's reference in line 12 to Doctors' Commons, in London. Also known as the College of Civilians, Doctors' Commons was the legal forum for England dealing with civil law, including matrimonial law. The name refers to the buildings used by these lawyers, located south of St Paul's Cathedral (*OED*). This was a London reference: legal proceedings for matrimonial disputes in Scotland did not go through Doctors' Commons, and, though divorce was possible in Scotland it was relatively rare and was handled through Scottish courts (cf. M. Anderson, *Female Playwrights and Eighteenth-Century Comedy: Negotiating Marriage on the London Stage*, 2002, p. 173).

Many eighteenth-century Scottish women poets wrote songs, usually as here new words to traditional airs, but this is the only song Craik included in the Beinecke manuscript. *The Soldier's Joy* was a popular Scottish fiddle tune. Burns had used it for the opening song 'I am a son of Mars', in his cantata 'The Jolly Beggars', though it seems unlikely that Craik would have known that, and his son of Mars is a veteran of the other ranks, not an officer and marriageable gentleman. The tune had been included in Campbell's *A Collection of the Newest and Best Reels and Minuets* (1778), MacGlashan's *Scots Measures* (1778), Aird's *A*

Selection of Scotch, English, Irish and Foreign Airs (1782) and other collections (Dick, *Songs of Robert Burns*, 1903, p. 445; McCue, *OERB*, IV: 581).

—Jove summon'd a committee lately on high,
To determine a point that had puzzl'd the skie;
The subject arose from we mortals below,
Who the joys of a Soldier demanded to know.—

5 —He first call'd his Daughter, bid Pallas draw near,
For wisdom like hers must of course make it clear,
But she sneering replied, 'tis no business of mine,
To Mars, Bacchus, Venus, the task I resign.'—

—'*Your business!*—says Venus, and spoke with
disdain,
10 '*Your disciples*, no doubt, are a numerous train!—
'To wisdom's dull precepts few mortals incline,
'While each day *Doctors' commons* bears witness
to *mine*.'—

—That's true cries out Bacchus, come Mars come
along,
The case in dispute must to we three belong;
15 Then the joys of a Soldier we'll quickly define,
And pronounce they consist in *War*, *Love* and *Wine*.

MS pp. 40–41.

1. **Jove**: Jupiter, god of thunder and king of the gods.
5. **Pallas**: Athena, goddess of wisdom.
8. **Mars, Bacchus, Venus**: deities of war, wine, and love respectively.
12. *Doctors' commons*: see headnote.

TO A GENTLEMAN
WRITTEN AFTER RIDING THROUGH A
MOUNTAINOUS PART OF THE COUNTRY

Despite the title, this is a poem about *not* writing a poem about the mountainous Scottish landscape. As the opening lines make clear, the gentleman to whom it is written was in Italy or had recently been there; it was Craik herself who had been riding in mountainous parts of Scotland and was now asked to write about it. A clue to the gentleman's identity comes in Craik's contents list in the Beinecke manuscript, where the poem is titled 'To Doctor M:'. There were at least two doctors known in the Dumfries area with surnames starting in M. One was Dr William Maxwell (1760–1834), friend and physician to Robert Burns. Helen Craik's will includes a small legacy to Dr Maxwell, and his father, James Maxwell of Kirkconnell, had ties with both the Craiks and relatives of the Riddells. In 1745, James had left his estate in the hands of William Craik before joining the 1745 Jacobite rising; later, in 1758, he had married Mary Riddell. But Dr William Maxwell did not return from France to practice in Dumfries till 1794. Another local candidate might be Dr James Mundell (1759–1801), a former naval surgeon, who subsequently set up practice in Dumfries, and who treated Burns both at Ellisland and in Dumfries. Neither Maxwell nor Mundell is known to have travelled to Italy. Given that the poem must have been written by 1790, to be in the Beinecke manuscript, but could have been written many years before that, other Dr M.s are possible, and a third candidate might seem to be Dr John Moore (1729–1802), friend and correspondent of both Burns and Mrs Dunlop; he had travelled in Italy in 1775–76, and his book *Views of Society and Manners in Italy* was published in 1781. However, Moore also seems unlikely, because he was so much older than Craik, he was married, and there is no known connection between him and the Craiks of Arbigland.

————————

—From Italy's enchanting scenes
Fit subjects for poetic themes,
Where all is elegance and ease,
And Nature forms her works to please;—
5   Just while description charms the Soul,
And the mind's eye commands the whole,
You turn,—and with mischievous spite
Mid Scotia's mountains bid me write:—
—With wit and ev'ry grace at hand,
10   How cou'd you make the strange demand?—
—For tho some idle lines I trace
The humble rhyme ne'er rose to verse,
But tyrant man's superior pow'rs
Must shine at the expence of ours,
15   And, 'tho too oft against our will,
We're doom'd to be obedient still.—

—Yet to assist me much I fear
No friendly Muse will venture near,
Melpomene with streaming eyes
20   From such dread precipices flies,
And vows the tragic sword or draught,
Not half so frightful to the thought.—

—Here Calliope, and Clio too,
Find little in *their* way to do:—
25   The first protests no sound she hears
But what with horror rends her ears,
Screach Owls and Ravens flutt'ring round
All sense of harmony confound.
And Clio thinks a hist'ry wrote
30   Of all she sees not worth a Groat.—

—Ev'n Thalia gaily tripping near
Shrinks back with more than comic fear,

For well she knows to miss a step
Inevitably breaks her neck;
35   And then adieu for ever after,
To all her future scenes of Laughter.—

—If, to contemplate too the skies,
Urania *here* shou'd raise her eyes,
Chance may a double gift bestow
40   And make her touch the shades below.—

—One Muse alone by Nature made
Seem'd form'd to give my wishes aid;—
For each steep precipice is found
A cure for Cupid's deepest wound
45   And once, if properly applied,
No second doze need e'er be tried—
A sight so strange I long'd to view,
And to the brink Erato drew.—
Prepar'd I stood to see her flight
50   And hear her bid the World good night.—
—When, with a sneer, she turn'd around,
And told me easier cures were found,—
That mankind now were wiser grown,
And scarcely Cupid's pow'r was known.—
55   *Convenience* too with *Gold* agreed
To heal where e'er he chanc'd to bleed:—
The cure was radical she said,
And *now no Lover* joins the dead;
For, ere the Grave they can attain
60   *Hymen* or *Time* has broke their chain,
Of course no leaps are ta'en from hence
And Love's a jest to men of sence.—

—In short each Nymph excuses found,
Not one appear'd propitious round.—
65   Since *aid* nor *talents* are decreed

Say,—shall the *Will* supply the *deed*?
What *more* to please you can I do,
The Muse and *genius* absent too.—

MS pp. 42–46.

8. **Mid Scotia's mountains:** While this may be a generalised reference
   to riding in hill country in the southwest or the Borders, most
   Scottish mountains are north of the central belt.
8. **bid:** Craik's manuscript reads 'bids'.
11–12. ironic teasing use disclaiming poetic pretension, c.f. 'To
   Captain Riddell'.
19. **Melpomene:** muse of tragedy often depicted holding a tragic
   mask in one hand and a sword in the other.
21. **And vows the tragic sword or draught:** i.e. suicide.
23. **Here Calliope, and Clio too:** Calliope: muse of eloquence and
   epic poetry, known also for her voice. Clio: muse of history
   and, in a few mythological accounts, of lyre playing.
24. **Find little:** Craik's manuscript reads 'Finds'.
30. **Groat:** Scottish fourpenny.
31. **Thalia:** muse of comedy and idyllic poetry.
38. **Urania:** muse of astronomy.
48. **Erato:** muse of poetry. Craik's manuscript appears to read 'Erata'.

THE Rᵀ HONᴮᴸᴱ: THE EARL OF CAITHNESS TO MISS D:

John Sinclair, eleventh Earl of Caithness (1756–1789), had succeeded to the title on the death of his father, William Sinclair, the tenth earl, in 1779. His suicide ten years later, on 8 April 1789, aroused widespread interest in the contemporary press. One newspaper reported:

> WEDNESDAY John Sinclair, Earl of Caithness, after breakfasting at the Mount coffee-house, retired to his apartments at the west end of the town, and shot himself. Lord Caithness was a nobleman, who to great good-nature added an uncommon portion of mental abilities. He was, however, unhappily addicted to the fashionable and prevailing luxuries of the times; and his affairs were much deranged.— His fortune was 2000£, a year, besides what he derived from his rank as Lieut-Colonel. His debts amounted to between 5 and 6000£, and he lately sold an annuity, on his half pay. [. . .] Lord Caithness was to have been married to Miss Dehanney, the daughter to an eminent West-India Planter, on the very day on which he committed the desperate action, that put a period to his existence. Some accounts say that the father of the young lady refusing his consent, occasioned this act of horrid desperation; previous to the perpetration of which he sent his servant with a letter to Miss D. affirming, that without her his life must be miserable. To this letter a favourable answer was returned by Miss D. but the servant on entering his Lordship's apartment found him a shocking lifeless corpse. The Coroner's jury brought in their verdict Lunacy (*Bath Chronicle*, 16 April 1789, p. 4).

The *Gentleman's Magazine* was more discreet: 'The cause of his lordship's putting an end to his existence has been attributed to

disappointment in a matrimonial adventure; but the accounts
of it are variously related' (*Gentleman's Magazine*, 65 (April
1789), 375). In his privately printed 'Reminiscenses' [*sic*], Joseph
Mitchell of Inverness wrote that Sinclair 'paid his addresses to,
and won the affections of, a Miss Dehenny', assuring her father
that 'although his estates in Caithness were not of much value,
he possessed besides these a valuable property in the county of
York'. Upon learning of Sinclair's deceit, Mr Dehenny upbraided
the earl who 'being a proud man felt the truth of Mr Dehenny's
rebuke, and in a fit of insane remorse committed suicide'. Miss
Dehenny remained unwed, rejecting all other suitors thereafter
(*The Highland Monthly*, 1 (1889–90), 367–68). Neilson refers
to these verses as an instance of Craik's 'painful taste . . . for
suicidal and murderous subjects' (Appendix II, p. 205).

—Ere *this* firm hand procures eternal rest,
And stills the raging tumult in my breast:—
Ere friendly Death resigns me to repose,
And the *last* scene on curst existence close:—
5   —While thus o'er Life's extremest verge I bend,
And *Hope* and *Sorrow* both approach their end;—
Ere the sad force of black Despair is shown,
And dull Oblivion claims me for its own:—
While bleeding Mem'ry dwells on former scenes,
10   Which once alas! Supplied us happier themes;
From icy death this fleeting hour I steal,
To soothe those evils you are doom'd to feel,
To bid calm comfort *now* propitious be,
And prove *your* friend, how e'er averse to *me*.—

15   —Then ere deep anguish veils each reas'ning pow'r
Remember sorrow rends *this heart* no more,
No more the pangs of stern *repulse* I fear,
Ev'n Disappointment cannot reach me *here*!—
The Grave a balm for ev'ry woe supplies,

20   And gives that peace th' unfeeling World denies.—
    —Affliction's victim,—fortune's fav'rite care,
    Alike their portion of the Tomb must share;
    Today—*tomorrow* our best Friends may claim,
    The period diff'rent, but the lot the same.—

25   —Then cease to grieve—tho Nature might decree
    A future course of circling years to me,
    What cou'd alas! The fatal gift contain,
    But *disappointed hopes* and *lengthen'd pain?*—
    —The guiltless wretch depriv'd of mental ease
30   Finds Death but trifling when compar'd with these;
    Death!—'tis the privilege of humankind,
    The certain cure of a distemper'd mind,—
    Design'd us as a safe resource from Care
    When suff'ring Nature can no longer bear;
35   The *last*, best favour, pitying Heav'n cou'd give,
    Without whose *aid* we neither die nor live;—
    Ordain'd *with peace*, heartrending woes to crown,
    And make the tedious draught of Life go down.—

    —Yet ere to this vain World I bid adieu,
40   And fly existence since depriv'd of you,—
    The fatal tale how I have lov'd, how well,
    These ebbing veins in streams of gore must tell:—
    The crimson proof, from doubtful mist'ry free,
    Is legible to all, who bleed like me.—
45   —Full well you know no selfish views were mine,
    No knee I bent at Fortune's fickle shrine;—
    Love only fill'd my breast,—its deadly strain
    With Passion's force tore my devoted frame.—
    —You,—you alone, this throbbing heart possest,
50   With you I thought for ages to be blest,
    In fancy form'd a thousand Fairy schemes,
    Which Time and Chance have prov'd alas! Were
        dreams.

—'Tis o'er!—the ideal scene at length is o'er,—
Delusive Hope can charm the mind no more.—
55   The pangs of struggling Nature *now* are past,
This hour of blood and horror is my last!—
—I go!—farewell—a *long*, a *last* adieu!
Already Life recedes from fancy's view,—
This tube already tears thee from my breast,
60   —Let stern parental duty speak the rest.—

MS pp. 47–50. In Craik's contents list, the poem is titled 'Earl of Caithness'.

23. *Today:* Craik's manuscript reads *'To day'*.

38. tedious draught of Life: cf. 'nauseous draught of life', in John Wilmot, Earl of Rochester, *A Letter from Artemizia* (c. 1675), l. 45.

41. have lov'd: Craik's manuscript mistranscribes as 'hav'd', indicating that the manuscript is a fair copy.

54. Delusive Hope: The opening of Samuel Johnson's *Rambler*, no. 67, has 'Delusive hope still points to distant good', and l. 1 of Johnson's 'On the Death of Dr Robert Levet' has 'hope's delusive mine': Craik also uses the phrase in: 'The Indian Maid—Part Second—', l. 70 and in 'Helen: An Epistle to a Friend', l. 54.

59. *This* **tube:** barrel of a gun. Alexander Pope uses 'tube' to refer to a gun in *Windsor Forest*, line 129: 'He lifts the tube, and levels with his eye', as does Robert Burns in *Ode for General Washington's Birthday*, l. 1: 'No Spartan tube, no Attick shell'. Craik uses the term again in 'The Following Lines . . .', l. 7.

TO LADY—

In the poem, Craik counsels a titled friend who regrets having lost or quarrelled with a male acquaintance, with Craik playfully taking on the voice of a religious advisor giving standard advice. In Craik's contents list, the poem is titled 'To Lady E: D:'. E. D. is most probably Elizabeth Dalzell, née Johnston, who in 1775 married Richard, styled Lord Dalzell and grandson of Robert, Earl of Carnwrath. While Neilson does not reference this particular poem, he notes that his MS contains a charade introducing a high-ranking member of Craik's coterie circle, Elizabeth Dalzell:

> My *First* with some help is to Valley allied
> My *Second* the place where Queen Caroline died
> My *Whole* is a compound of wit sense and whim,
> No changeable Proteus more various can seem.

The '*Second*' is Zell, i.e. Celle in Hanover, and the '*Whole*' is Dalzell (see Appendix II, p. 206). It seems unlikely that Craik was counselling Lady Dalzell about a suitor or love affair, as she only took that name after her marriage, and by then Craik could hardly advise her to scope out multiple replacements if the break had been with a disappointed suitor from before her marriage. In addition to the charade, Craik has other poems addressed to a Mr, or Miss D: 'To Mr D: from Goat Whey Quarters'; and 'To Miss D—' (pp. 32, 91 in this edition).

—With pleasure I read o'er your Ladyshyp's Letter,
But think for a *Chaplain* you might have done
    better,—
There's some I cou'd mention more judgement had
    shown,
Who are ever correcting all faults,—but *their*
    own.—
5   For me—who of failings have fully my share,

I rather shou'd *borrow*, then *lend* you a pray'r:—
—But since for *one* Sinner *repenting*, 'tis said
There's *more* joy, than o'er *ninety* that never have
　　stray'd
Why thus for your morals express so much fear?
10　Corrupting of them is a common case *here*;
And we see that *above* (by the scriptures 'tis plain,)
Repentance will settle all matters again.—

—My orthodox knowledge thus having made
　　known,
Permit me to offer a word of my own:
15　Being told you are subject to fits of despair
Which by Laughter flies off, and evap'rates in air,
I gladly wou'd contribute all in my pow'r
To fix the *gay* humour, and banish the *sour*,—
—Of course to begin with the loss you deplore
20　May Providence send you a far better Corps;—
And then you can do, like most Nymphs in your
　　case,
Let a *new* one fill up in the *departed* one's place;
And *Variety*, all your philosophers tell us,
Is the surest receipt for forgetting the Fellows.—

25　—But grant that all this shou'd not radical prove,
Nor strengthen your Spirits, nor weaken your
　　Love;
The elegant ****** I think might ** ****
Than make your amends for the beautiful ****;
For surely your Ladiship will not deny
30　That few in the ****** can with ********* vie.—
—Besides you shou'd keep, as all good Gen'rals do
One Corps-de-reserve, if you cannot have *two*,
And then *on* the *floor* when the *foe* shall appear
You'll still have a ****** to guard you from
　　fear.—

MS pp. 51–52.

7–8. But since for *one* Sinner . . . : Luke 15. 7, c.f. 'To a Gentleman',
ll. 63–64, p. 132.

13. My orthodox knowledge: A favourite trope of Craik's, used also
in ll. 13–16 'To a Gentleman' and in l. 68 of her subsequent
poem 'To a Gentleman'.

20. a far better Corps: a new, or better, group of young officers
stationed in Dumfries.

23–24. And *Variety* . . . : proverbial saying; in *The Task* (1785)
Cowper writes 'Variety's the very spice of life' (ii.606) and in
The Rover (1678), Behn writes 'Variety is the soul of pleasure'
(ii.1). In 'To a Gentleman', Craik repeatedly refers to variety
in the same manner; c.f. ll. 6, 30, and 53, pp. 130, 131, 132.

32–34. *One* Corps-de-reserves: Craik is using military metaphors
to envision the ball as a battle of the sexes.

LINES WRITTEN UPON A BLANK LEAF OF MR BURNS'S POEMS

This short tribute is the only one of Craik's poems to be widely known, because it appears, untitled and unsigned, on the title-leaf of the first (poems) volume of Burns's Glenriddell manuscript, but a calligraphic title-page is not a blank leaf, and it was not written specially for the Glenriddell Manuscript. In Craik's contents list for the Beinecke manuscript, the poem is titled 'Lines on Mr Burns's Poems'. The copy of Burns's 1787 Edinburgh edition for which it was written survives in the Mitchell Library, Glasgow; there Craik has inscribed it on a blank leaf, signed 'H. C.', with the date October 1789. There are, therefore, four manuscript copies of the poem, extant or reported, collated below: (1) the Beinecke MS, used for the text; (2) Craik's copy of 1787 in the Mitchell (collated as *Mitchell*); (3) the Glenriddell Manuscript in the National Library of Scotland (*Glenriddell*); and (4) the Neilson MS, collated here from the text printed by Neilson (*Neilson*; see Appendix II). The Glenriddell manuscript was prepared by Burns for presentation to Robert Riddell almost contemporaneously with Craik's preparation for Riddell of what is now the Beinecke manuscript, and both manuscripts have the same binding with Riddell's crest. For an authoritative transcription of *Glenriddell*, see Nigel Leask (ed.), *Oxford Edition of Robert Burns* (2014), I, p. 175. Leask's suggestion that the *Glenriddell* title-page and some of the other transcribed poems in that manuscript are in Craik's hand can now be confirmed by the hand in Beinecke. Because these lines on Burns were first known to Burnsians from the Glenriddell manuscript, where they are unsigned, Craik's authorship was unknown for many years; Henry Bright left the poem unattributed (*Some Account of the Glenriddell MSS.*, 1874, p. 6), as did James Gibson (*Bibliography*, 1881, p. 265), but Scott Douglas commented that it was 'probably by Roscoe' (Scott Douglas (ed.), *Works of Robert Burns*, V, p. 461). By the time of John Gribbel's Glenriddell facsimile (1914), the poem was being correctly credited to Craik. The punctuation in this manuscript differs slightly from that in the other sources.

———————

—*Here* native Genius *gay*, *unique*, and *strong*
Shines thro' each page, and marks the tuneful
    song,—
Rapt *Admiration* her warm tribute pays,
And *Scotia proudly* echoes all she says;—

5   Bold *Independence* too, illumes the theme,
And claims a manly privilege to Fame.—
—Vainly O Burns! Wou'd rank and riches shine
Compar'd with inborn merit *great* as thine,—
These Chance may take,—as Chance has often
    giv'n,
10   But pow'rs *like thine can* only come from
    Heav'n.—

MS p. 53.

2. thro': *Beinecke*; through *Mitchell, Neilson, Glenriddell*.
3. Rapt: *Beinecke, Mitchell, Neilson*; Wrapt *Glenriddell*. Neilson (1924) comments that this misspelling indicates that *Glenriddell* was a careless later copy from one of the other sources.
4. *Scotia*: Neilson states that Glenriddell reads 'Scotland', but that is not the case.
7. and: *Beinecke, Mitchell*; or *Neilson, Glenriddell*.
10. *can* only come from Heav'n: cf. Henry Mackenzie's description of Burns as 'this Heaven-taught Ploughman', in *The Lounger*, 97 (9 December 1786).

TO A LADY SENT WITH A FEW FLOWERS, IN RETURN FOR SOME BEAUTIFUL ARTIFICIAL ONES

This poem, accompanying Craik's gift of bog myrtle and a few carnations, plays on the contrast of the natural against the artificial, and the brevity of nature against the permanence of art. Ostensibly, Craik privileges the artificial flowers over her own natural ones, yet she does so in a way that makes clear the contrary valuation. Craik treats both the bog myrtle and the carnation as being natural, rather than, as Shakespeare does in *The Winter's Tale*, IV.4.80–108, seeing carnations as artificial cultivars, hybrids of the gardener's art. In Craik's contents list, the poem is titled 'To Miss H: with some Flowers', though who Miss H. is remains unidentified.

———————

    —The beauteous Flow'rs you lately sent
    Deserve no trifling compliment,—
    In them gay elegance I view,
    In them I see what *taste* can do;
5   There *Art* with *Nature* proudly vies,
    And form'd *by you* can Time despise.—

    —Say *how* shall I the gift repay
    With Flow'rs the offspring of a day?—
    Mine soon neglected, wither'd lie,
10   *Yours* ever bloom and never die:—
    —Tho not by *Art* immortal made,
    Mine bloom 'tis true, but quickly fade,
    While *yours* to latest Time shall show
    What I to *Taste* and Friendship owe.—

15   —But tho unequal far my pow'rs
    Ere to repay such gifts as yours,

Yet some return I wish to make,
Which not from *Art*, but *Nature* take.—
'This Myrtle sprig, I heard her say,
20   'To gentle ***** with care convey,
'*From Art* they both alike are free,
'And both have *all their* charms from *me*:—
'—Venus,—such is her high behest,
'Assigns it to adorn her breast,
25   '—She swears more Cupids pearch upon it,
'Then e'er on Gypsy hat or bonnet,
'And bids each Swain when you appear,
'Of Myrtle boughs and Love beware.'—

30   —More I wou'd send, but Boreas chose
To crush Pink, Jassamine, and Rose;
His boist'rous breath my pow'r defied,
And *almost* each Carnation died.
The few that now remain I send,—
35   A trifling offering from a friend:—
But *when* that friend gives *all* her store
Say—what cou'd you yourself do more?—

MS pp. 55–56.

19–28. Nature's speech in which the addressee is compared to a
    sprig of myrtle.
19. **Myrtle sprig**: the native bog myrtle or sweet gale is a small flow-
    ering shrub prevalent throughout much of Scotland. Because
    of its scent, sprigs were regularly tucked into hat bands to
    ward off midges.
20. The name of Craik's addressee, presumably a first name, must
    be a monosyllable.
23. **Venus**: goddess of love.

25. **pearch:** variant spelling of perch.

26. **Gypsy hat:** wide-brimmed straw hat with large flaps on the side tied with ribbons under the chin that was popular during the early nineteenth century.

30. **Boreas:** god of the north wind.

31. **Pink:** the pink, or *Dianthus deltoides,* from the same species as the carnation, is native to Scotland; it is named for its small size rather than its colour, which can be either white or pink often with a dark centre and stripes on the petals. Prior to the eighteenth century, pink, in Scots, referred to something very small.

33. **Carnation:** *Dianthus caryophyllus.* While carnation was often used to cover both carnations and pinks, Craik appears to be contrasting the pinks, which had been destroyed in the storm, with the carnations, some of which had survived.

A CHARADE

This is the second of two charades that Craik included in the Beinecke manuscript; in her contents list, the poem is titled 'A Charade—on Fortune', identifying the solution to the puzzle. A charade was a literary riddle popularised in eighteenth-century France in which clues are given separately to each syllable of a word and then to the word as a whole (cf. *OED*). Charades could be purely literary, as here, or, as in Victorian times, with each syllable acted or mimed. For Craik's other charades, see her earlier one on 'nothing' (pp. 48–50), and those on 'Dalzell' and 'Nothing' in the Neilson manuscript (Appendix II, pp. 206, 211).

  —Of Gender, Number, Case or Time,
  My *First* can little boast,
  Yet such its use in prose or rhyme
  It never can be lost.—

5 —In all that's sung my *Second's* found,
  It justly claims a share;
  For tho compos'd alone of sound,
  True harmony is there.—

  —My *Whole*, in ancient times we're told
10 Was held supremely great;
  An Heathen Goddess too enroll'd,
  And near allied to Fate.—

  Tho faithless, giddy, blind and vain,
  Fantastic, restless found,
15 Yet so bewitching is her reign
  A welcome guest she's own'd.—

  —Her vot'ries first to fraud gave birth,—
  She breaks the Lover's vows.—

Lays waste the hapless Indian earth,
20   Yet still creates no foes.—
—*Virtue* alone her sway denies,
And scorns the fickle Pow'r;
For virtue fortitude supplies,
How e'er she smile or low'r.—

MS pp. 57–58.

1–4. My *First*: for.

5–6. My *Second's*: tune.

9. My *whole*: fortune.

11. An Heathen Goddess too enroll'd: Heathen Goddess: Fortuna, goddess of fortune typically depicted with the wheel of fortune; enroll'd: i.e. rolled around, as in the wheel.

12. And near allied to Fate: Fortuna came to be associated, in classical times, with Tyche, goddess of fate.

13–14. faithless, giddy, blind and vain: Fortuna is conventionally represented as blindfolded and liable to sudden change. Cf. Shakespeare's *Henry V*, where Pistol describes 'giddy Fortune's furious fickle wheel, That goddess blind', and Fluellen responds that Fortune is 'turning, and / inconstant, and mutability, and variation' (*Henry V*, III.6.26–38).

19. Indian earth: i.e. East Indies.

TO INDIFFERENCE

Craik's tone and octosyllabic couplets in this attractive short poem seem to echo or allude to Milton's early poem 'Il Penseroso', on the pleasures of solitude, though contrasting with Milton's sense of philosophical ambition.

—*Now* farewell to Cupid's power,
His fatal charms deceive no more!—
For ever hence adieu the train,
Of *fancied* joys, but *real* pain.
5   Which poor mistaken mortals prove,
Who trust in thee deceitful Love.—

—But come *Indiff'rence*! Peaceful, blest,—
Henceforth be my *only* guest,—
Thou ne'er heartfelt sorrows gave,
10   Nor wounds that fester to the Grave.—
Time, nor *Chance*, nor deepest woes,
Interrupt *thy* calm repose.—
Pure thy state, serene and free,
Tears nor anguish follow thee:—
15   Come blest *Apathy* divine
I for ever *now* am thine.—

MS p. 59.

8. **Henceforth:** to be stressed on the first syllable.

15. **blest *Apathy* divine:** wordplay on the common and root meanings of apathy. In Platonist, Aristotelian, and Stoic philosophy, the divine nature is incapable of suffering, while Craik welcomes as blest or divine, not the absence of suffering, but of feeling. Cf. also Milton's conclusion to 'Il Penseroso': 'These pleasures Melancholy give, / And I with thee will choose to live' (ll. 175–76).

LINES WRITTEN IN A SUMMER HOUSE, UNDER THE INITIAL LETTERS OF A GENTLEMAN'S NAME

The summer house at Arbigland provided Craik with an escape from the confines of the house, a place to write poetry undisturbed, and also perhaps a place to meet people away from family scrutiny or interference. This poem is not an acrostic where the first or initial letter of each line would spell out the concealed name of the gentleman, but instead gives Craik's response to finding initials carved into the summer house. The unidentified youth or gentleman had carved or written his initials in the wood, and Craik must have left her poem there for him to discover when he returned. The summer house at Arbigland is also mentioned by Neilson in connection with a quite different poem, which he (or Arnott) suggests in a footnote was a variant version of Craik's 'Fair Helen' (Appendix II, p. 204 n.).

—————————

—May the Youth none of Life's dire vicissitudes
    prove
Whose initials appear so conspicuous above,—
—May his hopes be successful,—his fears ever
    vain,
May *Pleasure* exclude each intrusion of *Pain*—
5   May he still be possest of *the heart* he holds dear
May *Fortune* attend him, and Friendship be near—
And when from existence in time he shall turn
May *Remembrance* shed tears of esteem o'er his
    urn.—

MS p. 60. In Craik's contents list, the poem is titled more briefly 'Lines written under the Initial Letters of a Gentleman's name'.

1. **the Youth:** surely an indication that these lines are not addressed to a suitor of Craik's.
5. *the heart* **he holds dear:** again, not, presumably, Craik herself, who promises he will be remembered with esteem, rather than love.

TO CAPTAIN RIDDELL

This is the second poem in the Beinecke manuscript addressed to
Robert Riddell. It is a prefatory dedication for Craik's narrative
poem 'The Maid of Enterkin'; see the following pages for a
prose summary and for the poem itself. Riddell had apparently suggested the topic of the poem to Craik: see l. 26 in this
dedication, and cf. Neilson, Appendix II, p. 204. Riddell and
Craik, like Riddell's friend William Tytler, seem to have shared
an interest in post-Culloden Jacobite-related songs and stories;
Craik's immediate source is dealt with in the headnote to the full
poem. In the Neilson manuscript, 'The Maid of Enterkin' was
the opening poem on pp. 2–10, written in the 'principal hand',
but this prefatory poem to Riddell came later in that MS, at
p. 42; Neilson printed twelve lines from the poem, without
lines 7–10 or 15–24, but the text of those lines showed no
substantive variants between the two manuscripts.

—While timid Hope succeeds well grounded fears,
The trembling Maid of Enterkin appears,
And begs no stern, no criticizing brow
O'er her poor Lines a judging eye may throw;—
5   —Too well she knows no merit they *can* claim
Where shines a Burns's never dying strain;—
Such vain presumptive thoughts cou'd ne'er arise,—
'Tis for *Indulgence* she alone applies;—
And prays no cold contempt be deem'd her due,
10 For want of *Genius thus* expos'd to view;—
—Alas! No mount Parnassus *here* is seen,
No crystal Helicon's inspiring stream!—
On barren Criffel Laurels ne'er wou'd grow,
Nor Solway in poetic numbers flow;
15 But Nature free from polish'd rules of art
Pours out the feelings of a grateful heart.
Tho while she owns your Favours ill repaid,

Still from Indulgence must solicit aid,—
For her weak Talents kind allowance plead
20 And beg the *Will* may *now* supply the *deed*—
—She wish'd to please—for *that* each effort made,
And *prompt Obedience* was, at least, display'd,—
O then let *Friendship* o'er your *judgement* rise,
And guard her faults from *Observation's* eyes.—
25 —And while with Candour you the tale peruse
Whose mournful theme you gave the weeping Muse,
May Pity still her sovereign sway maintain,
Nor kill the Maid of Enterkin *again*.—

MS pp. 61–62.

2. **The Maid of Enterkin:** here, a reference to the poem, rather than to its heroine.

6. **Where shines a Burns's never dying strain:** an indication that Craik was writing this preface after she became aware that Burns was a neighbour and frequent guest of Riddell's at Friar's Carse.

11. **Parnassus:** mountain in central Greece, typically referred to as the home of poetry in literature.

12. **Helicon's inspiring stream:** springs of Hippocrene and Aganippe, which were believed to be the home of the Muses and source of poetic inspiration.

13. **On barren Criffel Laurels ne'er wou'd grow:** Criffel is the most prominent hill on the north side of the Solway, located in Kirkcudbrightshire, some two-and-a-half miles south of New Abbey. Craik's show of false humility in front of male readers or critics was common for female poets of the era.

15–16. **But Nature free from . . . :** Craik similarly privileges nature over art in 'To a Lady Sent with a few Flowers'. See head-note, p. 66.

26. **Whose mournful theme you gave the weeping Muse:** Craik credits Riddell with giving her the story.

THE MAID OF ENTERKIN
[PREFACE]

As noted in Craik's dedicatory poem to Robert Riddell (the previous item), Riddell had suggested to Craik that she should write a poem about this story, set a few miles north of his home at Friar's Carse. His apparent source, a tale that appeared in the *Scots Magazine* for October 1781, is treated more fully in the headnote to the poem itself (next item). Craik's prose summary given below is largely a précis of the magazine source, apart from a last sentence explaining the point in the story at which the protagonist is speaking. While Neilson discusses Craik's poem at some length, without identifying any source, he does not indicate that this prose preface was in his manuscript, nor does he quote from it: see Appendix II. Craik later included the prose preface, together with the whole poem, in her first novel, *Julia St. Pierre: A Tale of the French Revolution* (1796), III, pp. 345–49, though that part of the novel was not included in the truncated 1848 reprint. The prose preface shows several differences of phrasing between the novel and the Beinecke manuscript, as indicated in the notes below.

—The following Lines were occasioned by an incident said to have happened in the neighbourhood of Enterkin.— A Gentleman having fought *with* his Friends, but *against* the Laws of his Country, the event of Rebellion drove him a fugitive among barren Mountains.— During a seclusion of fifteen years his sole pleasure was to perform the part of a double Parent to an only Daughter.— In a Town whither paternal indulgence had suffered her to go, but whither a Parent durst not accompany her,—she was seen, and followed to her retirement, by a Man who *said* he was in Love.— To him the person of her Father was known, and, unless she would become the guilty pledge of her Parent's safety, *that* Parent was to be persecuted and betrayed.— By arts, which should not be mentioned but to curse them, her Father was driven to seek his Lodging, for three long Nights, under the covert of the surrounding snowy Hills.— The next, a miserable relic of cold and hunger, he crept over his own threshold—but to die!—his Daughter's reason fell a victim to the scene:— After mourning her Father, an *hour* for *every year* of his Life, amounting to Seventy-eight in number,—she rushed out of the Cottage during his funeral, and plunging into a neighbouring Pool put a period to her wretched exist-ence.—At the commencement of the following Lines she is supposed to be sitting, alone, by the Corpse of her Father, and far from any assistance.—

MS pp. 63–64. Variants from the later version of this preface in Craik's *Julia St. Pierre* are collated below as *Julia*. Specific verbal echoes from the magazine source are given as *Scots Magazine*.

The following lines . . . incident: This poem was written upon an incident *Julia*.

neighbourhood of Enterkin: a stream, and valley, on the western side of the Lowther Hills, in north Dumfriesshire, flowing into the Nith some six miles north of Thornhill.

fought *with* his Friends, but *against* the Laws of his Country: an exact quotation from the *Scots Magazine*.

among barren Mountains: far from the joys of society, the gayer scenes of earlier days, his sole pleasure, during a seclusion of fifteen years was *Julia*.

a double Parent to an only Daughter: parent and instructor to an only and motherless daughter *Julia*. The phrase 'double Parent' is from the *Scots Magazine*.

whither: whether *Julia* (twice).

The next: On the fourth *Julia*.

victim to the scene: victim to the terror of the moment *Julia*.

her Father: this ill-fated father *Julia*.

Seventy-eight: the *Scots Magazine* source suggests the father would be eighty-eight, not seventy-eight (thirty hours plus two days, or forty-eight hours).

At the commencement of the following Lines . . . assistance: the story in the *Scots Magazine* was narrated long afterwards, by a male narrator who had stumbled on the distraught heroine. Craik's preface gives the whole, but her poem is the heroine's desperate soliloquy before the magazine's narrator has appeared.

sitting, alone, by the Corpse of her Father, and far from any assistance: be sitting, by the corpse of her Father—unknown and unassisted *Julia*.

THE MAID OF ENTERKIN

Robert Riddell's estate at Friar's Carse lay in Nithsdale just off the road north from Dumfries to Sanquhar and the Enterkin valley where the story is set, and it was Riddell who suggested the story to Craik as a topic for her poem. In Neilson's manuscript, 'The Maid of Enterkin' was the first item, suggesting she saw it as one of her most significant works, and Neilson's first article about the Craik poems was titled 'The Maid of Enterkin'. If Craik had published the poem, contemporary readers would probably, given the history of the Enterkin area, have seen the story as about a Covenanting fugitive in the 1680s. However, Craik has kept the time-period vague, omitting the clues given in her source (excerpted below), and so leaving it ambiguous whether the poem is set in the 1680s or in the mid-eighteenth century, telling the tale of a Jacobite fugitive and his daughter in the years following the defeat of Prince Charles Edward Stuart and the Jacobite army at the Battle of Culloden in April 1746.

The narrow valley of the Enterkin burn, on the west side of the Lowther Hills, some six miles north of Thornhill, and fourteen miles north of Riddell's home at Friar's Carse, provided a pass up into the hills and an alternative route across towards Edinburgh. In the 1670s and 1680s, the area had been a Covenanting stronghold, when government forces hunted down those who still asserted the independence of the Presbyterian church against Episcopal and royal control, killing or executing many of those whom the authorities captured. When Craik was writing, the name 'Enterkin' would first evoke the dramatic clash in the Enterkin pass in July 1684, when Covenanters ambushed a small party of dragoons escorting some Covenanting prisoners to Edinburgh for trial and rescued the prisoners who scattered into the hills to isolated hiding-places, lying low till they were discovered or betrayed; see Robert Wodrow, *History of the Sufferings of the Church of Scotland*, 2 vols (Edinburgh: Watson: 1721–22), II, p. 448; Daniel Defoe, *Memoirs of the Church of Scotland* (1717), pp. 189–93; Defoe, *A Tour Thro' the Whole*

Island of Great Britain, 3 vols (London: Strahan, 1724–1727), III, pt 2, Letter XII, p. 64.

However, in 1781, a story set near Enterkin had appeared in the *Scots Magazine* that provides a much closer match to Craik's poem. The magazine story refers, not to a Covenanter, but to a Jacobite who had been hiding for fifteen years in the hills above Enterkin following the defeat at Culloden. The dates make the reference quite explicit: when the tale was published, nineteen years had passed since the events in the story, which occurred therefore in the early 1760s, and the fugitive had been in hiding for fifteen years before that, so since 1746. The story, unhelpfully titled 'An Affecting Tale', was the second instalment of an anonymous series, *The Country Curate*, first published in the *London Chronicle* in October 1781, but then reprinted in the *Scots Magazine* (the version used here) and other periodicals.[1]

At the time of the story, the narrator, then a young student, had been walking from Dumfries to Edinburgh and got lost in a snow storm in the Lowther Hills, eventually spying a glimmer of light from a ruined cottage. Breaking in, and on the verge of collapse, he finds an old man lying dead, and his dishevelled daughter crying inconsolably:

'I am an harmless maiden', she cried, when the tumult of her grief permitted her to cast a troubled eye towards me;—'let me alone—I shall soon follow my father!' . . . he has been dead these thirty hours—I have reckoned them—I will bewail him an hour for every year of his life—and then I myself will die unlamented. Alas, I have two days yet to survive . . . . You see my poor father stretched on an humble bed; in his youth he was accustomed to one more stately. I was three years old, when

---

[1] 'An Affecting Story, from The Country Curate', *Scots Magazine*, 43 (October [i.e. November], 1781), 536–38; reprinted from *London Chronicle* (9–11 October, 1781); also in *Edinburgh Magazine*, 54 (7 November 1781), 138–41; *Weekly Miscellany*, 17 (29 October 1781), 100–04.

he changed domestic tranquillity and private honours for
the hazardous occupations of a camp. He fought with his
friends—but against the laws of his country. The event
of rebellion drove him a fugitive among these mountains.
My mother, it seems, would not follow either his defection
with her wishes, nor his fallen fortunes with her love. His
only pleasure remained in this hovel, to act to me a double
parent's part. And in a seclusion of fifteen years, he had
both learned himself to forget the world, and taught me
to despise it. Half year ago, in town whither paternal
indulgence had suffered me to go, but whither a parent
durst not accompany me, I was seen, and followed to my
retirement by a man, who said he was in love but that
could not be,—for he was a villain. To him the person of
my father was known;—by his means he is now cold as
the clay. Unless I would become the dishonoured pledge
of a parent's safety,—such was the audacious proposal
made!—that parent was be persecuted and betrayed. By
arts, which should not mentioned but to curse them, father
was driven to seek his lodging, for three long nights, under
the covert of these snowy hills: the next, a more miserable
relic of cold and hunger than you, he crept over his own
threshold—but to die. No mortal has since entered this
cottage—'tis far to any house . . . . I resolved to do the
duty of brother, of a Christian, of a man: To see the old
man laid in a grave,—and his daughter separated from
sorrow. Little preparation was needed for the first— two
or three herdsmen were procured and though 'Dust to
dust' was not said, it was significantly meant, and the
consignment was equally secure. In the latter intention I
was prevented by a rashness I sore dreaded, but against
which my anxieties arose too late to guard. Whilst I bore
the father's head to the distant church-yard, and laid it with
sighs in the ground, only two women bore his weeping
child company in the cottage, and their observation she
easily eluded, it was but a little way to the period of earthly

sorrow.—The pool was nigh,—and late floods made it deep. The frost had but yet usurped its borders—the middle was left for the victim of despair.—There I found her at my return—I buried her beside her father, and *the world has not appeared to me the best that may be* ever since. It is now nineteen years since this happened to me, and yet I often seek the solitary corner; and when no distresses more near oppress me, shed a tear to the memory of Lucy Watson.

Scots Magazine, 43 (October 1781), 536–38.

For her poem, Craik changes the voice in the tale, from a male narrator, an outsider, recounting the events many years after they happened, to a female speaker mourning her fugitive father's death while the ending of the story is still unknown. Craik was sufficiently proud of the poem to include it later, without any substantive revision, in her first novel, *Julia St. Pierre: A Tale of the French Revolution*, 3 vols (London: William Lane at the Minerva Press, 1796), III, pp. 345–49, where it is read aloud by M. de Villars to Julia and her friend Miss Rutland, who are reduced by his reading to tears and silence.

  —Friendless,—alone,—with ev'ry woe opprest
  E'er fired the brain or agoniz'd the breast.—
  No pitying heart this sinking Frame to save,—
  No hand alas! to ev'n prepare the Grave!—
5 —While that poor clay wrapt in a Parent's form,
  Now snatch'd at length from keen misfortune's
    storm,
  There to my view,—before my streaming eyes,
  In mould'ring, cold, inanimation lies.—
  —Oft filial Duty bending o'er the scene,
10 From *Reason* torn, to *Frenzy* gives the rein,
  And wildly wand'ring from its darling care,
  Finds *Hope* and *Peace* absorb'd in stern Despair.—

¶

—Finds Hope and Peace!—ah me! too truly said,
Each cherub form with my poor Father fled;
15   Once blest indeed, their genial influence shone,
And left no pang for rank or riches gone,
Patience and *Virtue* ev'ry want supplied,
Nor calm *Content* her chearful aid deny'd.—
—And are they gone?—is nothing left behind
20   But the sad privilege to curse Mankind!—
—Good Heav'ns how chang'd!—what horror
     meets my eyes!
From smiling *Love* can such deep anguish rise!
Love!—No!—'twas *Vice* from Hell's black centre
     driv'n,
For Love like thine is enmity with Heav'n,—
25   —Remember thee!—yes Wretch, while Life remains,
Till freezing Death usurp these throbbing veins;
'Yes, till this heart forgets to beat and grieve,
'Live *there* thy image,—but destested live!'—
May vengeful *Conscience* no *Remorse* restrain,
30   For great my mis'ry,—tho no triumph thine.—

—But ah!—calm *Reason now* resigns her sway.—
Distraction's pow'r my hurry'd thoughts obey;—
In vain for Comfort ev'ry look I strain,
Grief rends the heart, and burns around the brain,
35   Ideal Phantoms swim before my eyes,
And from lost Mem'ry all connection flies;—
—Haste! haste my Father!—far from hence remove,
For Treach'ry comes disguis'd like smiling Love!
O Quickly fly!—yon snowy hills attain,
40   We'll meet above them, ne'er to part again;—
—Not rise!—Nay then, . . . ah me! depriv'd of breath
What Victim *here* lies sacrificed to Death?—
A Parent's form the lifeless image bears,
But burning Madness dries the source of tears.—

45   —A Parent's form! . . . again Reflection beams,
And fixt Despair succeeds Distraction's dreams,
Dispels th' unequal pangs that Madness feels
And through the breast, with double anguish steals.—

—O my lost Parent!—thou at length art blest
50   No legal Villain *now* disturbs thy rest
Through chilling snow, and Winter's ruthless storm
No more a wand'ring Exile doom'd to roam.—
In Death's kind arms secure from insult laid,
The mean *Informer* cannot reach the Dead.—
55   —In vain my loose, disorder'd Locks are torn,
In vain near *thee this* wretched Frame is thrown;
Cold,—silent,—heedless,—deaf to nature's part,
Thou views,—unmov'd,—a Daughter's bursting
        heart.
Distraction,—*Reason*,—mourns alike in vain,
60   Till mental suff'ring close the weary scene.—

—Tho *here* retir'd from ev'ry passing eye,
No friendly aid to share affliction nigh;—
No heart by mild Benevolence design'd
To sooth the tumults of a frantic mind;—
65   —Tho fainting mis'ry hope for peace in vain,
Yet *filial duty here* shall fixt remain:—
Shall o'er thy Corse, for ev'ry suff'ring year,
One hour assign, to sad Remembrance dear;
Nor tir'd with mourning,—thy hard fate bewail,
70   Till the last trace of worn existance fail;
Then calmly sinking by thy *mould'ring* clay,
A willing debt to grief and Nature pay.—

—Perhaps kind Chance some wand'ring step may
        send
To the lone Cot, where our poor ashes blend,
75   And while the scene each fixt attention claims,

While *these* sad *Lines* the source of Feeling drains,
The shelt'ring Grave *Compassion* may assign,
And our cold Frames to kindred earth resign.—
—What tho no solemn 'Dust to Dust' be said,
80   The last sad office thus humanely paid,
Recording Angels shall applause bestow,
Well-pleas'd to find *some Pity still* below.—

MS pp. 65–69. Neither the text given in Craik's novel *Julia St. Pierre* (1796), nor the short passage (ll. 73–82) quoted in Neilson's article, show any substantive variants from the Beinecke text. References in these notes to '*Scots Magazine*' are to Craik's source, the 'Affecting Tale', excerpted in the headnote above.

4. **No hand alas! to ev'n prepare the Grave!:** when the poem takes place, the daughter is alone, before the *Scots Magazine* narrator stumbles into the cottage.

27–28. **'Yes, till this . . . but detested live!':** cf. Edward Lovibond, 'Julia's Printed Letter to Lord —', in *Poems on Several Occasions* (1785), p. 21, ll. 43–44.

37. **Treach'ry comes disguis'd like smiling Love:** 'a man, who said he was in love, but that could not be for he was a villain': *Scots Magazine*.

50. **legal Villain:** by contrast with the father, an outlaw but an honourable man.

51–52. **Through chilling snow, and Winter's ruthless storm / No more a wand'ring Exile doom'd to roam:** on the dual reference here, to the seventeenth-century Covenanters and the eighteenth-century Jacobites, see the headnote above.

55. **my loose, disorder'd Locks are torn:** 'she tore the lovely tresses from her head': *Scots Magazine*.

67–68. **for ev'ry suff'ring year / One hour assign, to sad Remembrance dear:** 'He has been dead these thirty hours . . . I will bewail

him an hour for every year of his life': *Scots Magazine*. The
phrase 'to sad remembrance dear' occurs in, e.g., Legrand's
'Aucassin and Nicolette', in *Fabliaux or Tales, Abridged from
French Manuscripts of the XIIth and XIIIth Centuries,* transl.
Gregory Lewis Way, 2 vols (1796), l. 660, and in an anonymous poem 'Lines Written in the Last Century', *Edinburgh
Magazine,* 18 (July 1801), p. 449 (l. 13).
79. **'Dust to Dust':** here the daughter uses this Biblical formula from
the burial service (from Genesis 3. 19) to express a future fear
that her father will lie unburied, while the *Scots Magazine*
narrator invokes it to show that the hurried informal burial
was still reverent: 'though *Dust to dust* was not said, it was significantly meant, and the consignment [i.e. burial] was equally
secure'. Craik also uses the phrase in her poem 'Charlotte at
Werter's Grave', l. 81.

THE FOLLOWING LINES WERE OCCASIONED BY A HUMOUROUS COURT MARTIAL, HELD, AND WRITTEN BY TWO OFFICERS ON SOME LADIES WHO HAD DISOBLIGED THEM

Like her song 'The Soldier's Joy' and the following poem 'To Miss D—', Craik's satire in this poem is directed at some of the young army officers temporarily stationed in or near Dumfries, attending balls and other social events in the town. As several Jane Austen novels illustrate, the arrival of a new regiment in a neighbourhood expanded the local pool of eligible but flirtatious bachelors. Officers enjoyed the cachet of ranking as gentlemen, and because they had generally purchased their commission they could be presumed to have some family money in their background. There is no indication in this poem, or elsewhere, that Craik was in any way interested or entangled in the two unidentified officers to whom this poem is addressed; when Craik and her friend rebuffed some unspecified invitations or advances, the officers had responded by writing a comic 'Court Martial', in verse, charging them with being disobliging; Craik's teasing rejoinder expresses mock-surprise that army officers should be able to write such good poetry, portrays the Greek gods in a jurisdictional dispute over their trespassing outside their profession, and predicts their colonel will send them off to drill recruits in Edinburgh.

    —Two youths on whom Phœbus much wit had bestow'd
      At length almost rival'd their Patron the God;
      Apollo perceiv'd it,—but seem'd not to know
      That spirits so daring were met with below—
5   —'Tho silent his rage, yet he saw in despair
      These sons of true humour encroach on his sphere;

Already in fancy his name was unheard,
No corner on earth a petition prefer'd;
To aid works of genius appear'd ne'er a summons,
10   But all had recourse to young ********, and
      ********.—

—The case it was hard, and enough to perplex one,
For thus to be serv'd, tho a God, it wou'd vex one;
—At length to stern Mars the whole tale he related,
How doom'd to oblivion poor Phœbus was fated;—
15   Complain'd that the Army so witty was grown
The wreaths from his forehead by Soldiers were
      torn;
Then beg'd some assistance to settle his reign
Nor let these usurpers insult him again.—

—The Pow'r of fell War with amazement was
      seiz'd,
20   To find that *his sons* had in *this way* displeas'd,—
The fact was, tho obvious, uncommon and new,
And he scarcely imagin'd the God had spoke
      true.—
—But proud in Apollo's defence to appear,
(For *malice* had whisper'd *no* friendship was *there*)
25   He shook his Spontoon,—swore a soldierly word,
And vow'd no Goose quill shou'd take place of a
      sword,
Then moments of leisure wou'd grant them no
      more
But doom'd them to drilling Edina's new Corps.—

—With marching, and drumming, and fifing
      confus'd,
30   Their talents for humour forgot or disus'd,
Phœbus thought himself safe, and applauded his wit,
That on such an expedient had luckily hit.—

But Bacchus, who *now* had a quarrel with Mars,
Nor lik'd all these marchings *from him* to the wars,
35　Stept forth on their side, and to aid them appear'd,
He held up a *Bumper*,—their spirits were chear'd,
Their genius once more shone resplendent and
　　　bright,
The *subject was tempting*,—they sat down to write,—
"'Tis *satire* cries Phœbus!—I *now* have you hollow
40　'Then tremble ye rivals of mighty Apollo,
'The work I confess may be taken for mine,
'True humour and wit so apparently shine;
—'But since at Apollo you daringly scoff,
'I'll hold in *my* turn, a *Court Martial* on both;
45　'Revenge shall each moment of leisure employ
'And fear, and suspicion reflection annoy.—
—'Then my sentence is *this*.—be *oblivion* your fate,
'The *reverse is* your *portion*, attended *with hate*;
'Your fame tho intrusted to three, or to four,
50　'May *Conscience* still multiply *up* to a *score*
'For,—short sighted mortals!—one syllable known,
'Must set you at variance with half of the Town.—
—'Two Women are destin'd your secret to hear,
'And a secret with Females what Man wou'd not
　　　fear?
55　'Of course may you constantly dread the *revealing*
'Of *what you confided* to ****** and Helen.'—

MS pp. 70–73. In Craik's contents list, the poem is given the short title 'The Court Martial'.

1. **Phœbus**: Apollo, god of the Sun.
10. Both of the officers have two-syllable names; the second name has to rhyme with 'summons', perhaps, Cummins.

13. Mars: god of war.

16. the wreaths from his forehead: Phœbus is typically represented wearing a laurel wreath and playing the lyre.

19. the Pow'r of fell War: i.e. Mars.

20. *his sons:* i.e. the two army officers; cf. Burns's song 'I am a son of Mars,' in 'The Jolly Beggars' (Kinsley, I: 196).

24. The parentheses appear to have been written in later.

25. Spontoon: Sometimes known by the variant spelling espontoon or as a half-pike, a spontoon was a type of pole-arm worn by subordinate infantry officers in the seventeenth and eighteenth century.

28. Edina's new Corps: Presumably a regiment or company with an Edinburgh ('Edina') affiliation.

30. Their: Craik's manuscript reads 'There', an apparent mistake in making a fair copy from another notebook.

33. Bacchus: god of wine and pleasure.

36. *Bumper:* cup filled to the brim with alcohol, usually for the purpose of a toast.

45–46. Apollo's punishment on the two officers is that they will never be famous as poets, because they will have to keep their authorship secret to avoid retaliation from the targets of their satire.

56. The second of the officers' confidantes, along with Helen Craik herself, had a two-syllable first name.

TO MISS D—

Like the previous poem on the 'humourous court martial', this verse-letter illustrates Craik's ironic enjoyment of the social life during visits to Dumfries, where landed gentry, relatively isolated on country estates in the area for much of the year, would stay for hunt week, or quarter sessions, or when the judges came on Circuit, and bring their families with them for the balls, assemblies, concerts, renewed friendships, flirtations, and marriage opportunities, that the town could offer. Unlike the previous poem, this one is from a year when William Craik had decided that he and Helen would stay home in Arbigland, either to save money or to preempt a rumoured flirtation. Baulked of attending herself, Craik writes to ask her friend to update her on this year's county gossip, while making it devastatingly clear that she could already predict who would be there and how they would behave. Craik has an additional poem addressed to a 'Mr D: from Goat Whey Quarters', pp. 32–34.

    —While you the Circuit pleasures share,
    And join the chearful parties *there*;—
    While Beaus in crouds your charms adore,
    And *Flatt'ry triumphs less* or *more*;—
5   Can you amid such scenes attend
    To the misfortunes of a friend?
    Who vainly hop'd alas! To view
    The Youths in *Red, Black, Yellow, Blue*,—
    —But Caution in grey Wisdom's guise,
10   Stept in and told a thousand lies—
    Like Envy chose to interfere
    And whisper'd in my Father's ear,
    That Women ne'er abroad shou'd roam,
    That all their bus'ness lay at home,
15   That Cards, Assemblies, Balls were evil

And under Scarlet lurk'd—the Devil.—
—All this and forty stories more
The Beldame told him o'er and o'er,
Imagin'd dangers made him see,
20   And from gay Balls excluded me.—

—Hard fate!—that spite of such temptation
I'm doom'd to combat Inclination!—
For hist'ry says from Eve to Helen,
We Women have a cross-grain'd feeling,
25   And from forbidden fruit wou'd fly,
If wiser Mortals *bid* us *try*.—

—Should *this* be *so*, my resignation
Deserves no little commendation;
Since yielding sure has double merit
30   That conquers Nature and the spirit;
For 'tho faint murmurs—at a distance,
Shews *all* we *dare* of stout resistance,
'Tis only meant the price to raise,
Of what we do *against* our choice;
35   And when we *grumblingly obey*
Strong Love appears,—*by what* we say.—

—Yet still I doubt 'tis very clear
That I against my will am *here*,
And gladly wou'd renounce the merit
40   Of striving to *subdue* the spirit.—
Have pity then on my condition,
And, to my woes give some remission;—
For Circuit news I long to hear,
And *what* worth writing happen'd *there*;—
45   —If any new peculiar grace
Your fancy fixt on G*****'s face,
Or if her mighty head and feather
Drew all your admiration thither?—

¶

 —Does Lady ******** seem inclin'd
50 To view the moss with willing mind?
 —For sure I think so large a jointure
 Through any Bog might make her venture.—

 —But tell me,—did she make appearance
 In di'mond Necklace, or in Earrings
55 And was the Laird's dear Hundred pounds
 Laid out on trifling caps and gowns!
 Those pounds that for some fifty years
 Have caus'd alternate joys and fears
 Those pounds from Lime might profit bring
60 But marriage is—a diff'rent thing.—

 —With *this* and such *important* matter
 Pray fill my Friend your future Letter
 And tell how *****'s gracious Bride
 Attention paid the Voter tribe
65 For she, by dint of sage reflection
 Foresaw their use at next Election
 Where if poor ******'s fairly beat
 Triumphant ***** mounts the seat
 And seven years hence returns again
70 To try his Int'rest on the plain.—

 —In order next proceed to tell us
 A word or two about the fellows—
 —Of smart bon mots who said the brightest?
 What Hero's head with drink was lightest?
75 —But *that* perhaps were hard to tell
 Where *most* seem anxious to excell
 For seventieth Regiment all agree
 At *swallowing* show alacrity.—

 —But say—did *******'s dame appear
80 Or was the Knight of ****** there?—

Is she from Censure free again?
And does the World from sneers refrain?
Or did the Room, when they came thither
Hear *scandal* and *small talk* together?—

85   —*By Curiosity* you know
Our sex were ruin'd long ago;—
And Eve to each succeeding Daughter
Left a large portion ever after,
Which I to my eternal sorrow,
90   Find *here* to day and *here* tomorrow,
Defying strength and reason too,
What Pow'r can such a plague subdue:
For when I think it fairly slain,
Up rises Banquo's ghost again.—

95   —Now kindly help to lay this spirit,
And loudly I'll proclaim your merit.—

MS pp. 74–79.

1. **the Circuit:** twice a year judges from Edinburgh visited Dumfries on circuit. The *Statistical Account of Scotland* noted the overlap between the legal and social calendars: 'The Justiciary Court sits here during the spring and autumn circuits. Assemblies are held at these seasons, and never fail to bring together a considerable display of elegance and beauty': see *Statistical Account of Scotland* (1793), V, p. 127, and introduction.

8. **The Youths in Red, Black, Yellow, Blue:** Craik's manuscript has an asterisked footnote '*Different Officers *then* in Dumfries—'. In 1768, the War Office issued a 'General View of the Facings etc. of the Several Marching Regiments of Foot' which specified the different colours to be used. The 70th Regiment of

Foot (see l. 77 below), stationed in Scotland in 1776–78, had black uniform facings. There were more regiments than colours, however, with red facings for the 33rd and 53rd regiments, black facings for three further regiments, blue for ten regiments, and yellow in varying shades for at least eighteen: see Hew Strachan, *British Military Uniforms 1768–1796* (1975), pp. 178–81.

18. **The Beldame:** Envy, personified as an elderly lady advising Craik's widowed father.

37. **still I doubt:** 'doubt' here means 'feel certain that'.

46. **G*****'s face:** unidentified; perhaps Gordon: the same number of asterisks follows G in Craik's poems 'To Sir W. G.: Baronet' and 'reperusal'.

50. **view the moss:** The Solway Moss or Flow is located in the city of Carlisle in Cumbria, England near the Scottish border. On 16 November 1771, the Moss burst due to heavy rains, flooding farms and settlements and causing a lake to form. A description of the event, written by Mr John Walker to the Earl of Bute, was included in *Philosophical Transactions*, 62 (January 1772), 123–27.

63. *****'s gracious Bride:** clearly the young wife of a prospective parliamentary candidate, but there were several parliamentary constituencies in the Dumfries area, and identification rests on when the poem was written.

77. **seventieth Regiment:** Following overseas service in Ireland and the West Indies, the 70th Regiment of Foot, which had traditionally recruited heavily in Glasgow, was stationed in Scotland from 1776 to early 1778 (when Craik would have been between twenty-six and twenty-eight years old). Previously light grey, the uniform facings were changed to black in 1768, and later the regiment's base was moved to Surrey, obscuring its earlier Scottish connection: Richard Cannon, *Historical record of the Seventieth or Surrey Regiment of Foot* (London: Parker, 1849), p. 3; P. H. MacKerlie, *An Account of the Scottish Regiments* (Edinburgh: Nimmo, 1862), p. 21.

78. *swallowing:* i.e. drinking.

94. **Up rises Banquo's ghost again:** in Shakespeare's *Macbeth*, Act
III, sc. 4, the ghost of Banquo, whom Macbeth had murdered,
appears and reappears during a state banquet to remind him
of his guilt.

LINES WRITTEN UPON HEARING A GENTLEMAN COMPLAIN OF THE INSTABILITY OF HUMAN FRIENDSHIPS

The subject of this short poem, who had forgotten an early friend-ship with Craik, and now complains of neglect, is unidentified. In Craik's contents list, the poem is titled from its first line, 'A youth with every virtue blest'.

———————————

—A youth with ev'ry virtue blest,
That e'er superior Man possest,
Of various ills complain'd.
He dwelt on fleeting Friendship's theme,
5   Pronounc'd Esteem an empty name,
And 'gainst Neglect exclaim'd.—

—With silent anguish ***** heard,
His worth his genius she rever'd,
And well his merit knew,
10   To heal the wounds by *Fancy* made,
She wish'd,—and something wou'd have said,
But fear'd it wou'd not do.—

—In cold oblivion's frozen shade
His mem'ry long had left the Maid,
15   For *newer* friends to range
But these he found, as *time* or *chance*
Led Fortune's ever varying dance,
Were likeways apt to change.—

—Yet still with melting eye she view'd
20   A youth so gentle, wise and good,
The prey of *discontent*,
And oft she wish'd some pitying Pow'r

Wou'd hush in time's propitious hour
The sighs his bosom sent.—

25   —But where apply?—to whom complain?
From fickle Friendship's fleeting train
Experience turn'd with scorn
One last resource alone remain'd,
Drawn from his own superior mind,
30   Array'd in Reason's form.—

—Let him to *Nature* be but just,
His *mental pow'rs* with *judgement* trust,
And *on himself* depend.
Then peace and happiness shall stand
35   Unmov'd by Fortune's changing hand,
Or by the varying Friend.—

MS pp. 80–82.

Instability: Written as 'Insability' in the manuscript, further sug-
    gesting that this is a fair copy.
7. A two-syllable name, possibly Helen.
13. cold oblivion: widely used in earlier eighteenth-century liter-
    ature. See, e.g., Samuel Cobb, *Poems on Several Occasions*
    (London: Woodward, 1710), p. 99; Robert Jephson, *Braganza:
    A Tragedy* (London: 1775), II.2.114; and 'Elegiac Verses'
    in *Scots Magazine*, 43 (1781), 598, l. 50. Cf. also Mary
    Robinson's *Walsingham* (1797), p. 166: 'And cold oblivion's
    reign return, / The torch of love shall chear'.

TO MISS M: M:

This elegy, on the cumulative effect of successive losses on the
Craik family and on Craik herself, describes the death of her
brother Adam, and the gap left by the death abroad of another
friend or relative in the East Indies. Adam Craik (1740–1782)
had drowned with five other men on 23 July 1782, when the
excise cutter they were in capsized in the Solway Firth, near
Flimby, on the Cumberland coast. Craik recounts his death
in her letter to James Grierson, Esq., dated May 1810: 'poor
Adam, perished, as you may recollect, with his servant [Jack]
crossing the Channel at Arbigland, in an open boat, to visit his
friends in Cumberland . . .', where she attributes the accident to
'A gale of wind, want of proper ballast, and unskilful boatmen'
(*Farmer's Magazine*, 12 [June 1811], 161; reprinted in Appendix
I). Because Adam was his father's only legitimate surviving
son, and heir to the Arbigland estate, his death also became
a turning point in Helen Craik's life. William Craik decided
that Arbigland would pass, not to his unmarried daughters or
to his daughters equally, but through his married daughter to
his grandson Douglas Hamilton. The friend who died in the
East Indies is unidentified, though the title of the next poem in
the Beinecke manuscript, Craik's 'Lines on the Death of J. H.
in the East Indies', provides initials.

    —*You* who request *this* mournful Lay,
    And wou'd the pow'rs of Grief display;
    Say,—shall warm Pity's tear attend
    The early Urn, the mould'ring Friend?—
5   Shall kind Remembrance heave a sigh
    For scenes recall'd to Mem'rys eyes?—

    —Yes—Pity shall her aid bestow,
    And o'er the theme in anguish flow,
    While sad Remembrance mourns their doom,

10   And sorrowing views th' untimely tomb.—
—For soft Compassion's feeling mind
To soothing Sympathy inclin'd,
Deplores Man's suff'ring state below,
Alive to ev'ry touch of woe,
15   And gladly wou'd relieve the pain
That throbs through Mis'ry's bursting vein;—
—Of course the wish'd for strain I'll try,
In spite of Nature's struggling sigh.—

—When western skies receive the Sun,
20   And busy Day his length has run;
When Evening takes her turn to reign
And brings Reflection in her train,
Along the lonely Beach I stray,
And give to Meditation way.—
25   —There former prospects rise to thought,
By strong imagination brought;
The gayer World's once cherish'd scenes
Usurp a while my waking dreams;
The view no pleas'd sensation brings,
30   It fleets like sublunary things.—
More serious subjects soon return,
And prove that Man was doom'd to mourn.—

—For *there* by Neptune's sea green side,
As musing oft I trace the Tide,
35   And think, while gazing o'er th' expanse,
On all the ebbs and flows of Chance,
To Mem'ry's painful province true,
Sad Recollection clouds the view;—
—Then, then around, through ev'ry scene,
40   What mournful objects intervene!
What horror meets the streaming eyes,
What deadly Phantoms round me rise!—
—A Brother's wat'ry Shade appears,

And points to six untimely Biers;—
45 While floating o'er the raging Main,
The fatal Wreck appears again;
And by the pow'rs of Fancy tost
Once more each struggling Wretch is lost
Once more they rise above the wave,
50 Then sink to fate's allotted Grave:—
—While o'er the ever dreadful scene,
A Parent's aged Form is seen;
Absorp'd in grief and silent woe,
Too deep for words, or outward show;
55 Resign'd she bends her weary head,
And joins the much lamented Dead.—

—Oft too along the winding way
Gay Humour's sportive Son wou'd stray,
While Echo from each neighbouring rock,
60 Retail'd the mirth inspiring joke.—
And when to distant regions borne,
We vainly hop'd his wish'd return,
Impatient friendship hover'd round,
And heard his voice in ev'ry sound,
65 And ev'ry breeze that curl'd the Main,
In fancy brought him back again.—

—But ah!—from India's deadly shore
The fav'rite youth returns no more.—
No chearful Humour's festive Song,
70 Shall list'ning Echo *here* prolong;
Life's sprightly torch is *now* exhal'd,
And Nature's early functions fail'd,
Too soon alas! he join'd the dead,
And wit's eccentric spirit fled.—

75 —O rigid fate of human kind,
To Disappointment's lot assign'd!

And doom'd by stern Misfortune's will,
To feel corroding anguish still,—
Ordain'd Life's dearest hopes to mourn,
80   And weep o'er some ill-fated urn.—

—By woes like these each comfort torn,
And to the World indiff'rent grown,
No more shall Fancy gild the view,
Nor *Thought* delusive joys pursue,
85   But bending at Retirement's shrine,
On Resignation hence recline.—

—Come Solitude then,—peaceful Friend,
On thee my weary steps attend,
On thee I bend a longing eye,
90   Well-pleas'd from public scenes to fly,
By Life's gay hopes no more inspir'd,
And most content when *most* retir'd.—

MS pp. 83–88.

28. Usurp: Craik's manuscript reads 'usurps'.

32. Man was doom'd to mourn: A variation of Burns's poem, 'Man Was Made to Mourn: A Dirge', first published in 1784.

33. Neptune's sea: Neptune, Roman god of the sea; counterpart to the Greek god, Poseidon.

43. A Brother's wat'ry Shade: Craik's brother Adam, drowned with five other men in a boat accident on 23 July 1782, in the Solway Firth (*Cumberland Pacquet and Ware's Whitehaven Advertiser*, 30 July 1782, p. 2).

44. six untimely Biers: Adam's servant, Jack, and four crew members, perished alongside him. For 'untimely bier', cf. Shakespeare, *Richard II*, v.6.52, and perhaps, more generally, Milton's elegy on the drowning of Edward King, and his 'wat'ry bier', in *Lycidas*, l. 12.

52. **A Parent's aged Form:** William Craik, 1703–1798, was seventy-nine at the time of Adam Craik's death. He died sixteen years later, in February 1798, at the age of ninety-five. The pronoun 'she' in line 56 suggests, however, that Craik was referring to her mother, Elizabeth (Stewart) Craik, whose death Craik credits to the accident: 'My poor mother never recovered from the shock occasioned by this most distressing accident, and followed him [Adam] to another and a better world in February 1787' (*Farmers Magazine, loc.cit.*).

57–74. These lines lament a second death, that of the unidentified 'J. H.' for whom Craik also wrote a separate elegy, 'Lines Written upon the death of J: H: in the East Indies' (next poem). The epigraph to 'Lines', from *Hamlet*, v.1.172–84, refers to J. H. as 'a fellow of infinite jest'.

58. **Gay Humour's sportive Son:** The phrase 'sportive son' is applied to Cupid in a song from Lewis Theobald's opera *Apollo and Daphne* (1726), reprinted in such eighteenth-century song collections as *The Lark, The Thrush, The Bullfinch*, etc.

59. **Echo:** nymph who, after angering Zeus's wife, Hera, was able to speak only the last words spoken to her.

61. **regions:** Craik's manuscript reads 'region's'.

67–68. **But ah! . . . The fav'rite youth returns no more:** i.e. J. H.

LINES WRITTEN UPON THE DEATH OF J: H:—
IN THE EAST INDIES—

In the eighteenth century, ambitious younger sons of landed families in the Dumfries area, as in Scotland generally, often sought to make careers or fortunes overseas, if not with the army or navy, then perhaps in North America, the West Indies, or with the East India Company. The J. H. of this poem remains unidentified, but Craik's sister, Mary Ann, married John Hamilton of Ellershaw, so one possibility might be a relative from his family. In the immediately preceding poem in the Beinecke manuscript, 'To Miss M: M:', ll. 57–68, Craik also references J. H.'s death. Neilson (Appendix II, p. 200) notes that this poem was inserted in his MS as two loose pages written in the principal hand, suggesting that the poem was written separately and that Craik had missed copying it into that manuscript at the relevant place.

—Alas poor Yorick!—I knew him, Horatio, a Fellow of infinite jest; of most excellent fancy:—Where be your gambols now; your Songs? your flashes of merriment that were wont to set the Table in a roar?

Poor Fellow!—short has been thy date
And soon from anguish free;
The chance or change of varying fate
No more can injure thee.

5   From burning climes and deadly shores
We vainly hop'd thee soon;—
—Alas! each Friend thy loss deplores,
And mourns thy early doom.

¶

The plaintive Muse, whose streaming eye
10   To grief must tribute pay,
Pursues thee through thy Indian skie,
Along the liquid way.

There views Consumptions's rapid speed,
And Humour's bursting sighs;
15   While in the Grave for ever laid,
His fav'rite Vot'ry lies.

Th' eccentric thought, the cheerful Song,
No more alas! is here;
Yet these sad Mem'ry shall prolong,
20   And vib'rate on the ear.

Poor Fellow!—Life's gay hopes from thee
Fled, like a morning dream,
Yet few cou'd more enraptur'd be
With pleasure's fleeting scene.

25   Thy Life of frolick, soul of whim,
For ever *now* must rest;
No more thy youthful Form is seen
No more is heard thy jest.

For thee, to fond Remembrance true,
30   The feeling heart shall mourn;
And poor Meridian weeping view,
In fancy still thy urn.

MS pp. 89–91. In Craik's contents list, the poem is titled 'Lines
written on the death of J. H.'.

Epigraph: Variation of lines spoken by Hamlet (v.1.172–84) in which he ponders the transitory nature of life.

16. **His fav'rite Vot'ry lies:** Humour's votary, i.e. J. H.; c.f. l. 58 in 'To Miss M: M:'.

31. **poor Meridian:** Craik's manuscript has an asterisked footnote, '*A name he usually gave one', perhaps his joking reference to her being at life's midpoint, just about to start her decline. Because J. H. is buried in India, Craik's reference to weeping beside his urn is only in imagination.

THE GHOST OF QUEEN MARY—
OCCASIONED BY A BEAUTIFUL POEM
WRITTEN AND SENT ME BY MR BURNS

Craik's poem about the return of Mary, Queen of Scots as a ghost or revenant is one of the most direct links between her poetry and Burns's. Burns's own poem 'Queen Mary's Lament' (later 'The Lament of Mary Queen of Scots on the Approach of Spring') was first published in his *Poems* (Edinburgh, 1793), but had been written by the summer of 1790, when Craik met Burns at Friar's Carse. The rehabilitation of Mary, a villain to Presbyterian historians, was largely due to the research of William Fraser Tytler, a friend of Robert Riddell and someone who had been friendly also to Burns himself. In Craik's letter to Burns of 26 March 1792, from Carlisle, she says she has been writing something 'by Q. Mary in her confinement' (Ewing 1938, letter 286), which she plans to send to him for comment, but it cannot be this poem, where Mary appears not during her long imprisonment, but after her execution in 1587. That later poem may have been written not only from Craik's identification with Queen Mary's plight after the murder of her secretary David Rizzio in March 1566, but from parallels with her own stay in Carlisle after leaving Arbigland; in 1568 when Queen Mary left Scotland for England, she was a prisoner in Carlisle Castle for two months before she was moved south. This poem, a more direct comment on Burns's poem rather than an imitation from it, does not match the description in the Carlisle letter. On attitudes toward Queen Mary in the circles round Burns and Craik, it is worth noting that Craik's friend Lady Winifred Maxwell sent Burns a snuffbox bearing a portrait of Queen Mary, and he thanked her by sending her a copy of his unpublished 'Lament' (see *Letters*, II: 88–89; 25 April 1791; on Craik and Lady Winifred, cf. 'Bird of Paradise', pp. 20–23 above).

—From the pure regions of a happier shore
I come!—no more an Exile drench'd in gore,
No longer destin'd to corporeal pain,
Nor doom'd a Pris'ner *where* I ought to reign!
5   No more ordain'd a faithless Sovereign's slave;
Condemn'd to curse the charms that Nature
    gave;—
No more by Queens or Subjects robb'd of breath,
Nor crush'd with mental suff'rings ev'n to death.—
—But from a pure, a bliss inspiring scene,
10   From skies where all is peaceful and serene,
I come!—for Thee I quit eternal day,
And downward glide my gratitude to pay.—
Yes Burns!—to thee whose ever tuneful Song
Might soothe Remembrance from each sense of
    wrong—
15   To thee my list'ning Spirit homage pays
And hears, with pride, the Heav'n taught Poet's
    Lays.—
—The Bard whose praise confers immortal fame,
To latest time shall consecrate my name;
Shall poor Compassion o'er the mournful tale,
20   Till ev'n the stern Elizabeth bewail,
And view with torture midst the injur'd Great,
A Sister Queen by her consign'd to fate.—
—False Woman!—loud reproach pursues thy
    crime,
And keen Remorse embitters deeds like thine;
25   Yet meek forgivness *now* shall close the scene,
Since Burns was destin'd to record the theme;—
Yes!—*now* I pardon since my native Land
At length unanimously right shall stand;
For sure applause the gen'rous Bard must bless,
30   Whose feeling Soul can can paint such deep distress

Ev'n the vain Queen with envy still shall see
A gen'ral tear in pity stream for me,
And own enrag'd, with rapture she cou'd bleed,
Had fate on Earth a *Burns* for her decreed.—

MS pp. 92–94. In Craik's contents list, the poem is titled 'Queen Mary's Ghost'.

2. **no more an Exile drench'd in gore:** Forced in 1567 to abdicate her throne to her infant son, Queen Mary fled Scotland in 1568 for exile in England, hoping for Elizabeth I's support and protection. However, as a potential Catholic replacement should Elizabeth be ousted, Mary was held in captivity for nineteen years before being executed on 8 February 1587.

4. *where* **I ought to reign!:** Mary had a claim to the English throne, as Henry VII's great-granddaughter.

5. **a faithless Sovereign:** i.e. Elizabeth I.

6. **the charms that Nature gave:** Comments on Queen Mary's appearance were numerous throughout her life, and she was widely considered beautiful and charming, especially in comparison to Elizabeth I.

16. **Heav'n taught Poet's Lays:** cf. Mackenzie's review referring to Burns as the 'Heav'n taught ploughman' (*Lounger*, 9 December 1786).

HELEN:
AN OLD SCOTS TALE

This short prologue and the poem that follows (next item) are based on a well-known ballad, 'Fair Helen' or 'Helen of Kirkconnell Lea', set in the Borders in the early sixteenth century, but thought to have been written much later. Burns had contributed a revised version of the ballad to *Scots Musical Museum* 2 (1788), song 155, with the first line 'O that I were where Helen lies!', though he commented to George Thomson that 'The old ballad "I wish I were where Helen lies"—is silly, to contemptibility.—My alteration of it in Johnson is not much better' (Roy, *Letters*, II: 220). On other precursors and the scale of Burns's revision, see Pittock, *OERB*, III: 47.

Craik's prose summary does not indicate the distinctive angle she takes on the story in her poem. The summary follows the account in Thomas Pennant, *A Tour in Scotland and a Voyage to the Hebrides, MDCCLXXII* (Chester: Printed for John Monk, 1774), I, p. 101, recycled in, e.g., *Critical Review*, 38 (1774), 21; and cf. the lengthy footnote giving Pennant's precis and the ballad itself, in Rev. Andrew Monilaws, 'Parish of Kirkpatrick-Fleeming', in Sir John Sinclair, ed., *Statistical Account of Scotland* (1794), XIII, pp. 274–77; 'Song LXVII. Where Helen Lies', and annotation, in Joseph Ritson (ed.), *Scottish Songs*, 2 vols (London: J. Johnson, 1794), I, pp. 145–47; 'Fair Helen of Kirkconnell', in Walter Scott, *Minstrelsy of the Scottish Border*, 2 vols (Kelso: printed by James Ballantyne, 1802), I, pp. 72–79; 'Fair Helen of Kirkconnell', in F. J. Child, *English and Scottish Popular Ballads*, 8 vols (Boston: Houghton Mifflin, 1888), II, pp. 207–12. Topographical references in Craik's summary can be confusing, because the Maxwell family had several branches, and several places carried the name Kirkconnell.

—The subject of the following Epistle took its rise from Helen, a young Lady of great beauty, a daughter of the family of Kirkconnell in Annandale,—at present the possession of Sir William Maxwell of Springkell Baronet.—She had been courted by two Gentlemen, one of whom told her that if he found her at any time afterwards in the company of the other, he would kill him.—She had a greater regard for the other, and walking with him on the pleasant romantic banks of the Kirtle, observed his Rival on the opposite side of the river, amongst the bushes.— Conscious of the danger to which her Lover was exposed, she leapt into his arms as if to screen him, (or endeavouring to protect him) from the attempts of his antagonist, who immediately firing shot *her* dead.—She having thus fallen a victim for her Lover, he drew his Sword, passed the river, and cut the murderer to pieces.—She was buried in the adjacent Church-yard of Kirkconnell,—after which the forlorn, disconsolate Gentleman is said to have gone abroad for some time,—returned,—visited her Grave,— stretched himself upon it, and expired.—He was buried in the same place.

—On the Tomb-stone are engraven a Cross with a Sword and Hic Jacet Adam Fleming, cut on the north-side of the Cross.—There is no date on the Tomb-stone;—but from different circumstances this event seems to have happened about the end of the reign of James the fifth, or to have ushered in *that* of the unfortunate, the beautiful Mary Queen of Scots.—

MS pp. 95–96.

The family of Kirkconnell: the Maxwells of Kirkconnell took their name from Kirkconnell Tower, in the parish of Kirkconnell, thirty miles north of Dumfries, up Nithsdale, almost into Ayrshire. However, in Craik's time the family's home was at Kirkconnell House, near New Abbey, Dumfriesshire, seven miles south of Dumfries and about eight miles from Arbigland. The events of the ballad, however, are set in yet another Kirkconnell, some twenty miles west of Dumfries, a parish amalgamated in 1609 with Kirkpatrick Fleming.

Sir William Maxwell: Sir William Maxwell 3rd baronet (1740–1804), of Springkell, in the parish of Kirkpatrick Fleming. Maxwell had succeeded to the baronetcy in 1760, and his son married the daughter of Patrick Heron, M.P. for Kirkcudbright.

banks of the Kirtle: Kirtle Water or Kirtle Burn is a small river in east Dumfriesshire, near the Solway Firth.

churchyard of Kirkconnell: the memorial to Adam Fleming (or Fleeming) is still in the old Kirkconnell churchyard, closed in 1609 on the amalgamation of the parishes. A modern marker near the cross suggests the ballad was not sixteenth century, but eighteenth century. Another modern marker on Fair Helen's grave gives the name of Fleming's rival as Richard Bell.

reign of James the fifth: the early sixteenth century. James V was king of Scotland from 1513 to 1542; he died aged thirty, shortly after the Scots were defeated by the English at the Battle of Solway Moss.

Mary, Queen of Scots: Mary, daughter of James V, succeeded to the Scottish throne as an infant in 1542, and was brought up in France; for Craik's attitude to her later forced abdication, imprisonment in England, and execution, see 'The Ghost of Queen Mary', pp. 107–09, above.

HELEN:
AN EPISTLE TO A FRIEND

Like Craik's other longer poems in the Beinecke manuscript, this retelling of the ballad 'Fair Helen' focuses on the inconsolable survivor who feels responsible for the death of a lover. Significantly, in light of Arnott's biographical theories about Craik's romance and the murder of the man involved, she retells this story from the viewpoint of the surviving lover Adam Fleming, not of his murdered love Helen. She adopted a similar perspective in her poems about the late Queen of Denmark, James Hackman, the Maid of Enterkin (a daughter blaming herself for her father's death), Charlotte mourning at Werther's Grave, and the final long Gothic poem in this manuscript, the Monk of la Trappe.

For a summary of the ballad story that Craik is retelling, see her prose preface (previous item), which has a headnote identifying some probable sources. The Beinecke MS provides the only known manuscript for this poem. Neilson records that Craik's version of the 'Fair Helen' story had been mentioned by Alexander Gardyne, but that he had not seen it himself, hoping that it was 'not lost beyond recovery' (Appendix II, p. 204). When Craik wrote 'Helen' is uncertain, though it must predate her preparation of the Beinecke manuscript for Robert Riddell in 1790. This poem should not be confused with a later and quite different poem with the title 'Helen, Written in the Summerhouse at Arbigland, Feb. 25, 1792' (see Appendix II, p. 217).

    —You ask alas! Why heaves the frequent sigh,
    Why from the chearful haunts of man I fly?
    Why o'er these long neglected scenes I rove,
    And lonely wander through the silent Grove?
5   Why nightly musing midst the peaceful dead,
    O'er some low mould'ring Tomb I bend my head?

And while on Kirtle's verdant banks I go,
Cast o'er its streams despairing looks of woe?—
—Ah me!—each question to deep horror leads,
10   And torn Remembrance o'er the subject bleeds!—
In vain ev'n Time a lenient hand supplies,
His soft'ning aid the pow'r of Grief defies:
Misfortune's wound still festers in my breast,
And soothing Death alone can give me rest.—
15   —O Love!—thou source of all my suff'rings here,
For thee descends Affliction's lasting tear;—
For thee to worldly pleasures early lost,
I turn from Life, a self-devoted Ghost;
And when sad friendship's mournful debt is paid,
20   Resign'dly seek the Grave's eternal shade.——

—In yon old ruin—mould'ring from the view—
This wretched Being first existence drew.—
There art and nature variously combin'd
To form my morals, and improve my mnd,—
25   —Gay Fancy smil'd around,—her partial eye
Saw future scenes unclouded with a sigh;
—Saw gliding Time in smoothe succession flow,
Nor dreamt that man was preordain'd to woe.—

—But woe approach'd in passion's vengeful form,
30   And Life's enjoyments bent beneath the storm;—
O Jealousy!—Thou bane of human peace
When shall thy agonizing tortures cease!—
When shall the wounds by thee inflicted close,
And suff'ring Nature sink to calm repose?—
35   —I lov'd!—good Heav'ns from Love what horror
       came!
Each soft sensation shudders at the name,
Reflection throbs o'er long remember'd pain,
And Mis'ry's tear attends the deadly strain,

—The stream,—the field,—each stone my grief
   renews,
40 While the sad tale this trembling hand pursues.—

—In early youth,—when happier prospects reign'd
One lovely Maid my sole attention claim'd;—
Wise were her thoughts,—by Reason's views
   confin'd,
And ev'ry virtue fill'd her gen'rous mind:—
45 Each look the feelings of her heart exprest,
'Her Form was beauty, by the Graces drest.'
Her charms, her wit, each gay Admirer sung,
And Approbation dwelt on ev'ry tongue.—
—Congenial manners, such as ours appear'd
50 On friendship's basis firm attachment rear'd;—
And oft the Moon, in yon sequester'd shade,
Has witness'd to the fervent vows we made,—
For one bright flame each youthful bosom fir'd,
And views of bliss delusive Hope inspir'd.—
55 —Gay hours of peace, and rapture, whither fled?
Are ye too number'd with the silent dead?—
—No more on me your genial influence shines,
Now all my hopes the clay cold Grave confines—

—A rival came,—ill-suited to the Maid,
60 No soft impression on her heart he made;
Neglected, scorn'd,—his sullen looks exprest
The gloomy passions rankling in his breast;
On me some unknown vengeance was decreed,—
As *more* successful, I was doom'd to bleed;—
65 His vows rejected,—by Distraction drove,
He trac'd our footsteps to the lonely Grove;—
—The Maid was warn'd some deadly scene to fear,
And oft in silence stream'd the conscious tear;
In vain I urg'd the mournful theme to know,

70   The fatal cause she still refus'd to show,
      Afraid resentment in my breast might burn,
      And ill-starr'd vengeance doom an early urn.—

      —As thus on Kirtle's winding banks we stray'd
      And apprehension ev'ry look betray'd,
75   Across the stream a thoughtful glance she threw,
      Then to my arms in quick distraction flew!—
      —The sudden scream—convulsive grasp of fear,
      The thund'ring tube that vibrates on the ear,
      All, all, announc'd my vengeful rival near!—
80   —The ground a flood of crimson horror shows,
      And my lost Helen's eyes for ever close!—
      —She falls!—Immortals!—what a scene was there!—
      Yet ev'n in death I seem'd her fav'rite care,
      Her freezing arms my wretched Frame surround,
85   As anxious *still* to ward the destin'd wound,
      As anxious *still* her dire esteem to prove,
      Ev'n tho the throbbing heart had ceas'd to move;—
      At length from me my fated Love was torn
      And to the Grave the bleeding victim borne.—

90   —But ah!—Description's pow'rs no more avail,
      No more my streaming eyes can trace the tale!—
      —The Grecian Painter's art the Muse bestows,
      And o'er the scene a timely mantle throws;
      While Guardian Angels shudd'ring turn away,
95   And give to stern Despair unbounded sway.—

      —But quickly rous'd from agonizing pain.
      Resentment takes its furious turn to reign;—
      I leap the brook,—assail my rival's Life,
      The vengeful sword decides the deadly strife
100   This vig'rous hand directs the well-aim'd blow,
      And sends the wretch to kindred fiends below.—

¶

—In distant regions,—wand'ring and forlorn,
From all enjoyment,—ev'ry comfort torn,
For years I hop'd oblivion to obtain,
105   But mem'ry still recur'd with double pain;—

—At length I feel the wish for home return,
A ling'ring wish, to weep o'er Helen's urn;—
I came,—you saw my soul with grief opprest,
And kindly strove to soothe my tortur'd breast.—
110   —Tho vain each effort by your friendship made
The source of anguish I have *here* display'd;
At your request the sad narration giv'n,—
And sure it claims a pitying tear from Heav'n.—
—O may you ne'er such deep affliction prove,
115   Nor feel the pangs of an ill-omen'd Love.—

—For me the term of rest is surely near,
Last night a well-known voice approach'd my ear.
The plaintive sound like dying murmurs came,
And feebly call'd on Fleming's fatal name,—
120   —I started!—look'd,—a Form etherial spied,—
The erring ball had pierc'd her tender side,
In bloody torrents pour'd the vital stream,
Which from *my* view she vainly strove to screen.
Through the cold hand, extended o'er the wound,
125   The crimson flood a ready issue found;
And bursting forth, in spite of all her art,
Once more display'd my Helen's gen'rous heart.
Her floating garments drench'd appear'd in gore,
And former scenes my wretched mem'ry tore.—

130   —She saw the anguish struggling in my eye,
She heard the bursting heart's oppressive sigh,—
Convinc'd her suff'rings must severe appear,

She view'd her Form, and dropt for *me* a tear.—
Then sadly sighing rais'd her languid head,
135 And thus—in broken accents,—faintly said,—

—'To shield *that* cherish'd breast from poignant
            pain,
'In Life,—in death,—my efforts have been vain!—
'What tho to save you I existence gave,
'The pangs you suffer'd far surpass'd the Grave;—
140 'And *here*, ev'n now, when I with peace repair,
'Sad Recollection dooms you to Despair,—
—'Ill-omen'd Helen!—still ordain'd on earth
'To give some deep, some dire affliction birth!—
—'Yet shall the scene on mortal suff'rings close,
145 'I come to guide you to divine repose.—
—'O Fleming!—lov'd!—ador'd!—for ever dear!
'For whom my ling'ring Spirit hovers here,
'I come to tell you grief at length is o'er,
'And weary Nature soon shall weep no more;
150 'I come to call you to a happier state
'Remov'd from all the varying turns of fate,
'Where no stern rival deadly vengeance shows,
'Where tears, nor blood, no more in anguish flows.—
—'What tho the lustre from my eyes is fled,
155 'My cheeks display the paleness of the dead,
'And from those lips which spoke my heart your
            own,
'The deep vermilion is for ever flown?—
'Yet joys more lasting on your steps attend,
'Which no short term of fleeting years can end;—
160 'Eternity's wide prospects shall disclose
'Superior views to Time or human woes;
'And this deep wound, by passion's dictates giv'n,
'Appear a fav'ring mandate sent from Heav'n,
'An *early* Passport to serener scenes,
165 'Above weak nature's most seraphic dreams.—

¶

    —'But see!—the east proclaims th' approach of
        day,
    'The silver Moon nor more prolongs my stay;—
    'Now summon'd hence to native skies I soar,
    '*Where* Love and friendship soon shall part no
        more.
170   —'Farewell!—to my sad Tomb once more repair,
    'I'll meet—and be your guardian Angel *there*.'—

    —She ceas'd,—she vanish'd!—by amazement
        chang'd
    A heavy stupor through my sense reign'd;—
    At length Time brought returning thought again,
175   But thought return'd, unoccupied by pain;
    More calm sensations sooth'd my tortur'd breast,
    And soft composure gave Remembrance rest.—

    —But *now* I feel Life's vital spring decay,
    And this vain world from me recedes away;—
180   Last night's dire vision was no empty dream,
    Produc'd by mis'ry's past unhappy theme;—
    The timely warning her mild Spirit gave,
    To smoothe my passage to the peaceful Grave,
    Where free from grief for once, I now repair,
185   And hope to join my faithful Helen *there*.—

    —Come then my Friend,—the last kind office pay,
    Consign *this* mould'ring Frame to kindred clay;
    In Helen's Tomb see my cold ashes laid,
    And pour a tear o'er each ill-fated Shade.—
190   —I go!—her beck'ning Ghost my stay arraigns,
    And freezing death is gliding through my veins.—
    Farewell!—on Life no ling'ring look I cast,
    But view, well-pleas'd, the tedious journey past.—

MS pp. 97–108.

2. **the chearful haunts of man:** Milton, *Comus, A Mask*, l. 388, with 'men', not 'man'.

7. **Kirtle's verdant banks:** Kirtle Water or Kirtle Burn is a small river in east Dumfriesshire, near the Solway Firth.

28. **man was preordain'd to woe:** cf. Burns, 'Man Was Made to Mourn: A Dirge' (1784).

46. **'Her Form was beauty, by the Graces drest':** Variation of the concluding lines inscribed on Lucy Lyttleton's monument written by her husband Lord Lyttelton: 'Her form each beauty of her mind express'd, / Her mind was virtue by the Graces dress'd' (1746).

51–52. **And oft the Moon . . . the fervent vows we made:** 'Irregular marriage', or marriage founded on mutual consent via a declaration of vows, was legal in Scotland until 1939, although not recognised by the Church. For more, see Eleanor Gordon, 'Irregular Marriage: Myth and Reality', *Journal of Social History*, 47.2 (Winter 2013), 507–25.

54. **delusive Hope:** The opening of Samuel Johnson's *Rambler*, no. 67, has 'Delusive hope still points to distant good', and l. 1 of Johnson's 'On the Death of Dr Robert Levet' has 'hope's delusive mind'. Craik uses the same phrase in 'The Indian Maid—Part Second–', l. 70 and in 'the Earl of Caithness', l. 54.

58. **clay cold Grave:** Craik uses the same phrase in 'Written by Charlotte at Werter's Grave', l. 85.

77–79. In her manuscript, Craik has right-hand brackets around these lines.

92. **The Grecian Painter:** Craik's MS provides a footnote to this line: 'The Painter who drew the sacrifice of Iphigenia, covered Agamemnon's face with his mantle, as unable to delineate so much affliction.—'; Timanthes of Cythnus (c. fourth century BC) is best known for his depiction of the sacrifice of Iphigenia, which represents the grief of the bystanders with the exception of Agamemnon, whose face was covered by a veil as he performed the sacrifice.

92. **bestows:** Craik originally wrote 'bestows', correcting to 'bestow', but the singular subject, 'Muse', and following rhyme word, 'throws', indicate that it should be 'bestows'.

149. **weary Nature:** cf. 'The Flower and the Leaf', translated by Dryden, in his *Fables Ancient and Modern* (1700), l. 31.

TO SIR W. G.: BARONET—
WRITTEN UPON HIS SENDING ME HIS
PROFILE SOME YEARS AGO

This poem is the first of two that Craik addresses to an old friend, whom she had known when he was an army officer, who had sent her a silhouette portrait of himself. The poem echoes the atmosphere in Craik's other poems about army officers stationed in Dumfries, 'The Soldier's Joy', 'A Humourous Court martial', and 'To Miss D—'. Craik recalls the officers' teasing, and appears still to be open to the possibility of a future marriage, but again she rules out, as she had done her earlier poem 'To a Gentleman' (pp. 38–42 above, which can be dated 1782), ever marrying for money: 'No empty rank, nor riches, e'er / Shall make me Hymen's fetters bear.—' (ll. 43–44).

Silhouettes, or 'shades' (cf. l. 1 below), were fashionable in Scotland in the later 1780s. They could be made by tracing the shadow that the sitter's profile cast on a paper background, or they could be drawn or painted in solid black, or snipped out from black paper. Small silhouettes made attractive gifts or mementos either framed or inserted in a locket. A well-known silhouette artist, John Miers (1756–1821), living in Edinburgh from 1786 to 1788, snipped out small silhouettes of hundreds of Scottish sitters, including Robert Burns, Burns's Edinburgh friends Agnes McLehose ('Clarinda') and Robert Ainslie, and others in his circle. In February 1788 Burns told Mrs McLehose that he wanted her silhouette by Miers 'to wear on a breastpin close to my heart', and he wrote to Ainslie in June the same year asking him to sit for Miers, because he planned to hang silhouettes of Ainslie, the poet Dr Blacklock, and his patron the Earl of Glencairn over the mantel in his new house at Ellisland: see *Letters of Robert Burns*, ed. Roy, I, pp. 227, 288, and Basil Skinner, *Authentic Likenesses* (Edinburgh: Oliver and Boyd, 1963).

Because the W. G. of this poem, and the one that follows, was a baronet, and because he was an army officer when Craik first knew him, his identity can be narrowed down. In the next poem, Craik gives both the first and last letters of his name (G****n), and the metre of the poem requires the name to be two syllables. There was a family of Gordons who were baronets in Kirkcudbrightshire, but they seem to have had no William in the relevant period. A more likely candidate, though he was older than Craik, and was married before they would have met, might be William Gordon (1736-1804), 7th Baronet, of Embo, in Sutherland, who entered the army in 1755, was a lieutenant in the 52nd Foot in 1773, succeeded to the baronetcy in 1786, and became a captain in the 19th Foot in 1787 (*Caledonian Mercury*, 11 October 1787, p. 1).

    —Say G*****, is an empty Shade
    By *you* the type of Friendship made?
    You who alone of all I knew,
    Have to her dictates still been true;
5   And scorning *Time* or *chance's* name,
    Through circling years have prov'd the same,—
    Or is it only meant to tell
    That in your thoughts I sometimes dwell?

    —The magic view to Mem'ry brings
10   A thousand painful, pleasing things;
    Calls to remembrance ev'ry scene,
    That in oblivion long has lain;—
    The baseless fabrick Fancy rears,
    And B*** with all his Corps appears
15   Once more I hear him loud exclaim
    'Gainst Hymen, if *ungilt* his chain;
    And acting well the Major's part,
    From Cupid's wiles protect the heart.—
    —But shou'd gay ******** appear,
20   Themes harsh as these no more we hear;

Relaxing discipline a while,
The stern Commander deigns to smile,
And while the ***** keeps in sight,
Poor Cupid gains a short respite.—

25 —There C*******l, whimsically nice,
Turns delicacy to a vice;
And tho possest of pow'rs to please,
Must still himself, or others teaze.—

—The old Dragoon's repeated jest,
30 Once more my wearied ears molest;
Again I hear the loud encore,
Demand the hum'rous Song once more.—

—Next these a train of youths appear.
Who scarcely claim the Muse's care.
35 Vain,—giddy,—thoughtless,—ne'er design'd
By Wisdom's rules to be confin'd.—
In silence let them pass along,
Tho ev'n the C— join the throng.
—The C—, yes, *whate'er you say*,
40 To Plutus I'll no homage pay;
His sordid Vot'ries scorning Love,
Their own tormentors justly prove.—
—No empty rank, nor riches, e'er
Shall make me Hymen's fetters bear.—
45 This chain is heavy, at the best
He often proves a fatal Guest.
And ev'n when due attentions shown
Repays our caution with a frown.—
—Congenial minds,—good-humour,—sense,
50 Forbearance,—patience,—competence,—
These,—these alone can only tell
If *peace* within his bound'ries dwell.—

¶

—Tho partial Heav'n to you assign'd,
A Part'ner of congenial mind,
55   Th' example vainly wou'd you quote,
For few can boast the envied lot;—
On few alas! such blessings fall,
For human joys are dash'd with gall;
And Disappointment's bitter sting
60   With wormwood mixes *pleasure's* spring.—

—Yet still tho Fate disasters send,
I'll grateful at her Shrine attend,
There warm acknowledgements shall show
What for your present gift I owe;
65   A gift to me for ever dear,
Which Friendship's hand shall guard with care
And which to latest time shall prove,
Esteem superior far to Love.—

MS pp. 109–13.

Profile: a silhouette or outline portrait, also sometimes called a shade
(cf. l. 1), usually drawn, printed, or snipped out in solid black.
9. The magic view: i.e. the profile.
13. baseless fabrick: In Shakespeare's *The Tempest*, Prospero remarks
on the 'baseless fabric of this vision' (IV.I.151). Craik also
uses the phrase in 'To a Gentleman', l. 28.
14. B***: unidentified.
16. Hymen: God of marriage.
25. C*******l: Churchill. In the poem following this, 'Lines
Occasioned by a reperusal', Craik fills in the asterisks; cf. l. 9.
29. The old Dragoon: unidentified but possibly another name
for Churchill; perhaps the officer had transferred from the
Dragoons into a foot regiment.

38. **the C—:** colonel or captain.

40. **Plutus:** God of abundance or wealth.

54. **A Part'ner of congenial mind:** Sir William Gordon of Embo married Sarah Westfield, 15 June 1760.

61. **Yet still tho Fate disasters send:** subjunctive: 'though Fate should send disasters'.

LINES OCCASIONED BY A REPERUSAL OF THE FOREGOING EPISTLE TO SIR W. G. BARONET,—WRITTEN SOME YEARS AFTERWARDS—

This poem is a follow-up to the preceding verse, as Craik reflects on the fate of the officers she had remembered as she had known them years before. In Craik's contents list, the poem is titled from its first line 'Pass but a few short fleeting years'. On the possible identification of W. G., see the headnote to the previous poem, though here (l. 31) Craik gives both the first and last letters of his name, not just the initial letter.

  —'Pass but a few short fleeting years,'
  What changes in the scene appears!—
  —Poor B*** at length to rest is gone,
  The Soldier dreads no more his frown;—
5 In Honour's field he bow'd his head,
  With many a gallant Warrior dead;—
  Th' unerring Ball cut short his breath,
  And undismay'd he sunk to death.—

  —Churchill, whose discontented mind
10 No common forms of Life cou'd bind,
  Weary of Britain's friendly shore,
  The Eastern World must next explore
  And quitting all to Nature dear,
  Without one parting pang or tear;
15 He burst from ev'ry human tie,
  Reach'd India's coast,—but just to die!—
  A sad example, doom'd to show
  What evils from wild passions flow.—

  —The old Dragoon, by Fate misled,
20 At Hymen's shrine a victim bled;

Felt ev'ry curse attends his chain,
And paid with *int'rest back again;*—
Till weary with eternal strife
He died!—and pleas'd *for once* his wife.—

25   —The undistinguish'd, flutt'ring train,
The weak,—the gay,—the young,—the vain,
By Life's vicissitudes entomb'd,
Or ne'er to Mem'rys honours doom'd,
No more Remembrance calls to view
30   No mark'd esteem their conduct drew.—

—G****n alone the same remains,
And every thought of change disdains,
Lets Fortune ne'er his smiles confine,
Nor heeds the turns of varying Time;—
35   —Warmly supports with guardian care
The mind in which he claims a share;—
From selfish views and envy free
Friendship! in him thy essence see;—
Long may he feel the genial flame,
40   Secure from malice, chance or blame.—

MS pp. 114–16.

1. **'Pass . . .'**: First line of 'Ode for the New Year, 1774', written
by William Whitehead (1715–1785), who served as poet
laureate in 1757, and set to music by Dr William Boyce
(1711–1779), who was sworn in as the Master of the King's
Band of Musicians in June 1757 (*Gentleman's Magazine*, 44,
January 1774, 37) (*ODNB*).

3–4. **Poor B*** . . . frown**: Unidentified. In the previous poem,
B*** is described as a 'stern commander', l. 22.

9. **Churchill:** In the previous poem, Craik leaves Churchill's name unidentified, describing him as a man who 'turns delicacy to vice', l. 26.

19. **The old Dragoon:** unidentified, but possibly another name for Churchill.

31. **G****n:** that is, William Gordon, the only officer of the group still alive and happily married.

TO A GENTLEMAN

This poem was written to the same addressee as Craik's earlier poem 'To a Gentleman', pp. 38–42, who had still not yet replied to the first poem she had sent. Because this poem is dated in the Beinecke manuscript as written in 1782, it also provides a date for the earlier poem. In addition, it confirms the longer timeline for Craik's poetry discussed in the introduction to this volume, and the need to question Arnott's dramatic account in 'The Romance of Helen Craik' of a sudden reversal in Craik's marital hopes happening only in 1792. In Craik's contents list, the poem is titled from its first line 'Too long has hope on patience lean'd'.

———————

    —Too long has *Hope* on *Patience* lean'd,
    And Expectation ling'ring seem'd,—
    One week run o'er,—no answer came,
    Another gone,—'twas still the same!
5   No mem'ry *now* remains of me,
    The whim has lost *variety.*—

    —O fleeting state of human joys,
    Which Lordly man in pride destroys!—
    —'The *heart* shou'd act no changeful scene,'—
10   And why not *Friendship* do the same?—
    Why must *neglect* our pleasures chill,
    And bid Remembrance ev'n be still?—
    With deep regret alas! I view
    That *you* the beaten path pursue,
15   With deep regret,—but no surprise
    I own can from your silence rise,
    Because unequal far my powers,
    E'er to keep pace with such as yours;
    Of course no wonder if I see
20   *Neglect* take place of *Memory.*—

¶

—But tho convinc'd your reason's good,
I'd fain pervert you if I cou'd.—

—'Tis true, through Life we often find,
Our Judgement to the right inclin'd,
25   Yet still a wish will sometimes rise
That o'er the bounds of *Judgement* flies;
Bids reas'ning Pride resign the field,
And Wisdom ev'n to trifles yield;—
Have you—but no—the case I see,
30   Ev'n *this* has lost variety.—

—But since our joys on earth are few,
Oft out of *reach*—but ne'er of *view*;
Let me once more your mem'ry try,
Nor heed Decorum frowning by;—
35   'What!—write *again*!—' she proudly cries—
'Such condescension he'll despise,
'No more your Cards he hopes to see,
'Hear *this*,—and learn to follow *me*.'—
—'Too plain appears the fact' she said,—
40   And of the hind *this* use I made,
Spite of unfeeling cold Decorum,
My grievances I'll lay before him;—
If no redress I can obtain,
But find my application vain;
45   From Pope I'll hence *reverse* the Song,
And think *whatever is—is wrong*.—

—18th June—'Twas *thus* some days ago I wrote,
For much I fear'd I was forgot;

—But lo!—another letter comes,
50   And confidence again returns;—
—Mankind shall henceforth blameless be,—

Who says they love *variety?*—
—Mistaken notion!—I'll aver
No man was ever known to err;—
55   —Now Pope,—the case is alter'd quite,
Whatever is,—is surely right.—

—One observation you'll allow,
Attend,—I'll quickly finish now:—

—In spite of what your sneers impart
60   'Of loving Sinners in our heart,'
The will of Heav'n we but obey,
When we to Sinners pardon say;
Nay stop,—the case is very clear,
Again I follow Scripture *here*,
65   *More* grace in Heav'n *one* Sinner gains
Than ninety-nine good Saints obtain;—
—Then ne'er *our* lenity arraign,
I'm orthodox you see again.—
1782

MS pp. 117–21.

9. **'The heart shou'd act no changeful scene'**: this seems to be a direct
quotation from a letter sent by the gentleman to Craik that she
had also referenced in her previous poem to him, where she
quotes 'Most men wou'd think your system strange / Which
says 'the *Heart shou'd never* change" (p. 39, ll. 45–46).

22. **pervert**: to turn aside and/or deflect (*OED*).

27. **reas'ning Pride**: See Alexander Pope's *An Essay on Man*, 1.4.11:
'In pride, in reas'ning pride, our error lies'.

37. **Cards**: small card bearing a person's name, title, and rank that was
left or presented upon paying a visit (*OED*). Conventionally,

a person would leave a card first and would not expect to be permitted to visit until receiving a card in response. Neilson notes that while '"card of invitation" was in full vogue from about 1770 . . . there are signs of its adaptation as a literary form or medium' (Appendix II, p. 209). Craik's previous verse was written in response to having received the gentleman's card. See p. 38, l. 11.

39. 'Too plain appears the fact' she said: the closing quotation mark is missing from Craik's manuscript.

45–46. From Pope: See *An Essay on Man*, 1.10.14: 'One truth is clear, Whatever is, is right'.

47–48. 18th June: Craik's poem appears to have been written in two different sittings, with the second section, prompted by a response from the gentleman, dated 18 June [1782].

55. the case is altered quite: Craik may be referring to Ben Johnson's comedy, *The Case is Altered* (1609); the exact phrase occurs in the broadside ballad, *The Jolly Widdower* printed for J. Blare c. 1664–1703.

56. *Whatever is,—is surely right*: See above note for ll. 45–46.

56. 'Of loving Sinners in our heart': Perhaps a direct quotation from a letter sent by the gentleman to Craik.

65–66. *More* grace in Heav'n . . . : Luke 15. 7. See 'To a Lady', ll. 7–8, p. 62.

68. I'm orthodox: Line 68 recalls ll. 13–16 in 'To a Gentleman', p. 38: 'Intent to show the weight I lay / On *what* our Saints and Parsons say: / Nay,—wishing too in such a cause / T' explain how orthodox I was'.

EPITAPH UPON THE HONOURABLE
MRS S—

While the Honourable Mrs S. is unidentified, the metre requires
that her first name be trisyllabic, and end in 'a', so perhaps she
was Eliza or Edwina. The courtesy title Honourable ('Hon.')
was prefixed to the younger sons of earls, and to the sons and
daughters of viscounts and barons, but here the 'S—' would be
the name of her husband, precluding tracking her identity from
the peerage that would have been held by her father. In Craik's
contents list, the poem is titled more simply 'Epitaph on Mrs S:'.

—————

 —Here lies sweet E*******a whose merit was such
 That none cou'd esteem, or applaud her too much;—
 The delight of her Husband, her Children, and
   Friends,
 Almost free from the failings our Nature attends.—
5 To censure superior,—with charity blest,—
 And more lov'd, and ador'd, than can e'er be
   exprest,—
 —When rich, o'er our hearts was her empire
   complete,
 And adversity came but to show her more great;—
 —This Stone, like most Tomb-stones, no flatt'ry
   conveys,
10 For our feelings bear witness to all that it says;—
 Long o'er the lov'd spot shall Remembrance
   attend,
 And the tear of affection in torrents descend.—

MS p. 122.

THE INDIAN MAID—A TALE—
INTENDED FOR A COMPANION
TO THE HARP

Craik's two-part poem recounts a legend set in the Caribbean in which Inkle, a seventeenth-century English merchant, seduces Yarico, an indigenous woman, after she rescues him from drowning, and then betrays her by selling her into slavery. The tale was first recorded in Richard Ligon's *A True and Exact History of the Island of Barbadoes* (1657, 1673, 1680, etc.), and became well enough known to be frequently recycled for children during the eighteenth century and to be made into an opera by George Colman Jr for the Haymarket Theatre, London, in 1789. The most influential retelling was by Richard Steele, the first to give the names of the two protagonists, in *The Spectator*, no. 11 (1711):

I was the other day amusing myself with *Ligon*'s account of *Barbadoes*; and, in answer to your well-wrought tale, I will give you, as it dwells upon my memory, out of that honest traveller, in his fifty-fifth page, the history of *Inkle* and *Yarico*. MR. THOMAS INKLE, of *London*, aged twenty years, embarked in the *Downs* on the good ship called the *Achilles*, bound for the *West-Indies*, on the 16 June 1674, in order to improve his fortune by trade and merchandize. Our adventurer was the third son of an eminent citizen, who had taken particular care to instil into his mind an early love of gain, by making him a perfect master of numbers, and consequently giving him a quick view of loss and advantage, and preventing the natural impulses of his passions, by prepossession towards his interests. With a mind thus turned, young *Inkle* had a person every way agreeable, a ruddy vigour in his countenance, strength in his limbs, with ringlets of fair hair loosely flowing on his shoulders. It happened, in the course of the voyage, that the *Achilles*, in some distress, put into a creek on the main of *America*, in search of provisions. The youth, who is the hero of my story, among others went ashore on this occasion. From their first landing they were observed by a party of *Indians*, who hid themselves in the woods for that purpose. The *English* unadvisedly marched a great distance from the shore into the country, and were intercepted by the natives, who slew the greatest number of them. Our adventurer escaped among others, by flying into a forest. Upon his coming into a remote and pathless part of the wood, he threw himself tired and breathless, on a little hillock, when an *Indian maid* rushed from a thicket behind him. After the first surprize, they appeared mutually agreeable to each other. If the *European* was highly charmed with the limbs, features, and wild graces of the naked *American*; the *American* was no less taken with the dress, complexion, and shape of an *European*, covered from head to foot. The *Indian* grew immediately enamoured of him, and consequently solicitous for his preservation. She therefore conveyed him to a cave, where she gave him a delicious repast of fruits, and led him to a stream to slake his thirst. In the midst of these good offices, she would sometimes play with his hair, and delight in the opposition of its colour to that of her fingers: then open his bosom, then laugh at him for covering of it. She was, it seems, a person of distinction, for she every day came to him in a different dress, of the most beautiful shells, buggles, and bredes. She likeways brought him a great many spoils, which her other lovers had presented to her, so that his cave was richly adorned with all the spotted skins of beasts, and most party-coloured feathers of fowls, which that world afforded. To make his confinement more tolerable, she would carry him in the dusk of the evening, or by the favour of moon-light, to unfrequented groves and solitudes, and shew him where to ly down in safety, and sleep amidst the falls of waters, and melody of nightingales. Her part was to watch and hold him awake in her arms, for fear of her countrymen, and awake him on occasions to consult his safety. In this manner did the lovers pass away their time, till they had learned a language of their own, in which the voyager communicated to his mistress, how happy he should be to have her in his country, where she should be clothed in such silks as his waistcoat was made of, and be carried in houses drawn by horses, without being exposed to wind or weather. All this he promised her the enjoyment of, without such fears and alarms as they were there tormented with. In this tender correspondence these lovers lived for several months, when *Yarico*, instructed by her lover, discovered a vessel on the coast to which she made signals; and in the night, with the utmost joy and satisfaction, accompanied him to a ship's crew of his countrymen, bound for *Barbadoes*. When a vessel from the main arrives in that island, it seems the planters come down to the shore, where there is an immediate market of the *Indians* and other slaves, as with us of horses and oxen.

To be short, Mr *Thomas Inkle*, now coming into *English* territories, began seriously to reflect upon his loss of time, and to weigh with himself how many days interest of his money he had lost during his stay with *Yarico*. This thought made the young man very pensive, and careful what account he should be able to give his friends of his voyage. Upon which consideration, the prudent and frugal young man sold *Yarico* to a *Barbadian* merchant; notwithstanding that the poor girl, to incline him to commiserate her condition, told him that she was with child by him: but he only made use of that information, to rise in his demands upon the purchaser.

For a fuller discussion of these sources, see Steven Epley, 'Alienated, Betrayed, and Powerless: the Legend of Inkle and Yarico', *Papers on Language and Literature*, 38.2 (March 2002), 200–22.

Craik's subtitle 'A Companion to The Harp' is explained by
her asterisked footnote in the manuscript, '*A Poem, written
by Mr Macneil'. Hector MacNeill (1746–1818), Scottish poet,
songwriter, and novelist, had worked for many years as a clerk
in the West Indies, before publishing his first book, *The Harp:
A legendary tale, in two parts* (Edinburgh: Peter Hill, 1789).
Though set in Scotland, not the West Indies, it told a story with
some parallels to Craik's poem, about a minstrel and his wife
who are caught in a storm. To save his wife's life, the minstrel
burns his prized harp, only for her to leave him for another man
the following morning. In Craik's poem, the story focuses on the
woman, and the betrayer is the man. In a note 'To The Reader',
MacNeill reported that his poem was based on the traditional
Gaelic proverb 'Smeirg a loisgeadh a thiompan ria', i.e. 'I'll never
burn my harp for a woman'. Supposedly, the proverb stems from
a Highland tale, which MacNeill says he heard from Mr Ramsay
of Auchertyre and which was later published as 'The Harper of
Mull' in James Anderson's periodical, *The Bee*, 3 (1791), 223.
Later, the tale was also put into song by Robert Tannahill, titled
'The Harper o' Mull'.

Because of Craik's reference to MacNeill, 'The Indian Maid'
must have been among the more recently written poems in the
Beinecke manuscript, dating from 1789–90, just before she
prepared the manuscript for presentation to Robert Riddell.
MacNeill's book was advertised as published at the beginning
of May: see *Scots Magazine*, 51 (April 1789), 190. It is also
the only poem in Craik's manuscript explicitly addressing the
issue of Caribbean enslavement. Some of Craik's family, like
their friends the Riddells, their neighbours the Oswalds, and
many other families in the West of Scotland, had derived at
least some of their wealth from Caribbean plantations. While
parliamentary efforts against slavery and the slave trade were not
successful till much later, the years from 1787, when Craik was
writing this poem, saw the first major parliamentary agitation
against Caribbean slavery, by Thomas Clarkson, Granville Sharp,
William Wilberforce and others, and the issue attracted support

also from the General Assembly in Edinburgh. Craik writes about the enslavement of a Caribbean indigene, rather than the trade from Africa, and her focus is on the Indian Maid's emotional anguish at her betrayal, rather than on her life afterwards; nonetheless, Craik's sympathies, surely unusual for a writer of her class in southwest Scotland in the late eighteenth century, might well have set her at odds with others in her family circle.

—What musing Form by Cynthia's light
There lonely wanders near the Sea,
And while yon Vessel glides from sight,
Cries 'have I left my home for thee!—

5 —'The Cave secure—my youthful friends,
'The shade beneath the Olive tree;—
'The joys which freedom still attends,
'And have I left them all for thee!—

—'And am I destin'd to despair
10 'A wretched Captive doom'd to be!—
'Yes!—he recedes whose selfish care
'Whose sordid mind has ruin'd me.—

—'But ah!—restrain these bursting sighs,
'Remorse shall thy avenger be;
15 'For faithless Inkle blindly flies
'From peace, from honour, and from thee.'—

—'Twas thus along the winding shore
A Maid forlorn was heard to wail;
And still her sable locks she tore
20 As still she ey'd the less'ning Sail.—

—Her Hist'ry sad Remembrance keeps,
And mourns Britannia's lasting shame;

For while the gentle Suff'rer weeps
Who shudders not at Inkle's name?—

25　—Three Moons have scarcely clos'd their reign
Since free from all the storms of fate,
She who now drags a galling chain
An Indian Queen appear'd in state.—

—The moss-clad seat was all her throne,
30　No ill-got wealth her fears betray'd;—
The humble Grot a Palace shown
Where gentle Peace tranquilly sway'd.—

—Yet deck'd from Ocean's wat'ry bound
Full many a shining gem was there;—
35　And flow'rs were plac'd in Conchs round,
To show the Maiden's taste and care.—

—Some Coco' cups in order laid
Her fav'rite Goat each morning fill'd,
The Fawns securely round her play'd,
40　No harmless Fawn was ever kill'd.—

—The bow and arrow guiltless hung,
'Twas there for state,—no wound it gave;—
The wildly warbled notes she sung
Re-echo'd through the sounding Cave.—

45　—Kind Nature healthy food supply'd,
She pluck'd it from each neighb'ring tree;
And frisking through their branches spy'd
The Squirrels sport with merry glee.—

—The Indian grass with feathers wove
50　Her pow'rs for *splendid* dress display;—
And o'er the fountain in the Grove
She smil'd to see herself so gay.—

¶

—Oft lightly dancing in the shade
With many a chearful Nymph and Swain;
55   The balmy air was vocal made,—
It seem'd the golden age again.—

—Oft seated on the verdant ground,
From care and apprehension free;
The little Songsters pick'd around,
60   Our fearless perch'd upon her knee.—

—Life's trifling wants *Content* kimle'd,—
Content had silver'd o'er the whole;—
The Maid was form'd with passions mild,
A feeling heart, and gen'rous soul.—

65   —No Envy reach'd her peaceful Cave,
No Slander steept her Couch in tears,—
No pang deceitful Friendship gave,
Till Albion's faithless Son appears.—

—And has the wretch of love avail'd
70   With heavy chains to burden thee!—
—Ah Inkle!—while her fates detail'd
May Conscience thy tormentor be.—
—Say,—why was Av'rice here employ'd
The crimes of polish'd Life to show?
75   Ah! Why so pure a scene destroy'd
For all the empty wealth below?—

—Can Gold a balm for vice supply,
Can Gold avert Remorse's sting?—
No!—Guilt shall swell the rising sigh,
80   And Mem'ry all its terrors bring.—

—O that from Britain's distant land
Thy sordid thoughts had never stray'd!—

Or wreck'd upon some neighb'ring Strand,—
Or *like thy own* some heart betray'd.—
85   —The ev'ning mild,—the smiling morn
No more the wretched Captive chears;
Now doom'd,—from ev'ry comfort torn,
To daily toil, and nightly tears.—

—As Thought strays roving o'er the Past
90   The sad reverse each feeling rends—
In bonds!—deserted!—left at last!—
—And is it *thus* each prospect ends!

—To *this* alas! Her only meed!
Was *this* her sole reward to be?—
95   —And canst thou make that bosom bleed
Who left her all for Love and thee!—

MS pp. 123–29.

The Harp: Craik's manuscript has an asterisked footnote here, '*A Poem, written by Mr Macneil'. See headnote.

1. **Cynthia's light:** moonlight; in Greek mythology, Cynthia is the virgin goddess of the hunt and the moon and is named for her birthplace, Mount Kynthos.

15. **faithless Inkle:** It was Richard Steele who gave the Englishman the name of Thomas Inkle.

37. **Coco' cups:** coconut cups.

66. **Couch:** in literary usage, a vague term implying that on which one sleeps (*OED*).

68. **Albion's faithless Son:** i.e. Inkle; Albion is a poetic term for Great Britain.

THE INDIAN MAID
—PART SECOND—

———————————

—The lightning flash'd,—the storm grew high,
And loud, and dreadful, roar'd the Main;—
The tow'ring billows lash'd the skie,
Then to the center plung'd again.—

5   —The trembling Maid with eager view
Beheld what chill'd her mind with fear;
For as the storm tremendous grew,
A shatter'd Bark came driving near.—

—The sails were torn,—the rudder lost,—
10   The Vessel drove before the wind;—
And as it reach'd the rocky coast,
Despair had seiz'd on ev'ry mind.—

—Alarm'd she flew,—she left her Grot
In hopes some wretch the side might gain;—
15   But ah!—ere near the fatal spot,
The Bark had sunk beneath the Main.—

—Transfixt with grief,—dismay'd she view'd
The awfull scene replete with woe,—
Then weeping turn'd,—her path pursu'd
20   With heavy heart,—opprest—and slow.—
—Thus musing as she trac'd the shore
And fast fell pity's streaming tear—
A Form that strove with fate no more
Came floating on its wat'ry Bier.—

25   —Her stupor fled,—she scream'd for aid,
She call'd on faithful Ora's name;—

'Come Ora!—come my friendly Maid
'Ah come!—support this dying Frame'—

—They chaff'd his temples,—rais'd his head,
30 And gently wrung his auburn hair;—
'His heart still beats!'—he was not dead!—
The vital Spirit flutter'd there.—

—They bore him from the stormy sea,
To wish'd-for warmth within the Cave;
35 But drench'd was ev'ry shrub and tree,
No heat the moisten'd branches gave.—
—Poor Yarico, who long essay'd
To light the blazing hearth in vain,
Her *only* change of dress survey'd,—
40 —The thought was but a moment's pain.—

—She snatch'd it from the shelt'ring wall,
Compassion's dictates to obey;—
—A silent tear was seen to fall,
As its last embers dy'd away!—

45 —The web thus destin'd to the flame,
Each fav'rite cup was next resign'd;—
—A struggling sigh unbidden came,
And mark'd their value in her mind.—

—Mistaken Maid!—thy cares refrain,—
50 No more his guardian Angel prove;—
The cups, the web, are burnt in vain,
He merits not thy gen'rous love.—

—Restor'd to health—the faithless youth
Repaid each gift with treach'rous art;—
55 —He vow'd,—he swore, with seeming truth,
And soon alas! Obtain'd her heart.—

¶

But short was Pleasure's fleeting reign:—
Ere long his oaths, his vows forgot,
The world began its sway to gain;—
60   He sigh'd to quit the peaceful Grot.—

—Oft Britain's wealth was held to view,
Life's polish'd charms to fancy brought;—
The splendid scene no envy drew,
For *he alone* employ'd her thought.—

65   —Yet still the wish for change remain'd,—
He languish'd still to cross the sea;—
And artful Love at length obtain'd
The fated Maid his guide to be.—

—Poor wretch!—reflect!—of flight beware,—
70   Delusive Hope in time restrain;—
But ah!—Life seem'd not worth her care
If doom'd from Inkle to remain.—

—The light Canoe,—at early morn
That oft for pleasure kim'd the wave,
75   Whose sides fantastic plumes adorn,
The gift a rich Admirer gave,—

—The light Canoe was soon supply'd
With fruit from ev'ry neighb'ring tree;—
—Her flight no pitying bosom, spy'd,
80   Lest weeping, friends averse shou'd be.—

—She kiss'd her Goat,—she left her Cave,—
The tear stood swimming in her eye,
And many a parting look she gave,
And many a deep prophetic sigh.—

¶
85   —She view'd th' approaching shore with pain,
        Yet knew not *why* was fear'd the sight;—
        False Inkle sooth'd her mind again
        With magic schemes of new delight.—

        —'The Cave secure,—her youthful friends—
90   'The shade beneath the Olive tree;
        'The joys which freedom still attends,
        'And has she left them all for thee!'—

        —O'er gliding waves they gently bound,
        And gain'd at length the nearest Strand;—
95   —The sordid Planters crouding round
        Observ'd them as they reach'd the Land.—

        —Say Britons!—shall I now proceed
        Or in oblivion wrap the scene?
        For sure each gen'rous heart must bleed
100   As they peruse the mournful theme.—

        —The faithless wretch whom nought cou'd bind,
        Tho she preserv'd his fleeting breath;
        The friendless Maid to sale resign'd,
        To chains!—to mis'ry!—worse than death!—

105   —She started!—look'd!—she burst in tears!—
        Implor'd him to reverse her fate;
        She urg'd a *future* Mother's fears,
        She urg'd her unborn Infant's state.—

        —But Av'rice deaf to Nature's cries
110   No pow'r, no human tie restrains.—
        Of course her price must higher rise,
        For he has doom'd them both to chains.—

¶

 —'And has the wretch of Love avail'd
 'With *double* bonds to fetter thee!
115 —'Ah Inkle!—while her fates detail'd
 'May Conscience thy tormentor be.—
 —'Is *this* alas! Her only meed!
 'Was *this* her sole reward to prove?—
 'And canst thou make that bosom bleed
120 'Who left her all for thee and Love!'—

 —Unmov'd he hears!—his Vessel sails—
 It lessens!—fades!—the view is o'er!—
 'He's gone' she cries!—despair prevails.
 The hapless Maid can bear no more!—

125 —And see! From yon tremendous steep
 How wildly now she eyes the Main!—
 —Ah see!—she plunges in the Deep,
 No more alas!—to rise again.—

MS pp. 130–38.

26. faithful Ora's name: Yarico's maid or attendant.

39–44. Her *only* change of dress survey'd: Yarico's fleeting reluctance to burn her dress echoes the minstrel's reluctance to burn his harp in MacNeill's *The Harp*. See note to 'The Indian Maid—A Tale', p. 138.

45. The web: refers to Yarico's woven grass dress, mentioned in l. 39.

46. fav'rite cup: for her 'coco' cup', see the previous poem, 'The Indian Maid—A Tale', l. 17.

70. Delusive Hope: The opening of Samuel Johnson's *Rambler*, no. 67, has 'Delusive hope still points to distant good', and

l. 1 of Johnson's 'On the Death of Dr Robert Levet' has 'hope's delusive mind'. Craik uses the same phrase in 'the Earl of Caithness', l. 54 and in 'Helen: An Epistle to A Friend', l. 54.

80. **Lest:** Craik's manuscript reads 'Least', a variant spelling or perhaps mistranscription.

117–20. **'Is** *this* **alas!... Love!':** these lines repeat ll. 93–96 from 'The Indian Maid—A Tale'.

128. **No more alas!—to rise again:** While Craik ends with Yarico's suicide, most renditions of the tale end with Yarico sold into slavery.

AN EPITAPH ON A FRIEND

Even more than Craik's earlier epitaph, on the Honourable Mrs
S—, this epitaph, though wholly positive about the deceased,
seems too crisp and clear-eyed to have been intended for an actual
tombstone. Craik's praise notably hinges on these women's ability
to maintain equanimity and independence through reversals of
fortune. In Craik's contents list, the poem is titled 'Epitaph on
Mrs M'; who Mrs M. is remains unidentified, but must be a
name of two syllables.

    —Here M: reposes whose merit was great
    For well she conform'd to each change in her
        fate.—
    Possess'd of no wealth that her own she could call,
    Two Orphans were just the sum total of all:—
5   Yet still unrepining no murmur was heard,
    For a *rational* conduct to pomp she prefer'd.—
    —Independent, and patient, she glided through
        Life,
    Free from fashion, and folly, and envy, and strife,
    Possesst of esteem, of good-wishes and praise,
10   In calmness and credit, she ended her days.—

MS p. 139.

THE MONK OF LA TRAPPE—A TALE

This brief note introduces Craik's final long poem in the Beinecke manuscript. Unlike her other prose prefaces, however, this one does not provide a summary of the story (for which see the headnote to the next item, the poem itself), just a note on the Gothic setting and Craik's bold assertion that her story is original, rather than being worked up from an earlier source.

———————————

—The circumstance of an unknown Lady, but seemingly of high rank, having been bled to death, in a warm Bath at Florence, by the orders of some People who were masked, is the only authentic incident in the following Poem,—all the rest is merely imaginary.—

—The Abbey of la Trappe is in the Diocess of Seez, between the Towns Mortagne, Verneuil and L'Aigle;—it is almost hidden from view by the Mountains and woods that surround it, and is remarkable for the strickness and austerity of the order.—Jean Bouthillier de Rancé instituted this frightful reform of la Trappe in 1664.—

MS pp. 140.

This **frightful reform**: cf. '*Rancé (Jean de Bouthillier)* . . . institua *la reforme effraiante de la trappe* en 1664': Voltaire, *Le Siecle de Louis XIV* (London: Dodsley, 1752), p. 452. Lady Mary Wortley Montague reports visiting the monastery of La Trappe, telling her correspondent that Bouthillier de Rancé, a French nobleman, started the order after finding his Parisian mistress dead and disfigured from consumption, passing 'the remainder of his days in the most cruel and disconsolate devotion' (Let. LVI 56.1).

THE MONK OF LA TRAPPE—A TALE—
WRITTEN BY HIMSELF, AND FOUND
IN HIS CELL

Like Craik's other longer poems in the Beinecke manuscript, 'The Monk of la Trappe' is told in the voice of the survivor after a love-match has been broken up by the murder of one of the lovers. It is the most Gothic of her longer poems in its settings and violence, and it is also the poem that most clearly foreshadows the five Gothic novels Craik would publish after she left Arbigland; indeed, she recycled the poem, in a prose retelling, as a rediscovered manuscript or suicide letter, in what is now her best-known novel, *Adelaide de Narbonne* (1800).

'The Monk of la Trappe' differs from her other longer poems also in not being based on an historical incident or newspaper report. In her prefatory note for the poem (see previous item), Craik was quite definite that this story was her own, a fiction that she had created taking only the briefest hint in an unnamed source for the manner in which her heroine would be murdered. In some respects, her hero's story echoes the life of Bouthillier de Rancé (1626–1700), a French aristocrat who, after finding his mistress dead, abandoned Paris for a life of austerity and silence in the remote monastery of La Trappe. It is not clear whether or how much Craik also knew two rather different recent tales about aristocrats who shared the same name as her hero. The less similar was an anonymous novel, *Italian Letters; or, the History of the Count de St. Julian* (London: Robinson, 1784), where the count, away in Spain on business for his friend the marquis, is supplanted in the affections of his fiancée Matilda by the marquis. Finding them married when he returns, the count fights a duel with the marquis and kills him, but finds that Matilda will have nothing to do with her husband's murderer. (For a summary of this novel, see *Critical Review*, 58 (1784), 211–13.) More intriguing, because its St Julien becomes a monk at La Trappe, is 'The Story of the Count de Saint Julien, Related by a Prior of the Convent of La Trappe', by George Keate (1729–1797), in his Shandean miscellany *Sketches from Nature, Taken and Coloured in a Journey to Margate*, 2nd ed. (London: Dodsley, 1779), I, pp. 167–207. Keate's story appeared also in, e.g., the *Westminster Magazine*, 7 (July–August 1779), 352–54, 408–11, and was subsequently included in *A Collection of Interesting Anecdotes Memoirs, Allegories, Essays, and Poetical Fragments; tending to amuse the fancy, and inculcate morality, by Mr. Addison* (London: printed for the Author, 1797), VI, pp. 132–54. Keate's story portrays St Julien, like de Rancé, as a dissolute Parisian aristocrat who becomes a monk at La Trappe, but describes how the Count had a son with his Parisian mistress, how their joint profligacy had cost him his fortune, how St Julien had been captured by Barbary pirates before reaching La Trappe, and how on his deathbed he is reconciled to the son who unknown to either of them has also become a monk there. Keate's account provided the subject for a painting 'The Death of St. Julien in the Convent of La Trappe', by the Italian émigré artist Antonio Zucchi (1726–1796), published as an engraving in 1784.

Whether or not Craik knew or had heard of Keate's story, the novel, or Zucchi's painting, the plot in her poem takes a quite different turn: her St Julian is a blameless hero, a devoted lover and husband, not a debauchee, and his struggles are caused by the evil deeds of others, not by any shortcomings of his own. Without mentioning Keate, Craik's assertion of originality might be designed to pre-empt accusations of plagiarism, but it also suggests she already, in the late 1780s, years before she would publish her first novel, felt she had the capacity to create original narrative fiction. In her poem, Craik's protagonist, St Julian, recounts the story of his first encounter with his future wife, Laura, the daughter of an aristocratic family in Florence. She was running away from a previously promised marriage to her father's choice of husband, Count Albert, to take refuge in a convent. St Julian saved her from a pursuing band of ruffians sent by the father, and he and Laura fell in love and secretly eloped, to be married in a dim-lit convent church, during a thunderstorm. As Laura feared, her brother sought retribution. St Julian was kidnapped by a group of masked men, who led him to an undisclosed location; Laura was there, and St Julian was told that he must kill her, as mandated by her father's dying wish, or be killed himself. St Julien refuses to kill her, so Laura slits her own wrists and bleeds to death in a tepid bath, thereby saving St Julian's life. St Julian thereafter enters the Abbey of La Trappe and writes a record of his ill-fated love in a memoir which he hides in his monastic cell to be discovered after his death.

As noted above, Craik embeds a condensed prose version of her tale in her novel *Adelaide de Narbonne*, set during the French Revolution. In the novel, however, St Julien's account is set within a third-person narrative frame; many years after the events told in the poem, an aristocratic female narrator, entering a Trappist abbey that has been pillaged by revolutionaries, stumbles into a blood-spattered cell, where she finds Father Ambrose (the St Julian figure), stabbed to death and lying beside a statue of a beautiful young woman, in which he has hidden his memoir of their love: *Adelaide de Narbonne, with Memoirs of Charlotte de Cordet. A Tale*, 4 vols (London: at the Minerva Press, for William Lane, 1800), IV, ch. XIII; or ed. Marianna d'Ezio (Newcastle: Cambridge Scholars Publishing, 2018), pp. 484–89.

—*Homme aveugle, dont l'ame, au monsonge asservie, Des souvenirs du Monde est encore poursuivie, Que l'aspect de ces Lieux dissipe ton Sommeil;*
  C'est où finit le Songe de la vie
  Où la mort commence le Reveil.—

   —From these lone walls, where gloomy silence
      reigns,
   And stern Religion drags self-destin'd chains;
   Where Superstition rears her wild abode,
   And tortures man, to please a gracious God;
5   Where while deep anguish tears the soul from rest

No aid appears in Pity's semblance drest;
No consolation meets the list'ning ear,
For soothing Friendship cannot reach us *here*,—
But wasting Mis'ry muses o'er its urn,
10   Till ling'ring Time his weary course has run;—
    —From scenes like these where heaves the lonely
        sigh,
Where all our comfort is——at length to die!
I turn,—Life's ebbing tide is nearly o'er,
And I, and sorrow, soon shall weep no more.—
15   —Unknown, unheeded, to the Grave I go,
And close a long, a dreadful train of woe.—
—Yet ere the Mansion of the peaceful Dead,
(*Where* Grief's pale subject rests his mould'ring
        head)
Ere it receives *this* fast decaying frame,
20   This bleeding victim at Religion's fane;
To save me from oblivion's dreary shade,
This last attempt expiring Nature made.—
—Tho speech deny'd,—these lines my woes shall tell,
I'll leave the sad memorial in my Cell.
25   Perhaps some future wretch opprest like me
The mournful tale with streaming eyes may see,
And while Affliction's heavy hand he feels,
And black Despair no ray of Hope reveals,
Here shall he view *what* I was doom'd to bear,
30   And ev'n confess *his* suff'rings less severe;—
Compar'd with mine each pang inferior find,
And own in Mis'ry I surpass'd mankind.—

—Tho not of Princely rank,—Saint Julian's name
Was once conspicuous on the lists of Fame;
35   —Brave,—learn'd,—aspiring,—eager for renown,
Success my early wishes deign'd to crown;—
—*This* Form a manly model seem'd design'd
And care paternal gave a polish'd mind.—

¶

      —Alas!—how chang'd my setting Sun appears

40   From *that* whose lustre shown on former years!

      Ah gay delusions!—*whither* are ye fled?

      Where *now* those hopes by sportive Fancy led!—

      —Gone!—vanish'd!—dead!—each worldly comfort
          lost,

      And wreck'd on stern Misfortune's rugged coast!—

45   —Am I the Being whose ambitious eye

      Saw Fortune at command propitious fly?

      Saw circling years increas'd enjoyment bring,

      And future prospects rest on Pleasure's wing?—

      —Reduced,—to *what?*—to digging here my Grave,

50   To the mean office of a menial slave;—

      To nightly vigils—and to gloomy Cells,

      Where forc'd *Restraint*—not *Resignation*, dwells;

      Where Time's dull wheel with heavy sameness
          turns,

      And silent anguish in the bosom burns.—

55   —But cease Reflection—from my view retire;

      Life's ling'ring torch with me must soon expire,

      The fleeting hours ordain'd my woe's to tell,

      Permit no time on vain regret to dwell.—

      —In Florence once,—where not unknown to fame

60   And led by fate's mysterious hand I came;—

      A ruffian Band had seiz'd the fairest Maid

      That e'er gay Fancy's magic art display'd.—

      I robb'd the villains of their trembling prey

      And bore my beauteous, fainting prize, away.—

65   —Pale,—dying,—breathless,—long absorbt in woe,

      No sigh was heard,—no tear was seen to flow;—

      My utmost efforts scarcely brought relief,

      And the hush'd Spirit seem'd releas'd from grief;—

      —At length her languid pulse reviv'd again,

70   And Life returning throbb'd in ev'ry vein;
     My gazing eyes a pleasing task pursue,
     And charms divine through deep affliction view,
     Not brighter she whom haughty Florence boasts,
     Whose name extends to earth's remotest coasts;—
75   Whose easy look,—whose fam'd proportions show
     The stretch sublime of human skill below:—
     —*Her Form alone* attracts the wond'ring eye,
     No *mental* pow'rs the Sculptor's art supply;—
     But *here* in this unrivall'd Maid combin'd
80   Expressive features, with a gen'rous mind;
     A soul and shape with charms celestial fraught,
     Alike by Pallas and the Graces taught.—
     While such confusion all her dress display'd,
     As lent superior beauty ev'ry aid.
85   —One bleeding Temple her white garment stain'd,
     Her veil disorder'd—torn,—and loose remain'd.—
     Her auburn hair in wild luxuriance flow'd,
     And all her figure marks of terror show'd.—
     —Recall'd at length to mem'ry's active pow'rs,
90   O'er her sad fancy apprehension low'rs,
     She prays me still her threaten'd hand to save,
     And talks of marriage, mis'ry and the Grave.—
     —To Grief's keen force I lent a patient ear,
     And strove alone to shield her mind from fear.—
95   —On Arno's banks—for deep retirement made,
     A Villa stood within the Orange shade;
     There I convey'd her,—from exploring eyes
     Far in the Grove the friendly mansion lies.—
     —In safety plac'd—convinc'd from danger free,
100 Returning calmness I with pleasure see;
     A flood of tears reliev'd her troubled breast,
     And thus the beauteous Maid her woes exprest.

     —'O gen'rous Stranger!—how shall I repay
     'Your timely aid on *this* ill-omen'd day!

105 'A wretched wanderer, forc'd from home to fly,
    'For ever exil'd from a Parent's eye,
    'What gifts are mine?—what favours to bestow
    'On him who snatch'd me from eternal woe!—
    'But strong impatience in your looks I view,
110 'And tho the theme must all my griefs renew,
    'Yet sure the sad recital is your due.—

    —'My family bears Medina's Princely name,
    'And from a race of ancient Monarchs came;—
    'Count Albert long had strove my heart to gain,
115 'But all his efforts met with cold disdain;—
    'His form,—his morals, drew my fixt distaste,
    'And his chief merit was in fortune plac'd;—
    'Superior views *this* youthful heart refin'd,
    'For my first wish was an accomplish'd mind;—
120 'But sanction'd by a Father's stern command
    'He persever'd to seize my trembling hand
    'To melt that Father ev'ry art, I try'd,
    'But sordid av'rice all my pow'r defy'd;
    'And oft he swore, if still reluctant found,
125 'His hapless Daughter was no longer own'd;
    'But from the roof paternal doom'd to roam,
    'A wretched outcast from her native home.—
    —'At length *this* ev'ning was ordain'd to prove
    'My filial duty,—and Count Albert's Love;—
130 —'The thought was death!—appall'd,—dismay'd I
        fled,
    'And chose the path that to a Convent led;
    '*There* fixt,—if Albert still pursu'd his claim,
    'A willing Vot'ry ever to remain.—
    —'How after trac'd,—or how my flight reveal'd,
135 'From each conjecturing thought remains
        conceal'd.—
    —'You know the rest,—I owe you more than Life,
    'For e'er condemn'd to be proud Albert's wife,

'Ere *thus* at Hymen's fane a victim made,
'The Grave had wrapt me in its peaceful shade.—
140 'But who are you to whom such gifts I owe,
'My only refuge in this world of woe?'—

—Brief let me be,—my name, my rank she knew,
And in our hearts a mutual passion grew;—
Her charms, her merit, more conspicuous shown
145 As op'ning time made worth unequal'd known;
And oft from Life's insipid round I stole
'To feast on Reason and the flow of soul.'—
—At length she deign'd our union to approve,
And with her hand repaid my ardent Love—

150 —Ill-fated vows!—ordain'd alas! to show
The utmost stretch of heart corroding woe!—
—Ah Laura!—doom'd *alike* thy breast to rend
The hated Lover or the favour'd friend!—

—Within the shelt'ring Grove a Convent lay,
155 Where by the moon's pale light we bent our way;
The Church soon gain'd,—its heavy portals close,
And each dim Lamp a sick'ning horror throws.—
—No sportive Cupids round the altar play,
No smiling Hymen sends a chearing ray;
160 No Censer sheds for us divine perfumes,
No anchor'd Hope to youthful fancy blooms.—
—But while the Priest devoted victims join,
Prophetic nature shudder'd at the shrine;
Recording Angels heav'd a mournful sigh,
165 And sculptur'd Saints had anguish in their eye.—
—The lengthen'd Isle a hollow murmur sends,
A deep'ning horror oer the scene extends.—
A sudden crash of thunder bursts around,
And gleaming Lightning flashes on the ground;—

170   While shrowded Ghosts, who from their Graves
        were thrown,
    Had to the altar for protection flown.—

    —Poor Laura sinking seiz'd my trembling arm,
    As her known refuge from surrounding harm.—
    My trembling arm can scarce her weight sustain,
175   For chill amazement stole through ev'ry vein.—
    —Slow from the shrine her fainting Form we led,—
    The gastly Phantoms pitying round us fled,
    And when our absence through the gloom was
        known
    The Church re-echo'd with a hollow groan.—

180   —I saw the scene had deep impression made,
    And to efface it ev'ry art essay'd;—
    —She view'd my efforts with a grateful eye,
    And from reflection kindly strove to fly.—
    —At length oblivion wrapt the deadly theme,
185   Or if remember'd 'twas but like a dream.—
    —Gay Pleasure then display'd his smiling store,
    And ev'ry day increas'd affection more.
    While Love and Friendship, strong as fate,
        combin'd
    To fix their sway in each congenial mind.—
190   Yet sometimes still a cloud wou'd intervene,
    And shade the glories of our brighter scene;—
    A struggling sigh from Laura's breast wou'd steal,
    And apprehension's latent force reveal;—
    —For tho her Parent, to remorse unknown,
195   View'd *mutual* duties and her fate with scorn;
    Tho crush'd with *more* than Nature well cou'd
        bear,
    Tho doom'd to evils in th' extreme severe,
    Yet oft, 'twas wish'd she had sustain'd the weight,

And left to Heav'n to judge of *what* was right.—
200   For well her Father's, Brother's heart she knew,
And from their vengeance dire presages drew.
Of course suspicion seiz'd her timid mind
And to the *future*, views of terror join'd.—

—One morn retiring ere the break of day,
205   Ill-omen'd Fear exerts a gloomy sway:
With sad forebodings Laura's heart was torn,
And mine felt horror, ev'n till *then* unknown.—
—We parted oft,—but still return'd again,—
And ev'ry moment brought succeeding pain,—
210   Asham'd such weakness shou'd my thoughts molest,
I rush'd at length from her devoted breast:—
That breast soon destin'd to corroding woe,
To ev'ry pang that vengeance dooms below!—

—As back to Laura, through the Grove I stray'd,
215   And musing stole along the silent shade,
Four Ruffians mask'd my lonely steps arrest,
And held their deadly weapons to my breast;—
—The odds was great!—a hasty glance I threw,
But no approaching aid appear'd in view;—
220   My trusty Rapier too was left behind,
For Laura's fears along possest my mind;—
And Laura's fears,—so oft,—so strong exprest,
Like Aaron's rod had swallow'd all the rest.—
—Unarm'd,—defenceless,—still I scorn'd to fear,
225   And soon resolv'd to sell existence dear;
—But 'yield they cry'd,—your Life at least is yours,
'And prompt obedience all the rest secures.'—
—In short,—resistance vainly I essay'd,
And back to Florence was with speed convey'd.—

230   —Swift through the streets the gliding Carriage flew,
And from assistance ev'ry prospect drew.—

  —'Twas late!—'twas dark!—the Moon no longer
   reign'd,
  And a dread silence my stern Guards maintain'd;
  Officious Mem'ry on the period prest,
235 And Laura's suff'rings soar'd above the rest:—
  I saw her weeping,—wretched,—and forlorn,
  From all she trusted,—all she valu'd torn!
  No hand to shield her from the storms of fate,
  No friend to soothe her *now* defenceless state!
240 —My rash despair once more their fears alarm
  And each Assassin *firmer* seiz'd my arm.—
  —But now the Carriage reach'd its destin'd round,
  And my Conductors drag me to the ground.—
  In vain with struggling I prolong the time,
245 Superior strength destroy'd each form'd design.—
  —Forc'd from the Carriage, I am led along,
  To scenes where death and horror round me
   throng.—
  —Scarce light sufficient one dim taper cast
  To guide my rough Companions as we past;
250 Yet transient views a spacious Dome display'd,
  And vague conjectures to the mind convey'd.
  But soon my eyes far diff'rent scenes disclose,
  And to its crisis Fate in anguish rose.—
  —Remov'd from aid—from all resource secure,
255 We reach'd at length a gloomy distant door
  There one appear'd, superior to the rest,
  And thus his solemn mystic words addrest.—

  —'In wars stern ranks, engaged in doubtful strife,
  'Your valour once preserv'd my threaten'd Life;
260 'Tho *chance* and *absence* kept us still unknown,
  'I for the gift repay you with your own;—
  '*This* I have sworn,—but mark what *more* I say,
  'My orders *now* admit of no delay.—
  'Your aid we ask for,—and your hand we crave

265 'For *one* whose conduct dug a father's Grave:—
—'A victim,—soon from worldly errors freed,
'Is at the filial shrine condemn'd to bleed;—
—'Approach!—behold *whom* justice dooms to
   death,
'Curst by a Parent's last expiring breath.'—
270 —I enter'd—saw a solemn scene display'd,
For some dread scheme of long plan'd vengeance
   laid.—
A gloomy light that by *reflection* shown
Serv'd just to make surrounding horror known.
And o'er the walls the Painter's art pourtray'd,
275 Expiring mis'ry in each form array'd.—
—*Here* Roman Portia's haughty soul retires,
Firm and unmov'd amidst consuming fires.—
There poor Monimia, by misfortune prest,
Drench'd the dire Bowl,—her look explain'd *the
   rest.*—
280 —Conspicuous stream'd Calista's vital flood,
And the dropt dagger reeking seem'd in blood.—
—A *skull*,—a *coffin*,—fixt the wand'ring eye,
And death's *last garb* in awful pomp lay bye.—
—A female figure on an urn reclin'd,
285 Absorb'd in grief appear'd her suff'ring mind;—
—Her silent anguish beggar'd outward show,—
She seem'd the patient monument of woe.—
—While from the sable veil that careless hung
A falling tear some deep affliction wrung.—

290 —For some sad moments the dire scene I view'd,
Then *thus* my Guide his mournful theme renew'd,
—'You see her *there*—by erring folly led,
'Who from a noble father weakly fled;
'Who left a husband in the bridal hour,
295 'And rashly trusted in a stranger's pow'r,
'An unknown stranger,—whose ignoble birth

'Compar'd with hers, scarce soar'd above the
    earth.—
'For which that father with his parting breath,
'Has *thus* consign'd her to the arms of death.—
300 —'Yet shall no menial hand inflict the wound,
'For stern revenge a fitter arm has found;—
'And since a Brother, nature's pow'rs restrain,
'*You* must obey, and open ev'ry vein—
'The tepid Bath will easier make them flow,
305 'And Life without a pang expiring go.—
  —'See *there* prepar'd the deadly weapons lie,
'Approach!—your fate is fixt,—you *must*
    comply.'—

  —At *this* the Mourner rais'd her languid head,
And breathless,—struggling with emotion, said,
310 —'O save me Stranger from their merc'less hands,
'A dearer Life than mine your aid demands!—
  —'Protect me!—save me!—' faster still she cry'd,—
And threw in haste the shading veil aside.—
  —Quick from our lips—'*Saint Julian!*'—'*Laura!*'
    —broke,
315 And shudd'ring Nature scarce surviv'd the
    stroke!—

  —In vain for language I each effort try'd,
The bursting heart all pow'r of speech deny'd!—
A dreadful feeling throbb'd through ev'ry vein,
Too deep for words—too poignant to explain.—
320 Dire *Observation* crowded o'er the whole,
And *Apprehension* harrow'd up the soul.—

  —Thus for a moment,—motionless,—forlorn,
Like some poor wretches just transform'd to stone,
We stood!—then rush'd into each other's arms,
325 Nor longer fear'd impending fates alarms.

—Poor Laura pour'd her sorrows in my breast,
And ev'n her Brother seem'd *for once* distrest.—

—But ah!—returning vengeance soon appears,
And crowding Ruffians rouse again her
   fears.—

330 —'Strike!—strike!—she cries—oblige us not to
   part.'
And grasp'd me closer to her beating heart;—
—At length by force superior overborn.
The wretched Laura from my arms is torn.—

—'And dare you rashly *still* my pow'r defy'?
335 Exclaim'd Medina with a threat'ning eye.—
'*If so*, I here retract the word I gave,
'And doom you *both* unpity'd to the Grave.—
—'From you,—and you alone, the stroke must
   come,
'Else half th' allotted task is left undone;
340 'Her father *thus* his dying will explain'd,
'And by the hand she lov'd, her death ordain'd.—
'Determine than to fill what fate decreed,
'Or sacrific'd to vengeance you must bleed.'—

—'Take back your promise,—I indignant cry'd,
345 'Your bloody pow'r is *now* with scorn defy'd;—
'I spurn *such* mercy from my inmost soul,
'Nor shall your force my firm resolves controul;—
—'For ere by me her vital stream is shed,
'I'll freely number with the silent dead.—
350 'But save *her* life—let mine your vengeance bound,
'And *thus*,—I bare my breast to meet the
   wound.'—

—Ah! spare *that* breast, poor Laura frantic said,—
'Tis *I* have err'd,—and I must go in the dead;—

'A father's curse o'er future days wou'd bend,
355 'And self-reflection my sad bosom rend.—
'Then stay Saint Julian!—rob not twice of Life
'Your unborn Infant, and your hapless wife;—
'Ah stop!—reflect!—you must not,—cannot save,
'The wretch a Parent destin'd to the Grave.—
360 —'Medina hear me!—that rais'd poniard stay,
'And see!—obedience shall his Life repay.'—

—She bared her arm,—approach'd the tepid
        flood,—
Then pausing—turn'd, *where* held by force I
        stood,—
Her look!—her silence—more than language spoke,
365 She sigh'd—and *thus* the solemn stillness broke.

—'At length the bitterness of Death is past,
'The world recedes!—the curtain drops at last!—
—'Misfortune's victim to the grave resign'd,
'Casts not one longing ling'ring look behind.'—
370 —'My woes are finish'd!—fears and hopes are
        o'er,—
'I go *where* Parents can oppress no more.—
'I go to *Him* who rules *this* checker'd plan;—
—'*Time* will explain *his* mystic ways to Man.—
'*This dreaded moment now* no terror shows,
375 'For sick'ning Nature sinks to calm repose.—
—'To die!—'tis rest!—'tis blest respite from pain!—
'Where peace resides I trust we'll meet again.—
'Convinc'd of *this*—convinc'd that *all is right*,
'The wounded Spirit takes its willing flight.—
380 —'See then my hand each throbbing pulse arrest!—
'See Life's *last* efforts struggling in my breast!—
'See the warm bath its ready aid supplies,
'See your lov'd Laura *now* with fate complies.—
'See from each vein bursts forth the vital stream,

385   'Ordain'd from death your cherish'd Form to
        screen;
    —'If so—I bow to Heav'n's all wise decree
    'I die Saint Julian!—ah remember me!'—

    —I saw her hand inflict the fatal wound,—
    I saw her drench'd in vital gore arround,
390   Deep,—and *more* deep, the luke-warm fountain
        grows
    As from each vein the crimson current flows—
    I saw her heart heave forth a parting sigh,
    And the last sparkle fading from her eye.—
    —No more I saw,—for nature's functions fail'd,
395   And worse than death my burning brain assail'd!—
    —Borne from the scene insensible away,
    To gloomy madness I became a prey;—
    And wildly wand'ring through a world of woe
    Led by Despair's relentless hand, I go.—
400   —Unheeded past the lapse of Time away,
    Unmark'd, by me, the night or chearful day;—
    A dreary darkness shrouded ev'ry view,
    And trustless *Apathy* to stupor grew.—

    —At length kind Heav'n bestow'd some pitying aid
405   And my sad steps to *this* Retreat convey'd;—
    The rules austere,—the gloomy silence round,
    My musing fancy soon congenial found.—
    Returning Reason slowly clear'd the mind,
    But Laura's suff'rings *still* remain'd behind;
410   In vain o'er Mem'ry wou'd Religion reign,
    Her fate,—her death,—made all its efforts vain;—
    I felt her still, resistless in my breast,
    And dire Remembrance robb'd each thought of
        rest.—
    —The scene is chang'd,—and these dim eyes no more
415   In fancy view her drench'd in vital gore.—

—But from a Heav'n, where happier prospects
    dwell
She seems to hover o'er my lonely Cell,—
—She points above—where suff'ring worth is
    crown'd,
Where Parents curse not, nor rash judgements
    wound.—
420 She calls me hence,—receives my parting breath,
And slow—and solemn—tolls the knell of death;
I bless the sound which wafts me to the skie
And from a world replete with anguish fly.
De Rancé come!—*congenial* feelings show,
425 With Hope's bright visions soothe the mind from
    woe;—
Assist me *now*,—to Laura guide my way
'And smooth my passage to th' realms of day.'—
Bid friendly Death his healing hand apply,
And wipe affliction from the Suff'rer's eye;
430 Absolve the wretch from human errors here,
And bear my Spirit to your happier sphere.—

MS pp. 141–67.

Epigraph: See François-Thomas-Marie de Baculard d'Arnaud's *Le Comte de Comminge, ou Les Amans Malheureux* (1764), a three-act verse play based on Claudine Guérin de Tencin's *Mémoires du comte de Comminge* (1735). Baculard set his drama in the monastery of La Trappe. Charlotte Lennox's English translation from Tencin was serialized in *The Lady's Museum*, I (1756), and also published in book form in 1756 and (with alterations) in 1764.

11. **scenes like these:** while it is tempting to hear this as an (inappropriate) echo of Burns, 'The Cotter's Saturday Night',

l. 163, both Burns and Craik were drawing from the general stock of eighteenth-century poetic phrases; cf. similarly 'Life's ebbing tide', l. 13 below, or the Miltonic 'weep no more', l. 14.

18. **mould'ring head**): Craik's manuscript has two sets of punctuation at the end of this line, a comma and a parenthesis.

20. **Religion's fane:** i.e. the monastery.

23. **—Tho speech deny'd:** Craik's manuscript has an asterisked footnote '*—The Monks of la Trappe never speak, unless on particular occasions—'.

33. **Saint Julian:** 'Saint Julien' or 'St. Julien' is a family or noble name, in Craik's story, in that by George Keate, and in the painting by Zucchi (see headnote); despite the Catholic references in the poem, it has nothing to do with being a saint, or with Saint Julian of Le Mans, a third-century French bishop who became a hermit, or St Julian the Hospitaller, who devoted his life to religion after killing his parents by mistake.

49. **digging here:** Craik's manuscript has an asterisked footnote '*—The Monks of this order prepare their own Graves—'.

58. **Permit:** Craik's manuscript reads 'Permits'.

63. **prey:** Craik's manuscript reads 'pray'.

73. **she whom haughty Florence boasts:** Craik's manuscript has an asterisked footnote '*—The Venus of Medicis, a celebrated Statue.—' The Medici Venus, a marble copy of an early bronze Greek sculpture, depicts a nude Aphrodite. Although initially displayed in Rome, the statue was sent to Florence in 1677 because it was considered lewd. Thereafter it became one of the marks on the Grand Tour. The base of the statue bears the name Cleomenes, a sculptor working in Athens during the first century BC.

82. **Pallas and the Graces:** Pallas, the daughter of Triton and raised alongside Athena; the three Graces are Aglaia (Brightness), Euphrosyne (Joyfulness), and Thalia (Bloom).

95. **Arno's banks:** Craik's manuscript has an asterisked footnote '*—The River which runs bye Florence—'.

109–11. **'But strong impatience . . .':** Craik's manuscript has a right bracket around these three lines.

147. **'To feast on Reason and the flow of soul'**: Alexander Pope's *Imitations of Horace* II.1.127–28 (*Poems*, ed. Butt, p. 617).

166. **Isle**: Apparent mistranscription of 'aisle'.

218. **The odds was great!**: Until the nineteenth century, odds was treated as singular.

223. **Aaron's rod**: Refers to the staff carried by Moses's brother Aaron. When the Pharaoh demands to see a miracle Aaron's rod becomes a serpent, swallowing all of the other rods which had been transformed into serpents by the Pharaoh's sorcerers (Exodus 7. 12).

231. **And from assistance . . .** : Craik's meaning in this line seems unusually opaque; most likely, she means that as the carriage races through the streets St Julian loses hope that help will come.

276–77. **Roman Portia's haughty soul . . .** : Portia or Porcia was the second wife of Brutus, as well as the name of Shakespeare's protagonist in *The Merchant of Venice*. Contemporary historians believed that Porcia committed suicide c. 42 BC by swallowing hot coals, while modern historians speculate that she took her life by burning charcoal in an unventilated room. French poet and dramatist Robert Garnier (1544–1590) published a series of rhetorical speeches under the title of *Porcie* (1568) which were dramatised in 1573; in them, Porcia is depicted as swallowing hot coals.

278–81. *There* **poor Monimia . . .** : Monimia was the heroine of Thomas Otway's play *The Orphan* or *The Unhappy Marriage* (1680), a stock piece on the stage throughout the eighteenth century. In the play, the orphan Monimia is raised by her guardian, Acasto, and is the object of affection for his two sons, Castalio (in Craik's summary Calista) and Polydore. Castalio secretly betroths himself to Monimia but is overheard by Polydore, who enters Monimia's room using the signal, 'three soft strokes on the chamber door', that Monimia and Castalio agreed upon. When Castalio tries to enter he is mistaken for Polydore and is turned away. When all is discovered the following morning, Polydore challenges Castalio to a duel and purposefully runs into his sword after which Monimia drinks poison and Castalio stabs himself.

283. death's *last garb*: i.e. a shroud.

362. the tepid flood: i.e. the bath.

369. 'Casts not one . . .': See Thomas Gray, 'Elegy Written in a Country Churchyard' (1751), l. 88.

403. trustless: the first syllable of this word is untypically difficult to interpret in Craik's manuscript and may be a copying error for 'listless'.

415. view: Craik's manuscript reads 'views'.

421. knell of death: Craik's manuscript has an asterisked footnote '*—A Bell tolls slowly, and at intervals, while the Monks of la Trappe are dying.—'

424. De Rancé: Craik's manuscript has an asterisked footnote '*—The Abbé de Rancé,—founder or reformer of the Order of la Trappe,—His retirement from the world was occasioned by a shock of a deep and melancholy nature.—' Cf. Craik's prefatory note (previous item).

427. 'And smooth my passage . . .': See Alexander Pope, *Eloisa to Abelard* (1717), l. 322 (*Poems*, ed. Butt, p. 260).

LINES WRITTEN UPON HEARING THAT A CIRCLE OF MR E***'S *INTIMATE FRIENDS* HAD RECEIVED THE ACCOUNTS OF HIS DEATH WITH THE UTMOST INDIFFERENCE

Mr E*** remains unidentified, but in Craik's contents list, the poem is titled 'Lines occasioned by Mr C: E:'s death', giving a further clue. The frequency of underlining in the manuscript, shown here by italics, suggest that the poem was written to be read aloud; the initial omission from the manuscript title of the words 'Intimate Friends Had Received', and their insertion above the line, suggest that Craik was copying into the Beinecke manuscript from an earlier manuscript.

———————————

—*Not one laugh the less,—one sigh the more*
Shall mark him gone, with whom they laugh'd before.

    —Unhappy Man!—is *this* the tribute due
    For hours of social mirth deriv'd from you!—
    Are *these the friends*, who in Life's happier day
    Warmly extoll'd *whate'er* you *chanc'd* to say?
5   Retail'd with glee each humourous word you spoke
    And found *superior* wit in ev'ry joke.—

    —Unhappy Man!—fond Nature's partial hand,
    Assign'd thee wit and humour at command;
    But doom'd that *wit* and *humour* ne'er shou'd do,
10   Without *some* morals and *some* prudence too;—
    These were withheld,—their loss supremely great
    At length determin'd *here* thy wretch'd fate.—
    Despis'd—deserted in thy utmost need,
    Those who *follow'd* once thy *haughty* lead.—

15   Plunged in distress,—the veriest wretch on earth,
        And black Despair succeeding former mirth;
        Say,—can thy errors, now for ever past,
        Be ev'n aton'd for, by such pangs at last?—
        —Or can gay wit, in Life's expiring hours
20   Deprive dire *Conscience* of its tort'ring pow'r?
        Remove the thoughts of *what* we *once* have been
        And hush repining o'er the *present* scene?—
        —Ah no!—Grief turns from trifles light as these,
        For consolation in the mind at ease;
25   *There* proves,—whate'er the Sceptic may contest,
        True Worth, and Virtue *only* can be blest.—

MS pp. 168–169.

Epigraph: The source for this is untraced.

5. Retail'd: To recount or tell again in detail; to repeat to others.
The *OED* dates the earliest usage of this sense of retail to
Shakespeare, *Richard III* (1597), III.1.77.

15. veriest wretch: Burns uses this phrase in writing to Clarinda
(*Letters*, I: 211; 19 January 1788), and in the song 'Farewell
Thou Stream,' l. 9 (*Poems*, II: 684).

LINES WRITTEN EXTEMPORE, OCCASIONED BY A PERUSAL OF MR B*****'S TRAVELS.—

Craik's last poem in the Beinecke manuscript comments satirically on a brand new publication. 'Mr B—' is James Bruce the Younger (1730–1794), of Kinnaird, Stirlingshire, who set out in 1768 to reach the source of the (Blue) Nile, reaching the source on November 4, 1770, and raising a toast (of water) to King George III. Back in London Bruce's achievement made him a celebrity; James Boswell published a short, and admiring account of Bruce's expedition in the *London Magazine* 43 (August-September, 1774), 388–91, 429–31. However, in the years after his return, critics were already debating whether Bruce had discovered the true source, had been the first to reach it, or even had travelled into Ethiopia at all; for discussion of these criticisms, see, e.g. the *Scots Magazine* 48 (April 1786), 165–71.

Boswell had remarked that 'the compiler of this Sketch . . . waits with impatience for a compleat account from Mr Bruce's own pen', but it would be another sixteen years later before Bruce, with the assistance of ghost-writers, published his own account, in five large illustrated volumes, as *Travels to Discover the Source of the Nile, In the Years 1768, 1769, 1770, 1771, 1772 and 1773* (Edinburgh: printed by J. Ruthven, for G. G. J. and J. Robinson, London, 1790). Despite being very expensive it was a great financial success; as Richard Sher points out, rather than being published by subscription, Bruce himself had funded production, with almost the entire print-run pre-committed to Robinson and other booksellers, and he had separate agreements for French and German editions (see Sher, *The Enlightenment and the Book* (2006), 242–43). Curiosity or gossip about Bruce's book led to sections being reprinted in magazines and newspapers, including the *Caledonian Mercury*. However, as Nigel Leask notes, alongside some early positive reviews, that more recent explorers questioned Bruce's credibility, old carping resurfaced, and Bruce's self-congratulatory anecdotes and the pretentious book-format attracted mockery, and he instances 'Peter Pindar's' satirical *Complimentary Epistle to James Bruce, Esq., the Abyssinian Traveller* (1790), which asserted Bruce 'put probability to flight' (Leask, in *ODNB*, 2004–06; *Complimentary Epistle*, p. 12). Craik's short poem about Bruce seems out of place, even anti-climactic, as the final item in the manuscript she was presenting to Riddell; the date Bruce's book was published means it was written the same summer that she was copying out the Riddell-Beinecke manuscript, and its inclusion may have been a last-minute decision.

When to explore the source of Nile,
B**** trudg'd o'er many a weary mile,
The useful deed atchiev'd at last,
And ev'ry strange adventure past,—
5   —Say,—what advantages cou'd rise,
From *all* he seem'd so much to prize—
—Why just the *sole* attainment got,
Was—*drinking water* on the *spot.*—
And learning thrifty ways to feast
10   On collops from the *living* Beast.—
While wond'ring Readers bless their fate
Which doom'd them *here* at home to wait;
Content o'er humble Port to smile,
Nor stroll for *water* to the Nile;
15   But far from danger, free from care
Enjoy in safety, better fare;
Nor wish,—midst Crocodiles to boast,—
That bloody Cat'rine was *their Toast.*—

—O B****!—once more abroad repair,
20   You're but suppos'd a *madman there*:
But *here* for *worse*, 'tis said you pass,
By ev'ry Briton term'd an Ass.—

¶

Then hasten back to cooling Nile,
And make Senaar's *bright* Damsels *smile.*—
25   —But shou'd your *wise* discoveries rot,
Once more in barren sands forgot,
E'en friendly let them *there* remain,
Nor pick our pockets *thus* again.—

MS pp. 170–71.

8. *drinking water*: at the second source, he filled a coconut shell
   with spring water and drank two toasts, to King George III
   and to Empress Catharine II of Russia, then at war with the
   Ottoman (Turkish) Empire, who was therefore being toasted
   as the protector of his Greek traveling companion: see Bruce,
   Travels, III: 596–57.
18. bloody Cat'rine: Catharine. Craik's manuscript has an asterisked
   footnote '* Empress of Russia'. See note 8 above.
24. Senaar's *bright* Damsels: Sennar, a city on the Blue Nile in Sudan,
   which then numbered some one hundred thousand people, was
   the capital of the Funj Kingdom of Sennar. Bruce, who had
   trained in medicine, gives a lurid (racist) account of treating
   the naked corpulent King's Ladies in Sennar, with bleeding
   and emetics, commenting that 'calling these the fair sex is not
   preserving a precision in terms', but also reporting that they
   had insisted on stripping him and been equally disgusted by
   his whiteness: Bruce, *Travels*, IV: 447–51; this passage about
   Sennar was reprinted verbatim in *Caledonian Mercury*, 24
   June 1790, p. 3.
28. Nor pick our pockets *thus* again: the five-volume quarto illustrated set of Bruce's *Travels* cost a hefty £5 5s., i.e. a guinea
   a volume: see Creech's advertisement in *Caledonian Mercury*,
   6 May 1790, p. 1; Sher, p. 242.

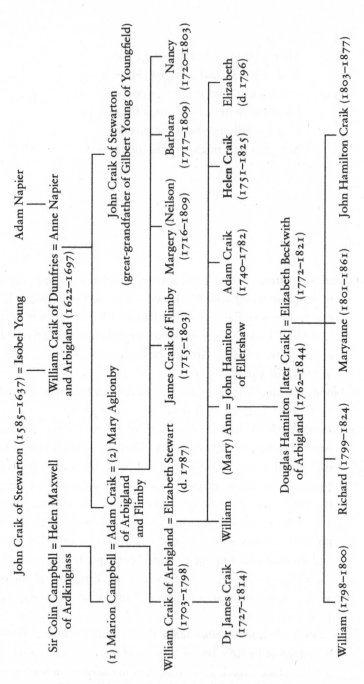

Fig. 4: The Craiks of Arbigland and Flimby

APPENDIX I:
HELEN CRAIK'S MEMOIRS
OF HER FAMILY

IN 1811, *The Farmer's Magazine*, a Scottish monthly published in Edinburgh, published a lengthy unsigned article on William Craik as an agricultural improver, based on material collected by Burns's friend, James Grierson (1753–1843), of Dalgoner, just north of Dumfries, and drawing also on 'a large body of material concerning Mr Craik' collected by Gilbert Burns, Robert's brother, 'from friends in the county of Dumfries and the stewartry of Kirkcudbright'.[1] Appended to the article were the two letters by Helen Craik herself given here, important as giving her own measured assessment of her father and family nearly twenty years after she had left Arbigland and moved to live with her cousins at Flimby in Cumberland. Ten years later, she sent a shorter letter, also given below, to the London-based *Monthly Magazine*, replying to comments on William Craik in an article about the American privateer and naval captain John Paul Jones, countering the allegation that he was William Craik's illegitimate son.[2]

(Endnotes for Appendix I can be found on pp. 191–95.)

1. Letter, Miss Craik to James Grierson, Esq., dated Flimby, 13 April 1810.

The contents of your very handsome and obliging epistle should have been instantly acknowledged, had not some unavoidable engagements interfered to deprive me of that pleasure.

As the sole and last survivor of my name and family, I cannot but feel extremely gratified by your kind and flattering attention to the preservation of my father's memory as an agriculturist. Accept then, Sir, my thanks on the occasion. The honour you confer upon him, must reflect back upon yourself; since you alone, of all his once numerous friends and acquaintances, have endeavoured to save from oblivion those exertions for his country's improvement, which, it cannot be denied, laid the first foundation for much subsequent advantage and prosperity.

I am truly concerned, however, to add, that after a minute examination of every written memorial connected with former days, now in my possession, aided by the utmost efforts of recollection also on the topic you mention, scarcely any circumstance worth communication has proved the result of my labour. What has occurred, nevertheless, is at your service. My father was born August 1703:—He was originally intended for the law; but upon his father failing in his promise of sending him to study at Leyden, (then the fashionable resort for that purpose), he succeeded to the Scotch estate of Arbigland, at that period considerably under 200*l.* per annum. Of a character and disposition always ardent and solicitous to make himself completely master of whatever he took in hand, he soon became distinguished in the agricultural line, at a period when the very meaning of the word, far less its practical possibility, was scarcely heard of in Scotland. As may be supposed, great were the difficulties he had to encounter. For many succeeding years the indolent obstinacy of the lower class of people was almost unconquerable. Amongst other instances of their laziness, I have heard him say, that, upon his first introduction of the mode of dressing the grain at night, which had been thrashed during the day,—all the servants in the neighbourhood refused to adopt the measure, and even threatened to destroy the houses of their employers by fire, if they continued to insist upon the business. My father speedily perceived that a forcible remedy was required for the evil: He gave them their choice of removing the thrashed grain in the evenings, or becoming inhabitants of Kirkcudbright jail; they preferred the former alternative; and open murmurings were no longer heard.[3] He has frequently told me, that he had laid out as much money, merely in draining the estate of Arbigland, (all of which required it greatly) as would have purchased the whole of it at his father's death. In regard to his system of improving land, that matter has been long sufficiently known in the south of Scotland, as likewise his alterations in the construction of the drill plough; which, though now not much used I believe, procured him, (1770), nevertheless, a valuable gold medal from the Society of Arts in London.[4] He was unwearied in his attention to his favourite object; and, for the greatest part of his farming life, was seldom later in his bed, during the summer season, than from three to four o'clock every morning,—usually breakfasting and dining in the fields, near his labourers, who did the same.

I am mortified that the above very trifling communication is all I can recollect at present on this subject,—nor do I now remember a single surviving human being qualified to add any further intelligence, unless Mr Maxwell of Carruchan, or Mr John Maxwell of Munches, could furnish it.[5] Have the goodness to excuse so long an intrusion on your time, with a detail too inconsequential to warrant the trouble it must have caused you: And believe me, Sir, your obliged and obedient servant, H. Craik.

II: Letter, Miss Craik to James Grierson, Esq.,
dated Flimby, May 1810.

I should ill repay the honour proposed to be conferred on my father's memory, were any apology judged necessary by me on such an occasion;—but the fact is, the female part of his family were never permitted to interfere, in the smallest degree, with those occupations and pursuits, which he considered as more particularly his own. The natural consequence was, we were kept in total ignorance of every transaction that came under this prohibited denomination. Nevertheless, some of your questions I feel competent to answer; and as it seems more the minutiae of what may prove connected with his public than his private life which you wish to obtain, there certainly can be no indelicacy attached to the very obliging solicitude expressed on that subject.

Our family is originally of English extraction. There is a Sir John de Creke buried in the churchyard of Westley Waterless, in Cambridgeshire, who died in the reign of Edward III.; but our branch came from Creke Castle, situated between Beverley and the city of York, where (though in the ever changing course of human affairs, some trifling variation in the spelling of the name has taken place) the family still exists.

The first person bearing the appellation, who settled in Scotland some time in the sixteenth century, was my father's great great grandfather; he held the rank of captain in a regiment quartered in Dumfries, and there married a woman sufficiently endowed with the good things of those days, to be distinguished by the title of 'an heiress'.[6]

What this gentleman's son was, I know not; but his grandson was grandfather to your deceased acquaintance. He married the daughter of Adam Napier, the youngest son of the famous Napier of Merchiston, and represented for some time the town of Dumfries, in the Scotch Parliament before the Union. I believe his name was William. He left two sons. Adam, the eldest, was father to mine: He succeeded to the estate of Arbigland. The other, John (uncle to my father), was, I think, grandfather to the late Mrs Young of Youngfield, and had Stewarton settled upon him by his father, as second son's portion. If I am not mistaken, it was this John Craik of Stewarton who joined with an ancestor of Sir Robert Lawrie's family in purchasing all the land they could possibly get hold of; in consequence of which, a common expression with the smaller proprietors in their neighbourhood was, 'God keep us from John Craik and Robert Lawrie!!'[7]

Stewarton certainly formed part of the Scotch estate, but I cannot call to mind how my father came to have any thing to do with it or its rents; it could not, however, be on his own account.

His maternal grandfather and grandmother were Sir Colin Campbell of Ardkinlass in Argyleshire, and Helen Maxwell, daughter to Sir George Maxwell of Newark. She was first cousin to the celebrated lawyer Sir George Mackenzie, King's Advocate for Scotland. Of her and her husband Sir Colin, I possess some interesting historical anecdotes, with which, however, I shall not at present trouble you.

Their daughter Marion (my father's mother) was a woman of very superior abilities, and much beloved by all who knew her; but her life proved a short one. She left only two children, both in early youth—my father, and a daughter who died soon after my grandfather's second marriage, and who, with myself, was named after Lady Campbell. It was the above Sir George Maxwell, who got what was called a *Lockerby wipe,* viz. one side of his face laid flat on his shoulder, in an engagement with the Johnstones at that place.

The estate of Arbigland was purchased by my great great grandfather, from Lord Southesk, in 1679.

Adam Craik my grandfather, and Miss Campbell of Ardkinlass, were married in Argyleshire, at Sir Colin Campbell's house in 1702. My father was born on the 26th August O.S. 1703, at Arbigland hall, as it was then styled; it stood upon a bank overlooking the sea, not far from where the garden is now placed; and certainly, in point of situation, much surpassed the present mansion. Allowing for the times in which it was built, I understand it was considered as greatly superior to any other gentleman's house in that quarter; but, like its former inhabitants, it has long been levelled with the dust. My father had it pulled down soon after his father's death, and removed the materials to the new dwelling.

He was originally intended for the law; but, as I mentioned in my last epistle, upon my grandfather failing in his promise of sending him to study at Leyden,[8] he renounced the profession, after having made no inconsiderable progress in it, and afterwards settled on a small farm called Maxwellfield, which his father gave up to him, in 1726: it was about a mile distant from Arbigland, I mean *old* Arbigland.[9]

The country was, at this period, so far removed from every idea of real civilization, that, to permit one's male guests to go sober to bed, was looked upon as the greatest possible failure in hospitality and good manners. My father, who, from his earliest days, always wished to take the lead in whatever he engaged with, was by no means behind hand on similar occasions. In hard drinking, hard riding, and every other youthful excess, few could equal his notoriety. I have frequently heard him say, that he felt a much older man, in constitution, before he was thirty, than afterwards at seventy and upwards.

In September 1733, he married my mother Elizabeth Stewart, only daughter of William Stewart, Esq. of Shambelly, in the parish of New-Abbey. He succeeded his father (who died at Arbigland) in 1736, at which time the estate was only about 173*l*. per annum. They continued, however, at Maxwellfield, where all their children were born, until the present house of Arbigland was habitable, into which the family removed in 1755.[10]

Samuel Johnstone was the name of the old overseer. What you say about him, is perfectly correct.[11] I cannot state the exact year in which the building of the new house commenced; but I know the drawing-room, and some of the other apartments, were not finished for many years after we dwelt in it. Long before that period, Samuel came to work in it as a joiner, and continued in the capacity of a head farm-servant with the family, until my father resigned his estate into the hands of the present possessor, when the latter turned off the good old man, who then went to reside in a small cottage at a little hamlet called the Borran, where his unmarried daughter (he had two and a son) kept house for him; but, as his real value was soon ascertained by his loss, he was afterwards recalled, and again reinstated in his former department and abode, which latter nearly joins the office-houses and Arbigland. On my last inquiries for him, I found he was no more. His family was a respectable one in Annandale, and formerly hereditary keepers of the Castle of Lochmaben. Poor Samuel! A worthier or honest man never breathed.

My father took an active and distinguished part in the great contested election of 1740.[12] I have heard him tell, that, sometime after that event, a number of the principal voters in the stewartry made him a voluntary offer of their services, in order to bring him into Parliament as their representative, free of all expense, too, during the time of the election; but prudential motives, of a pecuniary nature induced him to decline the intended honour.

Though the arrangement that prohibited those holding any situation under government (he was inspector-general of the customs, and the oldster officer, at his death, in the south of Scotland) from appearing as voters at elections of the above description, rendered his one [vote] of no use, yet he continued, as he had done from the year 1740, to be consulted and applied to, in every case of difficulty that occurred at such times; and was generally found to prove a sure and successful auxiliary to that side of the question whose interests he espoused.

Through the influence of the late Duke of Queensberry, and his invaluable friend the deceased Sir George Clerk, he might once have obtained the situation of a commissioner of customs at Edinburgh;[13] but he was then deeply engaged with his favourite agricultural pursuits, and too partial to country life, to think of exchanging it for the smoke and confinement of a town residence, even though that town was the metropolis of Scotland.

In 1764, he accompanied Sir George Clerk (then Mr Clerk) up to London, in order to give their joint evidence to government, on the propriety of adopting the worthy Baronet's judicious advice, in regard to purchasing the Isle of Man from the Duke of Athol, as the most likely means for suppressing the illicit trade of smuggling, then becoming ruinously prevalent on the south-west coast of Scotland.[14] This plan, in spite of Mr Grenville's long opposition, was finally acceded to, and has been attended with the best effects.[15]

I do not know that any particular cause (old age excepted) can be assigned for his deafness; but I have often heard him mention, that in consequence of getting a damp bed, during the election at Kirkcudbright in 1740, a giddiness, or what he called a swimming in his head, was brought on, and occasionally continued to distress him all his life. It is, however, rather an extraordinary fact, that he never had a common headache in the course of his existence, unless after hard drinking, in his earlier days;—those days when savage riot was considered as a proof of superior spirit, and brutal intoxication a test of the strongest constitution.

The latter part of his life had been systematically regular and sober. He was always an early riser; and, though but a bad breakfast man, he usually ate a hearty dinner; and, after a single dish of tea, and supping on milk and vegetables, retired to bed about ten o'clock. He took no wine, unless when in company, for many years; but, upon a slight paralytic attack, a few glasses of port were prescribed, and daily taken.

In May 1773, the late Earl of Selkirk, (whose father, the Honourable Basil Hamilton, had been my father's most intimate and cherished friend), with all that warmth of heart for which he was so remarkable, persuaded him to undergo the terrible operation of cutting for the stone,—a family distemper, of which my grandfather Craik died, and with which his son had long been afflicted.[16] His Lordship went to Edinburgh on purpose, in order to prevail with Mr Alexander Wood, then one of the first operators in that line, to undertake the business, and, with great difficulty, engaged him to leave his numerous patients in that quarter of the country, for the execution of this important affair at Arbigland. A stone of some size, I forget the weight, was extracted by that gentleman, with his usual success and high professional abilities. Nevertheless, for some hours after the operation, my father's life was supposed in much and immediate danger, and chiefly preserved by taking a copious and *first* dose of laudanum. Mr Wood had previously pronounced him a bad subject for the instrument, and was averse to the business: But my father's determination was not to be shaken; and the former declared, he never once found him shrink under his hands; and added, 'that he had never seen him surpassed for resolution and strength of mind, during a trial so painfully agonizing'. Mr Wood only remained two nights at Arbigland, but left another gentleman (who had accompanied him from Edinburgh) behind for the following three weeks.

Of the horse you mention, the recollection of what I have heard is very indistinct. I have been told, however, that he piqued himself, at one time, on having the best that could be procured. To the improvement of the breed of Scotch cattle, he was always particularly attentive. Formerly, he ploughed with oxen: Two of his rearing were so remarkable, at that time, for size and fatness, that they were exhibited for money, by the butchers who purchased them, as a public show in Dumfries.

I have heard my father say, that before the opera of the 'Gentle Shepherd' was finished, he won the three first acts of it in manuscript, at a game of cards, called 'three hand ombre', from Allan Ramsay, after having previously got all the poor author's little cash from him.[17] He had been a schoolfellow of Mallet the poet (then pronounced Malloch), but did not much like him.[18] Lord Kaims and he were likewise college companions, and the friendship continued through life.

He understood several languages well, and grammatically, viz. Latin, Greek, Hebrew, French, and Italian; and made some little progress in Spanish. He was a tolerable architect,—fond of chemistry,—read much on learned subjects,—and usually rendered himself master of whatever he set his mind upon.

My father had two sons and four daughters born in wedlock, of which number I alone survived him. William, of the former, died in childhood; the other, poor Adam, perished, as you may recollect, with his servant and four sailors, in crossing the Channel and Arbigland, in an open boat, to visit his friends in Cumberland. That melancholy, and ever-to-be-regretted event, happened on the 23d July 1782. His body came on shore some days afterwards, near a small village called Mowbray, situated between Allanby and Shinburness, in this county. We were solicitous that the corpse of his faithful servant, who had been long with him, might accompany his master's to Scotland; and the vessel that contained the latter, was consequently detained two days on this side, in hopes of his being found. At length, when expectation had almost ceased to exist, and the sloop just upon the point of sailing, poor Jack's remains came floating directly to the spot! They were both landed at the Carse, about a mile from Arbigland; and on the same day, conveyed from that place to the churchyard of Kirkbean. A gale of wind, want of proper ballast, and unskillful boatmen, were supposed to have caused this sad event. My dear brother was much beloved by all his particular friends; but his lot in life was not equal to his worth. He was upwards of forty years of age when we lost him. My poor mother never recovered the shock occasioned by this most distressing accident, and followed him to another and a better world in February 1787.[19] She died at Arbigland; as did my father, in February 1798, in his 95th year. In 1792, he resigned all of his property (except a small annuity of about 200*l.*, one half of which arose from his salary in the Customhouse) to the person whom he had previously appointed his successor,—the son of his deceased eldest daughter, by John Hamilton esq. of Eldershaw.

By my grandfather Craik's second marriage, 1713, with Miss Aglianby of Nunnery, one of the oldest and most respectable families in Cumberland, he had four sons and five daughters; of which number, three of the former, and four of the latter, survived him. John, the eldest, was born at Arbigland; all the others in Flimby, where four of them have likewise died since 1803. The second son of this union, James, was named after the brother of his father's first wife, Sir James Campbell of Ardkinlass,—a pretty sure proof of the estimation in which he continued to hold the memory of my father's mother!

With my worthy and much respected friends in Cumberland I came to reside in 1792; and on me has devolved the severe melancholy duty of laying their aged heads in the grave; where the remains of the last of its regretted members (my aunt Barbara) were deposited, in May 1809, in her ninety-second year.

About 500*l.*, received with his first wife, was laid out in the purchase of a small estate here by my grandfather. This little property, not exceeding 200 acres, sold, in 1807, for 16,504*l.* It had a fine wood upon it, and is full of coals. By his second marriage-settlement, in failure of his sons having male heirs, this estate was to go past his daughters, and rest with the eldest branch of the family. My uncles all died unmarried. The eldest branch was my father, who had departed this life before any of them did so; of course, his legal heirs succeeded to the above premises, though both in the female line,—being D. Hamilton Craik, in right of my deceased sister his mother, and myself. Between him and me, therefore, the above sum of 16,504*l.* was equally shared. Do not, Sir, conclude me an egoist, if I add, that with this money, and the handsome increase made to it by my late ever respected relatives here, I am now, thank God and them, in rather more than easy circumstances; and can say, what many richer people cannot say, that I am healthy, happy, and contented. A tolerably strong proof of the former is, that though now pretty far advanced in life, during upwards of eighteen years spent in Cumberland, it is a well known fact, that I have not once kept my bed a single hour for indisposition of any description whatever; and yet, in the course of the above period, I have had occasion to sit up through the whole of many an anxious night, by the sickbed of my dying relatives.

It may not, perhaps, be altogether improper to add, that one illegitimate son of my father's survived him. He was about six years old at the time of my mother's marriage, and always treated by her as if he had been her own child. He was educated in the medical line, and settled in America, where he married a very accomplished and amiable woman, of French extraction, by whom he had a large family. On his first going to that country, he was some years in the regiment commanded by Washington, then a Colonel in the British service, and with whom he formed a friendship that continued uninterrupted through life.[20] In both Marshall's and Ramsay's history of that great man, honourable mention is made of Dr Craik, as was also done by General Washington in his will.[21] Soon after the commencement of the American Revolution, the General appointed him 'Physician-general to the United States' besides paying all possible attention to the interest of his children. But the death of that illustrious man proved a heavy blow to their former fair prospects, his successors having pursued measures decidedly hostile to his former adherents. I have now, Sir, obeyed your injunction, of noting down all I can recollect from memory, or find marked upon paper. Had I understood, by your first epistle, that any information, except that merely connected with my father's agricultural pursuits, was required, what is now forwarded should then have been at your service. I wish, however, that the whole had proved more worthy of sending you. There is, unavoidably, so much said about grandfathers and mothers, that I greatly fear you will find the foregoing statement of facts very confined. Your own language and arrangement of the various articles, will, I doubt not, nevertheless remedy the evil. I will not, therefore, try your patience further on so tedious a subject, but remain,

Sir, your most obedient servant, H. CRAIK.

III. Helen Craik, 'To the Editor of the Monthly Magazine'
(1811)

Sir,

WHEN gross misrepresentations of any description, but more particularly of an individual nature, are laid open to public investigation, it then becomes the duty of those better acquainted with facts to detect the errors, by giving an authentic statement of what actually existed on the subject in question. In the 52d volume of the Monthly Magazine for Nov. 1821, an extract is published from MSS. denominated 'Stephensiana'; which extract is notoriously incorrect in almost every sentence. I allude to the article 'Paul Jones', in which nearly the whole detailed communication evinces the total misinformation of the writer. It is true, the error may appear a venial one, inasmuch as the general outline of occurrences, is, in some measure, preserved; but nothing ought to be considered as trifling that affects the cause of truth or common justice, where either the character or feelings of our fellow creatures are obviously implicated.

In the first instance, the late Mr Craik's Christian name was not *Robert* but *William*; in the next, there is no such place as Arbigglings in Dumfrieshire, or any where else in the south of Scotland. Arbigland, the real designation of the above gentleman's estate, is situated on the coast of Galloway, not sixteen miles from Dumfries, and certainly in annual amount, more than doubles the sum mentioned in the Monthly Magazine for November. Instead of dying in 1796, or 7, at the advanced age of 90, Mr Craik's decease happened in 1798, in the 95th year of his yet more prolonged existence. Why Mr Stephens should assert that Paul Jones was that gentleman's son by a female servant, is impossible now to discover. The woman in question was the wife of John Paul, Mr Craik's gardener, who remained upwards of forty years in his service. The master and these two domestics were both married in the same week, so far back as the year 1733, and the female to whom Mr Stephens so charitably alludes, had three daughters and one or two sons before the birth of the said Paul Jones actually took place. It was not late in life when Mr Craik succeeded to his father's estate of Arbigland, and his having ever been in the excise is equally false; he was, however, surveyor general of the customs, in which the latter mistake has no doubt originated. His legitimate son did not perish between Arbigland and Carlisle, for this conclusive reason, that the last mentioned place happens to be situated at some distance from the ocean. The fatal event occurred between his father's house at Arbigland and Allonby, on the opposite shore of Cuimberland, in 1782; neither was it a cousin, but the son of his eldest sister, who succeeded to the estate.

Should any further intelligence on the existing subject be deemed necessary, application may be made to the writer of the present communication, who happening to be the sole surviving daughter of the late Mr Craik, conceives herself fully as competent as Mr Stephens to answer any questions the occasion may henceforth require.

HELEN CRAIK.

Flimby Lodge, near Maryport,
Cumberland, Nov. 12, 1821.

Endnotes: Appendix I

1 'Account of William Craik, Esq. of Arbigland', *The Farmer's Magazine*, 12 (June 1811), 145–65; Helen Craik's letters appear on pp. 154–63.

2 'To the Editor of the Monthly Magazine', *Monthly Magazine*, 52 (December 1821), 418. Craik was replying to paragraphs about her father in 'Stephensiana, No. II', *Monthly Magazine*, 52 (November 1821), 329–30.

3 **Justice of the Peace:** Under Act Anent the Commissioners and Justices of peace introduced by James VI and I, Justices of the peace were established in the Parliament of Scotland in 1609. The office was meant to counter the power of the office of Sheriffs, which were then held hereditarily by landowners, dispensing criminal justice on a local basis.
   Kirkcudbright Jail: Built between 1627 and 1629, Kirkcudbright Tolbooth, in the county town some thirty miles from Arbigland, remained in use as a prison until the early nineteenth century.

4 **drill plough:** tool used for making holes to sow seed, with versions designed to contain seeds and drop them into the holes that were made. Jethro Tull is credited with inventing the drill in 1701, advocating its use in his *Horse-hoeing Husbandry* in 1731, although its use remained limited and improvements to it were regularly made. Craik's drill plow was 'drawn by one horse only, and sows four rows at once' (Rev. Edward Neilson, 'Parish of Kirkbean', *Statistical Account*, 15.VII, 1795, p. 124). Craik's plow, which was advertised in the *Caledonian Mercury*, 20 February 1768, was touted as being invented by Craik, although it appears that he improved M. du Hamel's existing barrel-drill by regularising the speed at which seed was discharged, thereby decreasing waste, as well as altering the drill so it could accommodate seeds of varying sizes (*London Review of English and Foreign Literature*, 1 (1775), 196–97). Of the plow, Craik says 'The saving, in seed, will be, in oats, above one half, and in all other grain above one third' (*Caledonian Mercury*, 20 February 1768).
   gold medal: The Royal Society of Arts was founded in 1754 and granted a Royal Charter in 1847. Though agriculture had not been included in the RSA's original scheme, the Society began awarding prizes for agricultural improvements in 1758. In 1761 the RSA began offering prizes for 'drill ploughs which should cut several furrows, deposit the seed, and cover the earth at one operation', the earliest of which was given in 1766 to Rev. H. Gainsborough. Craik, who describes to the Society his innovations in letters dated 4 January 1767 and 6 June 1767, received the gold medal for his improvements to the plow in 1771: see Henry Tureman Wood, 'The Royal Society of Arts. V.—The Society and Agriculture (1754–1830)', *Journal of the Royal Society of Arts*, 59 (3 November 1911), 1108–18.

5   **Mr Maxwell of Carruchan:** probably the elder George Maxwell of Carruchan (1738–1822), who would have known William Craik longer, though the date of Craik's letter means it could also be his son of the same name (1777–1821). The Maxwells' house and estate at Carruchan, is two miles south-west of Dumfries, in the parish of Troqueer, Kirkcudbrightshire. Craik mentions Carruchan in her poem 'A Card for J.M. Esq.' (Appendix II, p. 207).

    Mr John Maxwell of Munches: John Maxwell of Terraughty (1720–1814), who spent his early life as a skilled carpenter, was successful enough by 1754 to buy back the family estate of Terraughty, which had been sold after his father fell into financial difficulties. Subsequently, through his second marriage, he also acquired the other family estate of Munches, bordering the river Urr, in the parish of Buittle, Kirkcudbrightshire. In 1791, Burns addressed a poem to him on his seventy-first birthday. Maxwell's account of mid-eighteenth century agricultural conditions and improvement in the area, including brief comment on William Craik's success at Arbigland, was first published in W. M. Herries, *Report of the Stewartry of Kirkcudbright Agricultural Society for the Year 1810*, and later included in the *New Statistical Account of Scotland*, IV (1845), pp. 206–08.

6   **Great great grandfather:** John Craik (1585–1637), born in Stewarton, Dumfriesshire married an heiress Isobell Young (1593–1690), of Gulihill, Dumfries, with whom he had five children: Janet Craik (1613–?); James Craik (1619–1687); William Craik (1622–1697); Johne Craik (1624–?); and Thomas Craik (1635–?).

7   **Robert Lawrie:** Sir Robert Laurie (1708–1779), 4th Baronet, of Maxwelton, succeeded to the baronetcy on 23 November 1731, was elected as a Member of Parliament for Dumfries at by election on 19 June 1738, sat in the House of Commons from 1738–1741 and was known in the Burns circle. Craik is most likely referencing the first Sir Robert Laurie (c. 1641–1698) who was created a baronet of Nova Scotia on 27 March 1685. Both Laurie and Craik of Stewarton were appointed as commissioners of the sheriffdom of Nithsdale and Dumfries on 13 May 1685.

8   **Leyden:** By 1700, the universities of Leiden and Utrecht, both located in the United Provinces of the Netherlands, were the schools of choice for Scotsmen wishing to enter the legal and medical professions. See J. W. Cairns, 'The Origins of the Edinburgh Law School: The Union of 1707 and the Regius Chair', *Edinburgh Law Review*, 11 (2007), 300–48.

9   **Old Arbigland:** i.e. Maxwellfield. Craik settled on Maxwellfield, a small farm located on the Arbigland Estate, in 1726 and succeeded to the family estate in 1736, moving into the new Arbigland House in 1755.

10   William Craik designed Arbigland House himself in the classical Georgian style, with construction completed in 1760. Some speculate that

he was able to finance the project due to his involvement in smuggling brandy across the Irish Sea; cf. n. 14.

11 In a letter dated 1 November 1810, James Grierson, in response to the editor's inquiries about William Craik's agricultural achievements, writes: 'Mr Craik said, 1782, that, for thirty years together, the sun never rose while he was in bed; and added, what was still more extraordinary, that his overseer, Samuel Johnston, he never found in bed but two or three times' (165); Craik's avoidance of naming 'the present possessor' of Arbigland, her nephew Douglas Hamilton Craik, indicates her feelings about Hamilton Craik's inheritance of the estate.

12 **Contested election of 1740:** There was no parliamentary election for Kirkcudbright in 1740, but there was an election in 1741 when Basil Hamilton, 'a Jacobite with a strong local interest', defeated William Stewart, 'a Walpole Whig' (J. M. Simpson, 'Kirkcudbright Stewartry', *History of Parliament* 1716–1746, 1970, consulted online).

13 **Late Duke of Queensberry:** Charles Douglas, third duke of Queensberry and second duke of Dover (1698–1778) succeeded to the baronety in 1711 and married his second cousin, Lady Catherine Hyde (1701–1777). Under George I, Queensberry served as lord of the bedchamber (1721), vice-admiral of Scotland (1722), and privy councillor (1726). A dispute between his wife and the Lord Chamberlain, who refused to license John Gay's Polly, led George II to bar her from court and force Queensberry to resign his offices. From 1733 the duke served as a gentleman of the bedchamber to Frederick, prince of Wales and in 1734 played an active role in an attempt to elect opposition Scottish representative peers, standing as a candidate and voting in a peers' election for the only time in his life. Queensberry regained his place on the privy council, became keeper of the great seal of Scotland (1761–1763), and justice-general (1763–1768 (after the accession of George III.
Sir George Clerk: George Clerk (1715–1784), known after his 1735 marriage to Dorothea Maxwell (c. 1722–1793) as Sir George Clerk Maxwell, succeeded to the baronetcy of Penicuik in 1782. Clerk was a known agriculturist and Scottish landowner who was the king's remembrancer in the exchequer from 1761, a commissioner of customs in Scotland from 1763, and a trustee for improving fisheries and manufactures in Scotland (*ODNB*).

14 **Isle of Man:** In the eighteenth century, the Isle of Man lay outside the control of the British crown and became a hub for illegal trade, as a 'common storehouse for all manner of goods and merchandises that pay high duties in Great Britain or Ireland, or are prohibited into these kingdoms'. In 1755, losses to the British exchequer from the island's smuggling trade amounted to less than seven hundred thousand pounds per annum: Malachy Postlethwayt, *Universal Dictionary of Trade and Commerce*, 4th ed. (London: Strahan, 1755), II, s.v. 'Smuggling

in Relation to the Isle of Man'. Under the 1765 Isle of Man Purchase Act, known also as the Act of Revestment, the British Crown purchased the feudal rights of the Dukes of Atholl as lords and heads of state for seventy thousand pounds and an annuity.

Duke of Athol: John Murray, third duke of Atholl (1729–1774) succeeded his Uncle James Murray on 7 February 1764 and, through his marriage to his cousin Lady Charlotte Murray (1731–1805), the English barony of Strange and the sovereignty of the Isle of Man (*ODNB*).

Smuggling: As Commissioner of Excise from the Foot of Nith to Foot of Urr, Craik, entitled to one third of the value of captured illicit cargos, became wealthy from seizures (*Universal Scots Almanac for 1770*, Edinburgh: Ruddiman, n.d., 100). J. B. Blackett suggests that Craik himself may also have been involved in smuggling; a letter from the Excise Officer in Dumfries to Edinburgh notes that while the officer 'would not go so far as to say that the Laird was involved . . . many of his servants and horses were'.

15 **Mr Grenville's long opposition:** Craik is mistaken. The Duke of Atholl, not Grenville, was opposed to the purchase. George Grenville (1712–1770) entered Parliament in 1741 as an MP for Buckingham, eventually becoming Prime Minister on the death of Lord Bute on 8 April 1763. In his capacity as Prime Minister, Grenville negotiated and proposed the bill for the Crown's purchase of the Isle of Man. The bill passed 10 May 1765. Grenville was dismissed by George III the same year.

16 **Cutting for the stone:** the surgical removal of kidney or bladder stones known today as lithotomy. In the 1700s, bladder stones were typically removed by cutting into the perineum and opening up the bladder and bladder neck, a procedure developed by Jacques de Beaulieu and taken up by Johannes Rau in Amsterdam and William Cheselden in London (Roy Porter, 'Hospitals and Surgery' in *The Cambridge Illustrated History of Medicine*, ed. Porter, Cambridge: 1996, pp. 219–20). The surgery was said to be so painful that it was considered 'cruel and imprudent to subject the Patient to so severe and dangerous an Operation, without absolute Necessity' (*A General System of Surgery in Three Parts*, 4th ed., translated into English from the Latin by Dr Laurence Heister, London: 1950, sect. 5, p. 103).

late Earl of Selkirk: Dunbar Douglas, born Dunbar Hamilton, (1722–1799), 4th Earl of Selkirk, succeeded to the title on 3 December 1744, on the death of his great-uncle, since his own father, Lord Basil Hamilton (1696–1743), William Craik's friend, had died earlier. The Earl, Lord Lieutenant of Kirkcudbright, was a representative peer for Scotland from 1787; both he and his son Lord Dear were agricultural improvers and fellows of the Royal Society of Edinburgh.

Alexander Wood: Wood (1726–1807) studied medicine at Edinburgh, becoming a fellow of the Royal College of Surgeons from 1756, settling in practice in Edinburgh, and being elected Deacon (President) of the Incorporation of Surgeons there from 1762–1764 (*ODNB*).

17 **three hand ombre**: 'A trick-taking card game for three people using 40 cards' where players bid for the right to nominate a trump suit (*OED*). An English version of the French l'Hombre, the game was popular from the late seventeenth to the nineteenth century; it is frequently mentioned in literature of the period, as in Pope's *Rape of the Lock* (1712, 1714), and a proposition in Parliament to limit the stakes of the game to five pounds was ridiculed in high society.

Gentle Shepherd: this story is not recorded in any of the Ramsay sources, but assuming its truth, since Craik left Edinburgh for Maxwellfield in 1726, it seems more likely to have been manuscript for the 1725 edition than for 1728.

18 **Mallett**: David Mallet (c. 1705–1765); Scottish poet and dramatist.

19 **My poor mother**: Elizabeth Stewart, daughter of William Stewart of Shambellie (d. 1787).

20 **one illegitimate son**: Dr James Craik (c. 1730–1814). Craik studied medicine at the University of Edinburgh and served as a surgeon in the West Indies for the British Army in 1750. In 1751 he resigned his post and immigrated to Norfolk and later Winchester, Virginia where he opened medical practices. In 1755 he was named Washington's chief medical officer. In 1777 Craik joined the Continental Army upon being offered a position as a medical officer. He rose to the title of chief hospital physician of the Continental Army on 6 October 1780 and chief physician and surgeon of the army on 3 March 1781. Craik served in the army until 23 December 1783. Helen Craik does not mention William Craik's rumored second illegitimate son, John Paul Jones. She denies that rumour in her later letter to the editor of the *Monthly Magazine*, printed below.

21 **Marshall**: John Marshall (c. 1755–1835), fourth Chief Justice of the U.S. Supreme Court, had served with George Washington (and so with James Craik) in the Continental Army, published his five-volume *Life of George Washington* between 1804 and 1807. Marshall mentions Craik as Washington's physician and notes he was present at Washington's death bed.

Ramsay: Dr David Ramsay (1749–1815), who had served as a combat surgeon during the Revolutionary War, published his *Life of George Washington* in 1807. His account of Washington's death and Craik's attendance follows Marshall's.

his will: Washington bequeathed his bureau to Craik, writing: 'To my compatriot in arms, and old & intimate friend Doctr Craik, I give my Bureau (or as the Cabinet makers call it, Tambour Secretary) and the circular chairóan appendage of my Study' (*George Washington's Last Will and Testament*, 9 July 1799, item 19: www.mountvernon.org, accessed 11 September, 9 2023).

APPENDIX II:
GEORGE NEILSON,
SAMUEL ARNOTT, AND
'THE ROMANCE OF HELEN CRAIK'

THE LAST ATTEMPT at extended discussion of Helen Craik's poetry was in 1919 by the Scottish lawyer and historian George S. Neilson (1858–1923). Neilson had bought one of the three Craik poetry notebooks then extant, and he seems to have been in correspondence with the owners or previous owners of the other two, Adam Wood of Troon (the notebook now at the Beinecke), and Robert Henderson of Penicuik (the notebook Craik herself had given to Miss Staig of Dumfries). Neilson first published his discussion of Craik's poetry, reporting the contents of his own Craik notebook, in March 1919, in three separate articles at weekly intervals in the *Glasgow Herald*. After Neilson's death, they were republished in the *Transactions of the Dumfriesshire and Galloway Natural History Society*, the text given here. Neilson had given two talks about Craik to the Society, in 1919 using his *Glasgow Herald* material, and again in 1922, with further quotations from his own Craik notebook. After the second the chairman, Samuel Arnott, who had previously written about local ghost stories, suggested that one such legend could explain Craik's poems and her abrupt departure from Arbigland in early 1792. Neilson died soon after the second talk, and Arnott, working with Neilson's notes, wrote up his own dramatic account of her life, titling it 'The Romance of Helen Craik'. Given below are Arnott's original passage on the Arbigland legend, Neilson's three articles (treated as one long article on republication), and Arnott's follow-up. In Neilson's articles, parenthetical page numbers refer to the Craik notebook he owned, not to this edition.

I. From Samuel Arnott, 'Some Kirkbean folklore', *Transactions of Dumfriesshire and Galloway Natural History and Antiquarian Society*, 2nd ser., 11 (1894–95), 11–17.

. . . The next ghost we hear of with more detail, and the story is a tragic one with an ending in sharp contrast to that of the one just told. It is said to have haunted what is known as the 'Three Cross Roads', near Arbigland, a lonely spot, where, on a wild night, the dread feeling which was in these days felt in the deep darkness caused by the surrounding trees must have been intensified by the sound of the wind through their branches, and the roar of the waves of the boisterous Solway. The ghost was generally supposed to be that of a young man, and the tale is a romantic one, which, in the hands of an accomplished novelist, would form a thrilling narrative. As is pretty well known, Arbigland at one time belonged to a family of the name of Craik. Its then representative had a daughter who, it is said, had become attached to a young man named Dunn, who was in her father's employment as a groom or horse-breaker. One day a shot was heard, and soon after the lifeless body of Dunn was found near where the ghost was said afterwards to appear. In the eyes of the law, the sad occurrence was considered a case of suicide; but popular belief took an opposite view, and attributed it to the murderous act of one of Miss Craik's brothers, who had discovered the attachment between his sister and Dunn, and in his anger at the discovery, had taken the young man's life. It is said that Miss Craik was of the latter opinion, and that she left Arbigland and went to reside in England, never returning to the place so full to her of tragedy. The remains of Dunn were interred on the Borron Hill, and years afterwards disinterred by a man in the neighbourhood, the skeleton being, it is said, sent to Miss Craik. With the prevailing opinion regarding this ghastly tale, it is little wonder that the apparition of the unfortunate man was said to frequent the lonely spot where he met his death. It was hardly to be expected, however, that a haunted place like this should be deserted by the white ladies so familiar in ghost stories, and whose affection for Kirkbean seems somewhat remarkable, and one of my informants speaks of a white lady who was said to appear here also. The weight of the authority (if I am justified in using such a phrase in this connection) is, however, almost exclusively in favour of the tradition that the apparition was that of Dunn.

II. George S. Neilson, 'The Maid of Enterkin: Poems by Helen Craik and Burnsiana', *Transactions and Journal Proceedings of the Dumfriesshire and Galloway Natural History and Antiquarian Society*, 3rd ser., 11 (1923–24), 63–76.

15th February, 1924.

THE MAID OF ENTERKIN.
[POEMS BY HELEN CRAIK AND BURNSIANA.]
By Dr. George Neilson.

[Dr. Neilson made two communications to the Society on the Helen Craik manuscript, the first on March 21st, 1919, just before the third of his articles on the same subject appeared in *The Glasgow Herald*. In this contribution little more was given than appeared in these articles. The second communication was on 10th February, 1922, when further extracts and comments were made upon the same MS., particularly with reference to the social life of the period. Commenting on the change from lightness to melancholy, which appeared to take place, Dr. Neilson suggested that some profound tragedy had occurred in Miss Craik's life. In explanation of that, Provost Arnott told the story which follows Dr. Neilson's paper in this volume. These articles are reprinted by kind permission of the Editor and Mrs. Neilson from *The Glasgow Herald*, March 8th, 15th, and 22nd, 1919.—Ed.]

Relatively little is extant in the original to prove the actual contact and atmosphere of literature which surrounded Burns, the air without which the poet could hardly have lived. This rarity intensifies the examples such as the correspondence with Lapraik and David Sillar. Its noblest manifestations, however, are his own collective copies of his pieces lovingly written for the fit audience, though few. Frequently appealed to as critic of performers of far inferior grade he revealed his native generosity by over-appreciation. Specialists may recall the few cases in which the actual script submitted remains. Not quite so rare, yet rare and precious enough are the poetry books containing references to or quotations from Burns. Perhaps 'The Maid of Enterkin' opens a fresh vista.

It is the initial item of a little quarto manuscript volume which came into my possession some years ago, containing 172 pages, measuring about 8 inches by about 6¼ inches, the paper being without other distinguishing sign than a watermark ruling of eight lines. The first two and the last nine pages are blank. Pages 3 to 13 and 68 to 70 are written in what may be styled the principal hand, and of the remainder certainly 136, probably 141, are in a rather inferior copyist's hand. 'The Maid of Enterkin' occupies pages 2 to 10: it is a tragic poem about a melancholy 'incident said to have happened in the neighbourhood of Enterkin', that wonderful, steep, grassy cleft in the Lowther Hills to which Dr John Brown devoted a famous and beautiful essay. So perfect in spelling and punctuation is the initial poem that all presumptions favour its being the author's autograph, and an extremely neat script it is. On page 13 the same precise and beautiful hand gives us a ten line tribute to Burns, and on pages 68 to 70 sets forth a Troqueer local poem of particular interest to be examined in due course. Inside the book, when I purchased it, but on a separate sheet, folded as two quarto pages measuring 10 ¾ inches by 8 ¾ inches, were verses written in the precise principal hand on 'The Death of J. H. in the East Indies'. This separate sheet is watermarked with a crown over a hunting horn surmounting 'G. R.'. The suggestion it conveys is that the lines on J. H. are intended to be copied into the book, although this has not been done.

Of the Enterkin poem it may be enough to quote the lugubrious close of the speech of the maid over her dead father, herself about to die.

—Perhaps kind *Chance* some wand'ring step may send
To the lone Cot where our poor ashes blend;

And while the scene each fixt attention claims,
While these sad Lines the source of *feeling* drains,
The shelt'ring Grave Compassion may assign,
And our cold Frames to kindred earth resign.
—What tho no solemn Dust to Dust be said,
The last sad office *thus* humanely paid
Recording Angels shall applause bestow,
Well pleas'd to find *some pity still* below.—

Little wonder that an admirer of the poetess should have remonstrated in verse with her for her choice of dismal themes

'Where Madness Murder Horror dwell'.

The little poem on page 13 following a longer piece on the death of 'Mr C. E.' will at once arrest the attention of Burns students, and it is printed precisely as written:—

—LINES WRITTEN ON A BLANK LEAF OF MR BURNS'S POEMS—

Here native Genius, gay, unique and strong,
Shines through each page, and marks the tuneful song,—
Rapt *Admiration* her warm tribute pays,
And *Scotia* proudly echoes all she says;
Bold *Independence* too, illumes the theme,
And claims a manly privilege to fame.—
—Vainly O Burns! wou'd rank or riches shine
Compar'd with inborn merit great as thine!
These *Chance* may take as Chance has often giv'n,
But pow'rs *like thine can* only *come* from Heav'n.—

At present suffice it to note that apparently with some slight verbal incorrectness these lines appear in a scribe's hand-writing as the motto prefixed to the famous Glenriddell MS. without any intimation of authorship. Scott Douglas ascribed it as 'probably by Roscoe'; the editors of the fine facsimile of

the Glenriddell MS. which the world owes to the munificence
of Mr John Gribbel, directly assign it to Miss Helena Craik of
Arbigland.

More intense and intimate in its Burns touch is a piece on
page 37 headed

'TO CAPTAIN R.'

and beginning thus:—

> On Solway's Banks a humble Muse
> Let Fancy's Pow'r prevail,
> And oft along the winding Beach
> Arrang'd some artless tale—

Deprecating adverse criticism and hinting that poems sent to
be examined are sent only because Captain R. has requested it,
the poetess appeals for kindly treatment:—

> —Oft wou'd she by the gliding wave
> Her idle thoughts rehearse,
> But merit ne'er presum'd to claim,
> Nor dreamt they rose to verse.—

> —As sad or cheerful prospects shone
> Unbidden came the rhyme;
> No flatt'ring hopes of Fame in view,
> But just to *pass the time*.

> —The partial friends wou'd sometimes smile,
> And think the page might do,
> Yet much she fears the judging eye
> Of Coila's Bard and You.—

This introduces Burns as poetical censor and friend. Another
poem on page 42 is even more specific:—

TO CAPTAIN R——LL
WITH THE MAID OF ENTERKIN

While timid Hope succeeds well grounded fears
The trembling Maid of Enterkin appears,
And begs no stern, no criticizing brow,
O'er her poor Lines a Judging eye may throw—
Too well she knows no merit they can claim,
Where shines a Burns's never dying strain.

Alas no Mount Parnassus here is seen,—
No crystal Helicon's inspiring Stream!
On barren Criffal Laurels ne'er wou'd grow,
Nor Solway in poetic numbers flow.—

And while with Candour you the tale peruse
Whose mournful theme you gave the weeping Muse,
May *Pity* still her sovereign sway maintain,
Nor kill the Maid of Enterkin again.—

Putting these various intimations together, there can be no hesitation in identifying the Solway Muse. It was to Miss Helen Craik, daughter of William Craik of Arbigland, that Burns on August 9, 1790, wrote:—

> I inclose you two of my late pieces as some kind of return for the pleasure I have received in perusing a certain manuscript volume of poems in the possession of Captain Riddel.

A later letter of January 12, 1792, exhibits Burns not only as revising or willing to revise Miss Craik's lines but also as valuing high his opportunities of literary intercourse with her.
  'As to *Helen*', he writes,

> I shall certainly bestow my utmost attention on it, if possible that I can start a hint that may not have occurred

to you in smoothing a line or improving a thought. Now
that I have by removal to town got time and opportunity,
I shall often intrude on you with any assurance how sin-
cerely and respectfully I am, Dear Madam, your obliged
and obedient humble servant, Robt. Burns.

One may readily accept as probable a statement by that
industrious bibliographical commentator on the poets, Alex.
Gardyne, in his MS. Notes (in the Mitchell Library) that *Helen*[1]
was a poem concerning Helen of Kirkconnell, an eminently
likely theme of tragedy immortalised in the grand border ballad
of the Kirtle in Annandale narrating how the avenger pursued
the murderer to death and 'hackit him in pieces sma' / On fair
Kirkconnell Lea'. Possibly Miss Craik's poem is not lost beyond
recovery. To Captain Riddell, she tells us, her 'weeping Muse'
owed the suggestion of 'The Maid of Enterkin.'

There is no need to claim peculiar merit for her metrical
performances; the literary respect paid her by Burns and her
own modesty are warrant enough for attention to her books,
the forces and fashions of contemporary literature it reflects, its
intimations of a more or less poetic circle, the identification of
some of the figures which cross the scene, and finally the problem
of authorship presented by an enigmatic poem of banter in which
it is imperative to suspect the hand of Burns himself.

A noteworthy characteristic is the recurrent Werterism of Miss
Craik's poems. Goethe's romance written in 1774 had appeared
in translation, the 'Sorrows of Werter', in 1779. My manuscript
includes verses 'written by Charlotte at Werter's grave, 1779',
and another of Miss Craik's pieces bids us 'the sorrows of Werter

---

[1] A poem so entitled appears in each of the MS volumes by Helen Craik
owned by Mr Adam Wood, Skeldon, Dalrymple, Ayrshire, and by Mr
R. J. Henderson, Craigleur, Penicuik. In the former it is entitled 'Helen,
An Epistle to a Friend, p. 95'; in the latter, 'Helen, Written in the Summer
House at Arbigland, Feb. 25, 1792', which seems to be identical with
the verses printed, p. 80. *Ed. From Dr Neilson's Notes.*

deplore'. Burns sent Mrs Walter Riddell his copy of 'Werter' after the offence and quarrel of 1793. Whether fostered by 'Werter' or not, a kindred tragic sentimentality appears in Miss Craik's preference for suicidal and murderous subjects. Verses on the Earl of Caithness who shot himself in 1789, on Hackman's murder of Miss Ray in 1779, and on the mutual murder-suicide of Faldoni and Theresa in 1770 are instances of this painful taste. We can repeatedly sympathise with her rhyming critic, who wrote:—

> With powers so great how cou'd you Helen
> So hideous a subject, dwell on?

A word regarding the Glenriddell MS. motto will close the present instalment. The precise date when that was added as a sort of leading introductory note of homage to the contents of the priceless volume, mainly in Burns's own handwriting, does not seem to be known. The MS. itself, although Burns's preface to it is dated April, 1791, contains in Vol II. half a dozen letters written in 1793. Where did Captain Riddell, who died in 1794, get the motto? That Miss Craik might have got it from him is precluded by the significant error of the Glenriddell MS. which misspells 'Rapt' (line r above) and turns it into 'Wrapt.' Where she has 'Scotia' the Glenriddell MS. has 'Scotland'—on the whole the less poetic form. Her profuse italics fall with perfect aptness on the emphatic words of a little tribute to Burns which, while it may lack the supreme distinction necessary to justify its acceptance as an adequate inscription to a work of genius at a unique pitch of literary power, was at least felt by Captain Riddell to be worthy to grace the frontispiece of the poet's own autograph volume. The citations already made prove that the Captain had her verses through his hands, and that Burns himself was not insensible to her appreciation. Is further argument required for a conclusion which is no novelty that the checkered honours of the motto belong to the humble Solway Muse?

THE SOCIAL AND LITERARY CIRCLE, 1790–1793.

An amateur mannerism, current at the time, may be seen in Miss Craik's volume in sundry tame and easy charades on Fortune, Adam, and Woman. Mainly quite undistinguished one of the set introduces a star of the poetess's coterie:—

> My *First* with some help is to Valley allied
> My *Second* the place where Queen Caroline died
> My *Whole* is a compound of wit sense and whim,
> No changeable Proteus more various can seem.

The 'Second' is Zell (modern spelling Celle) in Hanover, where Queen Caroline of Denmark, sister of George III., closed her ill-fated days in 1775. The 'Whole' is Dalzell, being apparently the Lady E. D. of one poem and the 'Lady Elizabeth Dalzell' in a pencilled note to a piece 'on the death of a Brother'. Presumably she was the Elizabeth Johnston who married in 1775 Richard styled Lord Dalzell, grandson of Robert, Earl of Carnwath. The Craik circle closely touches that of Burns. Very odd is 'the humble petition of Margaret and Helen' (p. 46) into which an insertion in the principal handwriting (the words 'To R. O. Esqr. Sheweth') discloses the addressee. The initials need little ingenuity to interpret, still less when the gay petitioners bid him:—

> Wonder not Sir that we prefer this pray'r
> A poor Ten Thousand of your wealth to share,

archly adding:—

> We'll take ev'n Twenty Thousand if you please,

Mrs Oswald of Auchincruive had died in December, 1788, the subject of Burn's distressing Ode, and her heir, styled 'wealthy young Richard', is glanced at with adverse eye in Burns's second Election Ballad. It must be noted that Cavens, a seat of the

Oswalds, is a neighbouring residence to Arbigland in Kirkbean Parish. Lines 'To Lady W. M. Constable—with a Bird of Paradise' (p. 66) remind us that Burns also addressed verses to her.

One piece requires particular notice. It is on pages 68, 69, and 70 in the 'principal' hand, and its title is 'A Card from J. M. Esq': After certain explanations about the desirability of social gatherings the Card goes on thus from general head to specific application:—

> With this view Mr M****** his Compliments sends,
> And requests at K********* to meet with some friends
> He'll insure them a welcome if granting his boon
> They'll repair to the sign, when he *hangs out the Broom,*—
> From Cargen 'tis hop'd all the party attends,
> To cheerful good humour, 'tis said they are friends,—
> Goldie-Lee's beauteous Inmate he means to invite,
> To enliven the scene and enrapture the sight.
> On the Colonel's attendance he too must insist
> For the Broom shews there's wine and a party at Whist—
> Dalscerth's worthy owners if timely from Town,
> His endeavours to please with their presence shall crown.—
> Miss Maxwell, if she'll at the summons repair
> Of the strongest of Shrub shall have *fully* her share;
> And on Helen he'll gladly bestow his sweet wine
> To prevent her from scribbling nonsensical rhyme.—
> Captain Craik, who tho sober, from *hedging* is free
> Shall fill Bumpers as long as the Glass he can see,
> While Carruchan as usual exerts all his pow'rs,
> To preserve proper order and timely good hours
> For each Guest in particular, this Card has not room
> But in short, it announces he hangs *out the Broom.*—
> As a Landlord his merit has long been confest,
> And his friends shall acknowledge he now does his best.—
> 'Tis hop'd then in person they'll answer him soon,
> And the signal observe when he hangs out the Broom.

The exercise in identification these verses involve opens with the six dots after M and the nine dots after K in the indication of the inviter and his abode. Plainly it is James Maxwell of Kirkconnel, father of Dr Maxwell, Burns's friend, that is made to 'hang out the broom' in the mode once customary as the Card explains at Preston, which was the next house to Arbigland.

'In Preston as time immemorial has shown.' Preston at the foot of Criffel is styled in the old titles the 'Barony of Prestoun under the Fell', and is thus expressly associated with that most beautiful Galloway mountain known to Camden and beloved of Carlyle. It emerges from the obscurity of charter history as a commonty of horse pasture *super montes et fellis vocatos Crufellis.*

All the localities named lie between Kirkbean and Dumfries and the lairds of several of them appear in the correspondence or verses of Burns. Maxwell of Carruchan he valued and respected particularly. But the chief interest lies in the allusions to three personalities of the Burns coterie prominently seen for a moment of illumination in the playful but animated characterisations of the Card. 'Goldie-Lee's beauteous inmate' is a welcome and telling phrase, which sufficiently reveals the great contemporary impression made by Maria Riddell *nee* Woodley, the handsome and brilliant young wife of Walter Riddell, on her appearance as a new and dazzling light in the Dumfries firmament at Goldielea renamed, after her, Woodley Park, although ere long restored to its earlier title. The Riddells both at Friars' Carse and Woodley Park are inseparable from the life of Burns in his glory as master-poet, an association overcast at the end with poignant regrets due to the still mysterious quarrel not ended when Captain Riddell died in 1794. It was one more of the friendships of literature closing in severance and pain. No such distressing memory attaches to the guest who follows the radiant Mrs Riddell in the hospitable Kirkconnel's invitation. 'The Colonel' can be no other than the doughty old wooer of the Muses, Colonel De Peyster of Mavisgrove, afterwards the 'honoured Colonel' of Burns as volunteer, but now not long returned, hale, hearty, and jovial, from distinguished service with the Army at Fort Niagara and elsewhere in Canada as well as in what by fortune of war and politics had become the United States. And as for 'Helen', can one be far astray in believing that her own modest self-disparagement may be recognised in the twinkling humorous and sly allusion to her poetical proclivities? In the following line close after her comes Captain Craik—'the Captain' to whom as well as to old Mr Craik, deservedly renowned for his public spirit and enterprise in agriculture, Burns sent his greetings in his letter to Miss Craik. The agricultural connection, found a trifle oppressive, is rather skittishly glanced at in a poem 'To a Gentleman—from Newabbey—' appropriately located 'Where gloomy Criffald bleakly stands'. This perhaps explains the 'hedging' of Captain Craik. Surely, however, at any rate this Card of Kirkconnel's has served its turn in these flashes of passing light on the associates of Burns. A word may be in place to mention that the word 'Card' in the special sense of a 'card of invitation' was in full vogue from about 1770, as shown by the Oxford Dictionary of Dr Murray. But in addition there are signs of its adaptation as a literary form or medium. For instance, in 1781 the dedication of the 'Poetical Works of John Cunningham' (Apollo Press, Edinburgh) consisted of 'A card from the author to David Garrick, Esq.'. My closing article will embrace what is possibly a flash of Burns himself.

OLD AND NEW: 'A MONODY' TO DAVIE.

Indirect as may be the implications regarding the environment of Burns which Miss Craik's triflings with the Muses would warrant, direct contacts are not wanting. Lines addressed 'To a Lady—with a copy of Burnses Poems'—the spelling is that of the copyist scribe—although rather too apologetic about the rudeness of 'Our Poet's Lay' are emphatic about its charm and power of gift.

> If chance some luckless blot appears
> O may it be forgiven
> For rough the course that Genius steers
> Wild as the flash from Heav'n.

But it might be expected from the terms of Burns's letters to the poetess that signs should emerge of direct communication of some piece or pieces of his work whether finished or on the anvil. In this respect the spoil for future Burns editors is meagre, but there is some. First, there is a version of the impolitic inscription at Stirling extolling the Stewarts, and decrying the Hanoverian sovereigns, as well as of the bitter rejoinder ascribed to the Rev. G. Hamilton of Gladsmuir. Unfortunately the copyist has nodded badly in both versions, yet as it may be that they are the earliest rendering extant, it is desirable to give the script as it is, with all its imperfections on its head. The closeness of these versions to those in James Maxwell's 'Animadversions' published in 1788 may be such as to leave little dubiety about the source. Some reader may deduce the inferences from a collation.

WRITTEN IN A WINDOW AT STIRLING.
Here Stewarts once in Triumph reign'd
And Laws for Scotia's weal ordained;
But now unroof'd their palace stands
Their Scepter fallen to other hands.
The injur'd Stewarts line is gone,
A race outlandish fills the throne,
An Idiot race to honour lost
Who knows them best dispise them most.
                              B—

WRITTEN BENEATH.
Thus wretches rail when sordid gain
Drags in factions gilded chain;
But can a Man which fame inspires
When genius lights her highest fires
Can B—s disdaining truth and Law
Factions venom'd dager draw—
And skulking with a villains aim
Basely stabb his Monarchs fame
Yes B—s its o'er thy race is run

And Shades secure thy setting Sun
With pain thy wayward Fate I see
And mourn the Lot that's doom'd for thee
These few rash lines shall d— thy name
And blast thy hopes of future fame.

Burns in his American War Ballad was severe on Burgoyne's surrender in 1776. In one of Miss Craik's 'Charades' (page 58) the missing word has its various implications pointed out:—

'And many a gallant Soldier's skull
Of *this* and *this* alone is full
Burgoyne by numbers forced to yield
For *this* or worse resigned the field
And all our Troops on Yankee shore
Have just done this or litle more.'

The answer was 'Nothing'. In different strain, however, is a piece (page 153–54), 'The Soldier's Widow', which opens with the curlew screaming

O'er Saratoga's mournful plain,

and is in the orthodox pathetic vein. On the next leaf is a bright little song in a new handwriting of peculiar interest. Those who share with my friends, Mr J. C. Ewing and Mr H. S. Gladstone of Capenoch, the opinion that Captain Riddell as man of letters deserves better of his country will learn with pleasure that the song is in his bold and dashing script. Mr Ewing gave me among other valuable hints the clue to the unusual significance of this piece. It begins:—

When fame proclaimed with tongues in hundred
Gallant D—s sudden flight
Believe me girls the baggage blundered
For he'll be here this very night.

When this was written 'Gallant D—s' was only a subaltern. Time came in 1794 when an ambiguous toast proposed by Burns provoked captain Dods to such resentment as almost 'to end in a brace of pistols.' It seems in every way probable that the 'Captain' of Burns's quarrel was the 'Lieutenant' of Riddell's arch and laughing song.

A larger problem arises with a poem which the copyist, here a good deal more careful than usual, has taken evident pains to render distinctly and exactly. It is a piece that may require some critical construing, for its relationships to Burns in general diction, special vocabulary and easy epistolary style are patent, however, they are to be explained. The subject of the 'Monody' affords room for speculation, and perhaps it is well to say that 'the fatal 29th Decr., 1789', does not seem to be a date writ large and deep in the calendar of history. Inferentially its fatality is to be understood with reference to some private accident or episode of which 'Davie', was the unlucky cause.

A MONODY ON THE FATAL 29TH DECR., 1789.

Arms and the Man I scorn to sing,
The thread-bare tale is common
Coila thy chiefest succours bring,
My Theme is lovely Woman.
O Muse! if e'er ye heard my prayer
If ev'r I dearly prized ye
Had to my hand w' rhymin ware
To Sing that fatal Tyseday.

Not for your fauts, ye bony twa
This Sair mishap ye've got it
Your Virgin forms like virgin Snaw
Are taintless and unspotted,
For Your sweet Sakes it cou'd na be;
But thou, Unlucky Davie,
Thy Sins and Sinfu' Companie
Brought a' this Cursed Shavie.

Dispel your fears, ye lovely Pair
For a' the ills that's near ye
Angels are Heaven's peculiar Care
Misfortune dare na Steer ye
But Davie lad do thou repent,
E'er out again ye venture
Or Korah like ye'll meet a rent
Will send ye to the center.—

Had but the wheel within the wheel
Of our administration
Run wi' their Cargo to the deil
It wad been less vexation
But such a precious freight nae less
Than lovely Virgin Beauty
How cou'd even senseless iron and brass
Refuse to do its duty.—

In line seven 'Had' should, of course, have been spelt 'Haud'.
In line eight the form 'Tyseday' familiar enough in Scotland
though perhaps not in recorded use by Burns, will compel scrutiny. Its complete verification as correct by the rime is of final
importance in the verbal criticism. The 29th of December, 1789, it
is to be specially noted as a fact of the calendar, was as the poem
tells us a Tuesday. Nothing in the entire piece tells a plainer tale
of poetic power and confidence than line five; the writer proclaims
himself as one who knows that on other occasions than this the
Muse has heard his prayer and may hear it again. The unique
phrase 'Korah like' is—Burns et praeterea nihil; and 'center' is
used with obvious knowledge of the history of that fascinating
word in mediaval cosmogony and the derivative concepts of later
natural philosophy. It is legitimate to speculate whether the first
two lines of the last verse are a direct reference to politics. The
'Monody' apart from an obscurity of theme is a bit of first-class
composition, and can fearlessly encounter the cut and thrust of
the critics to whom it is now definitely committed.

III. Samuel Arnott, 'The romance of Helen Craik of Arbigland', *Transactions of Dumfriesshire and Galloway Natural History and Antiquarian Society*, 3rd ser., 11 (1923–24), 77–83.

In the course of a paper, entitled 'The Ghosts of Kirkbean', which I contributed to this Society, and which appeared in the *Transactions*, I referred to a tradition relating to the ghost of a white lady which was said to appear at a certain point on the road near Arbigland, Kirkbean, and which was reputed to have been habitually seen since the death by murder or suicide of one of the servants of Arbigland, who was alleged to have had an intrigue with Miss Helen Craik, the poetess, the daughter of Mr William Craik, the proprietor of Arbigland, a well-known man of his time. The tradition was quite a romantic one, but I attached no special importance to it, and it only assumed a different aspect when the late Dr George Neilson gave a lecture on Helen Craik to the members of this Society on 10th February, 1922. At that meeting I had the honour of being called upon to preside, and, in passing, I should like to say that it is with the deepest regret that we know the death of Dr Neilson, one of the brightest ornaments of our Society, made that his last contribution to our work. His illness, which followed almost immediately, prevented him from putting his lecture into permanent form for preservation in the annals of the Society. In the course of the lecture Dr Neilson made reference to the striking change in the tone of the poetry written by Miss Craik in later years as compared with her earlier verses. The latter were, as a rule, cheerful, almost sprightly, indeed, while those of her later years were of a melancholy kind, dealing largely with such subjects as murder and suicides. Dr Neilson also quoted from one of her poems, a portion of which I give later, written evidently in deep despondency, lamenting her banishment from Scotland, as if it were enforced and would for ever remain. At the close of the lecture I referred to the local tradition, of which Dr Neilson had never heard, as a possible indication of the cause of this change of tone and the depression into which the poetess had fallen. It had been my hope that Dr Neilson would have been able to make use of this tradition in preparing his lecture for publication, or as part of a later paper on the same subject, but, alas! that was otherwise decreed. I have been favoured by Mr Shirley with a perusal of Dr Neilson's material on which his lecture was founded, and from various pieces of information contained in the notes I have culled some interesting particulars, which appear to go a long way towards explaining the change in Helen Craik's poetry, and to confirm, to a certain extent at least, the tradition, not of the ghost, but of the belief that this was a spot where some dread deed had been consummated.

The tradition itself was related to me many years ago by two old residents of the parish of Kirkbean, who have been dead for a number of years, and who, though not contemporaneous with Miss Craik's residence at Arbigland, were in their early youth at the time of her death, and whose excellent memories yielded many stories of past days and of the people of the vicinity.

The tale was to the following effect, and it may be added that these two old residents agreed in every substantial particular.

There was employed at Arbigland a young man, whose name was said by my informants to be Dunn, but I heard another one from a different source, but had omitted to take a note of it. This man was a groom or horsebreaker—probably the former. Miss Craik is said to have formed an attachment to Dunn, and this was said to have been reciprocated by him and that clandestine meetings took place between them, apart from the numerous occasions on which they met in the ordinary course of life about a country house. It ought, I think, to be said that no hint of anything which would impugn the virtue of Helen Craik emerged in the tales, but that she was said to have been infatuated with the man. In some way the affair was brought to the knowledge of the Craik family, with the usual inevitable result.

When the discovery of the affair came to the knowledge of the family, their anger blazed out furiously. Then came the tragedy. According to the tale, Dunn was sent to Dumfries for a message on horseback, and about the time he was due to return the horse he had ridden came home riderless, and shortly afterwards the unfortunate man was found lying dead quite near Arbigland entrance, having been recently shot. There could only be two alternative theories of the cause of the tragedy. The man had either been murdered or had committed suicide. Public feeling was almost unanimous that it was a case of murder, and guilt was supposed to belong to one of the family. The police took up the matter, and inquiries were duly made by the Procurator-Fiscal of the Stewartry. In the end no proceedings were taken against anyone, it being attributed by the Fiscal to suicide. It was a common belief in the vicinity that the influence of Mr Craik, which was very powerful with the authorities, had been exercised to avert any charge of murder. In accordance with the feeling of the times, the body of the slaughtered man was buried on the sea shore at the precipitous promontory called Borron Point. Shortly afterwards, it is said, Miss Helen Craik disappeared from Arbigland, to which she never returned, and it was said that her face had been seen by someone belonging to the parish looking out of a window in Maryport. Some mystery attaches to the disposal of the body of poor Dunn. According to the tale related to me, it was removed from its lonely grave by a man living in a little hamlet called The Borron, near the point of that name. This man was called 'Umfrey Fenimore' by the people of the vicinity, and it was said that he retained the skeleton in his loft for some time, but that it was eventually sent to Miss Craik in England. Mr Shirley informed me the other day that the Rev. J. D. Cochrane, the present minister of the parish, had been told that the skeleton had been sold for anatomical purposes, but I can only give you what I was informed many years ago.

From the time of the burial of the unfortunate man a white lady was said to appear at night at the lonely spot where the tragic event took place.

One difficulty in following up this tale is that we have no reliable date at which this occurrence is said to have taken place, so that we might have a better idea of the probability or improbability of the tradition, which seems to have some connection with the doleful tones of Miss Craik's later poems.

Yet I think we can come to a close approximation of the time, and that we can put ourselves in a position to form a surmise at least of the period of the tragic deed. The theory of suicide seems to have very little to support it, nor can I, even in view of the certainty that there would be fierce resentment in the family at the intrigue, believe that any of its members lay deliberately in waiting for the return of Dunn and shot him in cold blood. If he was murdered it was probably done in a time of passion and probably after a heated altercation between man and man. In order to form an idea of who could have been alleged to be the perpetrator of the deed, we have to arrive within a reasonable conjecture as to the date of the affair, and this, I think, we may learn from the verses written by Miss Craik. Here are extracts from 'Lines Written in the Summerhouse at Arbigland in 1792'. This must have been about the time the gifted poetess left Arbigland never to return. The date is February 25th, 1792.

> Deprived of peace—to calumny a prey,
> HERE Helen wept her lonely hours away;
> Though guiltless, forc'd *imputed* guilt to bear,
> No justice destin'd—and no pity near.
>
> Forlorn! neglected!—happier prospects flown,
> And doom'd to expiate errors *not her own*,
> HERE oft to grief unbounded sway she gave
> And wearied heav'n with pray'rs to reach the Grave!
> The shelt'ring Grave!—that cure for human smart,
> The last sad refuge of a broken heart!
>
> *Scotia!* from thee my streaming eyes I turn,
> Now doom'd to rest in SOME far distant urn!
> Exil'd from all I valu'd!—country, home!

Near Solway's banks, no more, alas! to roam;
O'er youthful scenes where pleasure led the way,
Where fond *remembrance* oft shall ling'ring stray.

Affliction pours *this last*—this *parting* strain,
And proves WEAK REASON'S boasted efforts VAIN;
Alas! How VAIN!—torn!—from each comfort driv'n,
Thus robb'd of *all* save innocence and heav'n,
Can *her cold* precepts *mental* strength impart
When *outrag'd Nature* wrings the bursting heart?

Scotia, farewell! Long cherish'd Land, adieu!
Soon, soon on *thee* shall close my aching view!'
No more; but ah! let anguish speak the rest,
For *deep'ning* anguish rends my hapless breast,
I go!—sad Nature's *final* pang is o'er.
Scotia, farewell! *now fate can* wound *no more!*

In these despairing words, so full of deep feeling, and which cannot but touch all with any sense of compassion, do we not see that some crisis in the life of Helen Craik had come and gone, and that her departure from her beloved Scotland was an involuntary one? Does not this sad poem give at least some colour to the tradition current in the district round her beloved home? If we are to accept this as in any way confirmatory of the tale and of the period at which the tragic event of the murder or suicide took place, we are driven to the conclusion that no part could have been taken by her brother, Adam Craik, who was accidentally drowned near Flimby, on the Cumberland coast, in 1782, some ten years before. There was another member of the family, then in early manhood, to whom the death may have been attributed, but I do not purpose giving his name. He has long passed away, and we have no right to include his name in this connection without better proof than we can submit. What came of Helen Craik in the immediate time after she wrote this lament in the Summerhouse of Arbigland we cannot tell. She may have rented a house or taken lodgings, but it is possible that she may have gone to reside with her uncle, James Craik, and his sisters, Anne Elizabeth, Barbara, and Margery Neilson, who lived at Flimby Lodge, Cumberland. We do not know when she went to reside at Flimby Lodge, but we know that she died there on 11th June, 1824, in her 74th year, and was interred in Flimby Churchyard, the tombstone calling her 'Helen Craik of Flimby Lodge.' Her uncles and aunts predeceased her by some years, but all four were alive in 1792, when she probably went into Cumberland.

In two other poems, written, apparently at Flimby, Miss Craik reveals her personal feelings. 'Lines addressed to Miss Young on receiving a present of a Tartan Handkerchief from her Mother' display strong resentment at her relations and indicate that calumny had embittered her days in Scotland.

> MY LOVE FOR MY COUNTRY!!! from *whence must* it
>   flow?
> From falsehood—injustice—each species of woe?
> From *cunning's deep* fountain too *winding* to sound,
> From Avarice grasping at *all* seen around;
> From the *envy* of *some* who with malice pursued me,
> From the *coolness* of *Those* who mistakenly view'd me;
> From inhuman connections—from Nephews and Nieces
> *Who all for the best* tore my conduct to pieces;
> *Being* formed by *self-int'rest* with morals *so* civil
> As for sixpence to sell *half* their *kin* to the Devil;
> Yet that *once* they spoke truth must I think be confest
> Since THEIR WORDS I can echo "twas all for the best!!"*

* "'Tis all for the best,' said Mr H—— when the late Captain Riddell of Friars' Carse expostulated with him on certain *existing* circumstances; "'Tis all for the best,'

re-echoed the *Committee* of *Ways* and *Means,* and *for once* I completely *agree* with them.[2]

In her 'Lines Addressed to Miss Staig with the foregoing Poems' she expresses her appreciation of Miss Staig's constancy in friendship, as she does also of Miss Young and her mother in the poem already quoted, 'When the keen blast of slander near blighted the mind.'

You who *through chance* and *change* have *prov'd the same,*
Whose bosom glows with *Friendship's purest* flame,
Whose tongue ne'er stab'd *where* Fate *too heavy* prest,
Nor unreprov'd let pass th' unfeeling jest;

and describes the circumstances under which many of the verses were written.

If *wrapt* in *gloom* the pensive strain appears,
The *pen* that trac'd it *oft was steep'd* in *tears.*
With *tears* the page was often deluged o'er,
Forc'd from the bleeding HEART'S *half* broken *core,*
And *when deep* anguish THERE usurps the sway,
All else she *tinges* with her *sombre* ray—
Then ANNA!—*still* let *Friendship's pow'r* prevail,
And o'er *each error* throw *Indulgence'* veil.

One or two weak points arise in connection with the tradition. The leading one is that, if we take 1791 or 1792 as the time of the tragedy, Helen Craik was not then the young inexperienced maiden who, carried away by poetic feelings, and it may be inoculated by the sentiments of Robert Burns and the revolutionary

---

2 Anne Craik, sister of Helen Craik, married 4th June, 1758, John Hamilton of Ellershaw, their son, Douglas Hamilton Craik, born 1762, inherited the Arbigland estate, married, and had issue. Ellen Craik appears not to have had a niece, and but one grandniece. Captain Riddell of Friars' Carse died 21st April, 1794.

ideas of many in that age, would think lightly of social differences and distinctions, and would readily fall in love with a
handsome and attractive looking youth. In, say, 1791 she must
have been 40 or 41 years of age—not usually an impressionable
age. But it must be admitted that this is not a point necessarily
overthrowing any idea of the truth of the tradition. All history
and experience show us otherwise, although it must be stated
as casting some doubt on the tale. We can find no trace of her
ever being back in Scotland again, although she seems to have
been at Gilsland, in Northumberland, at a later period, and a
poem written in connection with a visit to that place, where she
stayed at Orchard House, reveals some lightening of the cloud
which had hung over her so long, and which had saddened the
lays she produced.

Whatever the truth or otherwise of the local tradition, it is
sad to think that this talented woman, whose friendship Burns
evidently appreciated, had her later years clouded with grief and
sadness—a cloud she should never have borne if we accept her
own words in the verses quoted above. Unfounded suspicion
may have poisoned the minds of her family, and the gloom of
her final years will seem only a proof of the words of her great
examplar in the worship of poesy:—

> Man's inhumanity to man
> Makes countless thousands mourn.

WRITINGS BY AND ABOUT HELEN CRAIK

WITH OTHER SOURCES CITED AND CONSULTED

(a) Manuscripts

Beinecke Library, Yale University, 'Poems by a Lady', by Helen Craik, MS Osborn c 375: a fair copy MS made by Craik for Robert Riddell, completed in 1790, and bound for him; owned in 1881 by James Wood, Troon (Gibson 1881); owned and exhibited in 1896 by Adam Wood, of Troon (*Memorial Catalogue*, 1898); referenced by Neilson and Arnott (1919, 1923–24) as the Wood MS; owned by E. W. M. Myerstein (1889–1952), who was researching its contents in 1947; subsequently sold Sotheby, 17–18 December 1956, lot 43; bought by Maggs; then to the James Marshall and Marie-Louise Osborn Collection, Beinecke Rare Book and Manuscript Library, Yale University; a related provenance file at Yale acquired with the MS has Meyerstein's notes, dated April 1947, and some earlier letters from Robert Henderson, J. C. Ewing, and others, about the interrelationship, and location, of the three Craik MS notebooks.

Ewart Library, Dumfries: a group of material from Lady Winifred Jardine, *née* Young, including transcripts of Burns's manuscripts given to Helen Craik and discovered in a lacquered cabinet after the death of Thomas Young of Lincluden, with other material relating to Helen Craik's family; the transcripts were made before the Burns MSS were sold at Sotheby's in 1913: see *The Scotsman*, 29 July 1913, p. 8; *New York Times*, 29 July 1913.

Lilly Library, Indiana University: provenance material from Hugh Dunlop, executor of John Henry Craik (1803–1877), Craik's great-nephew, relating to the Bemis/Lilly MS of Burns's 'Red, red, rose' and the Craik family.

Huntington Library, San Marino, CA: letter of Robert Burns to Helen Craik, 9 August 1790.

Mitchell Library, Glasgow: letter of Robert Burns to Helen Craik, 12 January 1792, MS.50/4; Craik's poem in her copy of Burns's 1787 *Poems*, call number 311219.

National Archives, Kew: transcript of last will and testament of Helen Craik of Flimby, 6 May 1825, as proved by her executors, 10 November 1825: record PROB 11/1705/149.; and transcript of will of James Craik of Flimby, 27 June 1796, as proved by his sole surviving executrix, Margery [Craik] Neilson, 31 January 1804, with an additional note

19 October 1807 transferring administration of James Craik's 'goods, chattels and credits' to Helen Craik, as sole executrix for Margery Neilson: record PROB 11/1403/281.

National Library of Scotland: in Robert Burns's Glenriddell Manuscript, vol. 1, NLS MS 86; facsimile (Philadelphia: privately printed [for John Gribbel], 1914; reprinted ed. Desmond Donaldson, Wakefield: EP Publishing, 1973); full transcription, in Nigel Leask (ed.), *Commonplace Books, Tour Journals, and Miscellaneous Prose* [*Oxford Edition of Robert Burns*, vol. 1] (Oxford: Oxford University Press, 2014).

Robert Burns Birthplace Museum (National Trust for Scotland), Alloway, Ayrshire: abstracts of letters from William Craik and Helen Craik to Robert Burns, prepared for James Currie: see Ewing, *Letters Addressed to Robert Burns*, 1938.

University of Glasgow Library, Archives and Special Collections: George S. Neilson papers, MS Gen 1114v, with copies of Neilson's 1919 *Glasgow Herald* articles.

Unlocated manuscripts

The Neilson manuscript: Helen Craik's own working poetry notebook, titled from its opening poem 'The Maid of Enterkin'; includes a version of 'Helen' dated 25 February 1792; given or bequeathed by her to her executor, Gilbert Young of Youngerfield (d. 1828); owned by his son, Major Thomas Young of Lincluden (d. 1896); inherited by Major Young's daughters but not included in the Sotheby's sale in 1913; later owned by George S. Neilson (1858–1923), and described by him (Neilson, 1919, 1923–24); not among the Neilson papers in the National Library of Scotland; no subsequent record.

The Henderson manuscript: given by Craik to her friend Miss Anne Staig of Dumfries; given by Miss Staig to General Goldie of Goldielea, thence to his daughter Miss Margaret Goldie, thence to her niece Mrs Starke, and thence to her husband James Gibson Hamilton Starke, J. P., of Troqueer Holm, Dumfries; sold at Dowell's, Edinburgh, 4 November 1908, lot 110, when the contents were described as dating from '1788–1811'; bought by Robert J. Henderson, of Penicuik, who described it in correspondence as having the first three leaves excised, and starting with a poem 'To a Linnet' (see Meyerstein provenance research file at Yale); includes version of 'Helen' dated 25 February 1792; referenced as the Henderson notebook by Neilson (1919, 1923–24) but not described; no subsequent record.

Transcript of Craik's poem 'Lines Written at Sea by the late Queen of Denmark', reported in 1849 as among the papers of Sir Robert Murray Keith, formerly British envoy in Copenhagen: see Published Writing, and Smyth (1849), below.

(b) Published Writing by Helen Craik

Julia St. Pierre: A Tale of the French Revolution: A Novel, 3 vols (London: for William Lane at the Minerva Press, 1796); shortened version, in ten weekly illustrated eight-page penny numbers, possibly vol. 1 only, but apparently all issued (London: Edward Lloyd, 1848; print-on-demand repr., Gale/Cengage and British Library, n.d.).
—the 1796 Minerva Press edition listed as 'in press', *Reading Mercury*, 25 April 1796, p. 2, and again in *Staffordshire Advertiser*, 19 November 1796, p. 1. The three-volume 1796 edition (over 1000 pages, more than 170,000 words) includes Craik's poem 'The Maid of Enterkin', in vol. III, pp. 345–99; this is not in the Edward Lloyd edition (seventy-eight pages, with nine large woodcuts, under fifty thousand words; the first number, seven pages in the digitisation and British Library reprint, must have had an illustrated cover sheet lacking in extant copies).

Henry of Northumberland, or, The Hermit's Cell: A Tale of the Fifteenth Century, 3 vols (London: at the Minerva Press for W. Lane, 1800); 2 vols (Dublin: printed by William Fields, for P. Wogan [et al.], 1800); microfiche (Wildberg: Belser Wissenschiftlicher Dienst, 1989).

Adelaide de Narbonne, with Memoirs of Charlotte de Cordet. A Tale, 4 vols (London: at the Minerva Press, for William Lane, Leadenhall Street, 1800); 1 vol., ed. with an intro, and notes by Marianna d'Ezio (Newcastle upon Tyne: Cambridge Scholars Publishing, 2018).
—includes a prose re-working of Craik's poem 'The Monk of la Trappe', in vol. IV, ch. xiii.

Stella of the North, or, The Foundling of the Ship: A Novel, 4 vols (London: at the Minerva Press for Lane and Newman, 1802); microfiche (Wildberg: Belser Wissenschiftlicher Dienst, 1989).

The Nun and Her Daughter, or, Memoirs of the Courville family: A Novel, 4 vols (London: at the Minerva Press for Lane, Newman, 1805).

Letters, dated 18 April 1810 and May 1810, in 'Account of William Craik, Esq., of Arbigland', *Farmer's Magazine*, 12 (June 1811), pp. 154–63.

[*attrib.*] 'Verses, Suggested by the Subscription for the Mausoleum of Burns', *The Star* (London), 5 September 1815, p. 4.

'To the Editor of the Monthly Magazine', *Monthly Magazine*, 52 (December 1821), p. 418: correcting errors about William Craik in an earlier article on John Paul Jones.

'Lines Written at Sea by the Late Queen of Denmark', in Mrs Gillespie Smyth (ed.), *Memoirs and Correspondence (Official and Familiar) of Sir Robert Murray Keith, K. B.*, 2 vols (London: Colburn, 1849), I, pp. 299–300.

(c) Maps

Ainslie, John, *Scotland Drawn from a Series of Angles and Astronomical Observations* (Edinburgh: J. & J. Ainslie & W. Faden, 1789): maps. nls.uk/view/74400651.

Conder, Thomas, *A New Map of the Southern Part of Scotland* (London: A. Hogg, 1786): maps.nls.uk/view/216441494.

Ferguson, William, and John Gellatly, *Plan of the Estate of Arbigland lying in the parish of Kirkbean and the Stewatry of Kirkcudbright belonging to D. Hamilton Craik Esq.* (1835): maps.nls.uk/view/132293872.

(d) Other Sources

'Account of William Craik, Esq., of Arbigland', *Farmer's Magazine*, 12 (June 1811), pp. 145–65.

Adam, Robert Borthwick, *Autograph Poems and Letters of Robert Burns* (Buffalo, NY: privately printed, 1922).

Aitchison, Peter, and Andrew Cassel, *The Lowland Clearances: Scotland's Silent Revolution, 1760–1830* (East Linton: Tuckwell, 2003).

Anderson, Misty G., *Female Playwrights and Eighteenth-Century Comedy: Negotiating Marriage on the London Stage* (New York: Palgrave, 2002).

Arnott, Samuel, 'Some Kirkbean folklore', *Transactions of Dumfriesshire and Galloway Natural History and Antiquarian Society*, 2nd ser., 11 (1894–95), pp. 11–17.

———, 'The Romance of Helen Craik of Arbigland', *Transactions of Dumfriesshire and Galloway Natural History and Antiquarian Society*, 3rd ser., 11 (1923–24), pp. 77–83.

Backscheider, Paula, *Eighteenth-Century Women Poets and Their Poetry: Inventing Agency, Inventing Genre* (Baltimore: Johns Hopkins University Press, 2005).

———, *British women poets of the long eighteenth century: an anthology* (Baltimore, MD: Johns Hopkins University Press, 2009).

Barash, Carol, *English Women's Poetry, 1649–1714* (Oxford: Clarendon Press, 1990).

———, *Women's Writing and the Circulation of Ideas* (Cambridge: Cambridge University Press, 2002).

Barker, Nicolas, and Wendy Van Wyck Good, *Robert Burns: The Poet's Progress, A Bicentennial Exhibition* (Philadelphia: Rosenbach Museum and Library, 1995).

Behrendt, Stephen, 'Scottish Women Poets of the Romantic Period: Romantic Poetry, Women Writers, and Literary History's Blind Spots', in *Scottish Women Poets of the Romantic Period: An Electronic Archive* (Alexandria, VA: Alexander Street Press/ProQuest, 2007).

———, *British Women Poets and the Romantic Writing Community* (Baltimore, MD: Johns Hopkins University Press, 2008).

Blackett, James, 'Arbigland Estate Records', Kirkbean Parish Heritage Society—Arbigland Estate (2004): www.kirkbean.org/history/arbigland-estate-records [accessed 19 April 2023].

———, *Red Rag to a Bull: Rural Life in an Urban Age* (Wykey, Shrewsbury: Quiller, 2018).

Blakey, Dorothy, *The Minerva Press, 1790–1820* (London: printed for the Bibliographical Society by Oxford University Press, 1939 [for 1935]).

Bode, Christoph, '"Imaginary circles round the human mind": Bias and Openness in Mary Wollstonecraft's *Letters Written During a Short Residence in Sweden, Norway, and Denmark* (1796)', in Cian Duffy (ed.), *Romantic Norths: Anglo-Nordic Exchanges, 1770–1842* (Cham: Palgrave Macmillan, 2017), pp. 29–52.

Bricker, Andrew Benjamin. 'Libel and Satire: The Problem with Naming', *ELH*, 81.3 (2014), 889–921.

Bright, Henry A., *Some Account of the Glenriddell Manuscripts* (Liverpool: Womersley, 1874).

Broxburn, Tim, *Scottish Garden Buildings: From Food to Folly* (Edinburgh: Mainstream, 1989).

Bruce, James, *Travels to Discover the Source of the Nile, In the Years 1768, 1769, 1770, 1771, 1772 and 1773* (Edinburgh: printed by J. Ruthven, for G. G. J. and J. Robinson, London, 1790).

Bruss, Elizabeth W., 'The Game of Literature and Some Literary Games', *New Literary History*, 9.1 (Autumn 1977), 153–72.

Bullard, Paddy, 'Describing Eighteenth-Century British Satire', in Paddy Bullard (ed.), *The Oxford Handbook of Eighteenth-Century Satire* (Oxford: Oxford University Press, 2019), 1–22.

Butt, John (ed.), *The Poems of Alexander Pope, A One-Volume Edition of the Twickenham Pope* (London: Methuen, 1963).

Cairns, J. W., 'The Origins of the Edinburgh Law School: The Union of 1707 and the Regius Chair', *Edinburgh Law Review*, 11 (2007), 300–48.

Cannon, Richard, *Historical record of the Seventieth or Surrey Regiment of Foot* (London: Parker, 1849).

[Caroline Matilda, Queen of Denmark], *Memoirs of an Unfortunate Queen, Interspersed with Letters Written by Herself* (London: Bew, 1776).

Carruthers, Gerard C. (gen. ed.), *Oxford Edition of Robert Burns* (Oxford: Oxford University Press, 2014–).
　Vol. 1: Nigel Leask (ed.), *Commonplace Books, Tour Journals, and Miscellaneous Prose* (2014).
　Vols 2–3: Murray Pittock (ed.), *The Scots Musical Museum* (2017).
　Vol. 4: Kirsteen McCue (ed.), *Robert Burns's Songs for George Thomson* (2021).

Chambers, R. W., and William Wallace (eds), *Life and Works of Robert Burns*, 4 vols (Edinburgh: W. & R. Chambers, 1896).

Chapman, Hester, *Caroline Matilda, Queen of Denmark* (New York: Coward, McCann & Georghegan, 1972).

Cowan, Edward J., 'Agricultural Improvement and the formation of early agricultural societies in Dumfries and Galloway', *Transactions of Dumfriesshire and Galloway Natural History and Antiquarian Society*, 3rd ser., 53 (1977–78), 157–67.

Craciun, Adriana, *British Women Writers and the French Revolution* (Basingstoke: Palgrave Macmillan, 2005).

———, 'Craik, Helen (1751–1825)', in *Oxford Dictionary of National Biography* (2004; entry revised 2011).

———, 'Craik, Helen', in Elizabeth Ewan and Rose Pipes (eds), *The New Biographical Dictionary of Scottish Women* (Edinburgh: Edinburgh University Press, 2018), pp. 98–99.

———, *Fatal Women of Romanticism* (Cambridge: Cambridge University Press, 2003).

———, 'The new Cordays: Helen Craik and British representations of Charlotte Corday, 1793–1800', in Adriana Craciun and Karl E. Lokke (eds), *Rebellious hearts: British women writers and the French Revolution* (Albany, NY: State University of New York Press, 2001), pp. 193–232.

———, 'Revolution, Romanticism and the Long Nineteenth Century', *19: Interdisciplinary Studies in the Long Nineteenth Century*, 2 (Open Library of the Humanities, April 2006).

———, 'Romantic spinstrelsy: Anne Bannerman and the sexual politics of the ballad', in Leith Davis, Ian Duncan, and Janet Sorensen (eds), *Scotland and the Borders of Romanticism* (Cambridge: Cambridge University Press, 2004), pp. 204–24.

Cunningham, Allan (ed.), *Works of Robert Burns*, 8 vols (London: Cochrane and M'Crone, 1834).

Davison, Carol Margaret and Monica Germanà, 'Borderlands of Identity and the Aesthetics of Disjuncture', in Davison and Germanà (eds), *Scottish Gothic* (Edinburgh: Edinburgh University Press, 2017), pp. 1–13.

Dawson, Bill, 'Questions around the Composition of "Tam o' Shanter"', *Burns Chronicle*, 130.1 (Spring 2021), 99–102.

'Deaths' [Helen Craik notice], *Cumberland Pacquet* (Whitehaven, 14 June 1825); also in *Dumfries Weekly Journal* (21 June 1825); *The Star* (London, 20 June, 1825), 4.

D'Ezio, Marianna, 'Introduction', in Craik, *Adelaide de Narbonne, with Memoirs of Charlotte de Cordet. A Tale*, ed. Marianna d'Ezio (Newcastle upon Tyne: Cambridge Scholars Publishing, 2018), pp. x–xx.

Defoe, Daniel, *Memoirs of the Church of Scotland* (London: E. Matthews, 1717), pp. 189–93.

———, *A Tour Thro' the Whole Island of Great Britain*, 3 vols (London: Strahan, 1724–27).

Devine, T. M. (ed.), *Recovering Scotland's Slavery Past: the Caribbean Connection* (Edinburgh: Edinburgh University Press, 2015)

_____, *The Scottish Clearances: A History of the Dispossessed* (London: Allen Lane, 2018).

Douglas, William Scott (ed.), *The Works of Robert Burns*, 6 vols (Edinburgh: William Paterson, 1877–79).

Draper, Nicholas, 'Scotland and Colonial Slave Ownership: the Evidence of the Slave Compensation Records', in T. M. Devine (ed.), *Recovering Scotland's Slavery Past: the Caribbean Connection* (Edinburgh: Edinburgh University Press, 2015), pp. 166–86.

Duncan, Ian, et al., 'Introduction,' in Leith Davis, Ian Duncan, and Janet Sorensen (eds), *Scotland and the Borders of Romanticism* (Cambridge: Cambridge University Press, 2004), pp. 1–19.

Dundas, Robert, *Memorial for Mary Craik, eldest daughter of the deceast Adam Craik of Duchrae, and Mrs. Winnifred Maxwell, her Mother and Tutrix, against Mrs. Jean Craik, and Mr. Stewart of Castle-Stewart, for his interest* (Edinburgh; 12 July, 1735).

Epley, Steven, 'Alienated, Betrayed, and Powerless: A Possible Connection Between *Charlotte Temple* and the Legend of Inkle and Yarico', *Papers on Language and Literature*, 38.2 (March 2002), 200–22.

Ewing, J. C., *Robert Burns's Literary Correspondents, 1786–1796: a Chronological List of Letters Addressed to the Poet, with Precises of their Contents* (Alloway: Burns Monument Trustees, 1938).

Ezell, Margaret, *Social Authorship and the Advent of Print* (Baltimore, MD: Johns Hopkins, 1999)

_____, *The Patriarch's Wife* (Chapel Hill, NC: University of North Carolina Press, 1987).

Ferguson, William, *Scotland 1689 to the Present* [*Edinburgh History of Scotland*, vol. IV] (Edinburgh: Oliver and Boyd, 1968).

Fulton, Henry L., *Dr. John Moore, 1729–1802: A Life in Medicine, Travel, and Revolution* (Newark, DE: University of Delwarare Press, 2018).

Galt, John, *Annals of the Parish*, ed. Robert P. Irvine [*Edinburgh Edition of the Works of John Galt*] (Edinburgh: Edinburgh University Press, 2020).

Gibson, James, *The Bibliography of Robert Burns* (Kilmarnock: M'Kie, 1881).

Gifford, Douglas, and Dorothy McMillan (eds), *A History of Scottish Women's Writing* (Edinburgh: Edinburgh University Press, 2007).

Gifford, John, *Dumfries and Galloway: The Buildings of Scotland* (London: Penguin, 1996; New Haven: Yale University Press, 2002).

Glover, Katharine, *Elite Women and Polite Society in Eighteenth-Century Scotland* (Woodbridge: Boydell Press, 2011).

Gordon, Eleanor, 'Irregular Marriage: Myth and Reality', *Journal of Social History*, 47. 2 (Winter 2013), 507–25.

Graham, Eric J., *Burns & the Sugar Plantocracy of Ayrshire* (Edinburgh: MPDB, 2014).

Gray, Peter, *Dumfriesshire Illustrated, etc.* (Dumfries: Maxwell, 1894).

Grenier, Katherine Haldane, *Tourism and Identity in Scotland, 1770–1914* (Farnham: Ashgate, 2005).

Hall, Mrs Matthew, *The Royal Princesses of England* (London: Routledge, 1858).

Hart, Francis Russell, 'Limits of the Gothic: The Scottish Example', *Studies in Eighteenth Century Culture*, 3 (1974), 137–53.

Hay, George, 'Scottish Post-Reformation Church Furniture', *Proceedings of the Society of Antiquaries of Scotland*, 88 (November 1954), 47–56.

Heister, Lorenz, *A General System of Surgery in Three Parts*, 4th ed., trans., (London: W. Innys et al., 1750).

'Helen Craik', in *The Bloomsbury Dictionary of English Literature*, ed. Marion Wynne-Davies, 2nd ed. (London: Bloomsbury, 1997), online.

'Helen Craik', in Susan Brown, Patricia Clements, and Isobel Grundy (eds), *Orlando: Women's Writing in the British Isles from the Beginnings to the Present* (University of Alberta; Cambridge University Press/Cambridge Core, 2008), online.

'Helen Craik', in Elizabeth Ewan, Rose Pipes, and Jane Rendall (eds), *The Biographical Dictionary of Scottish Women* (Edinburgh: Edinburgh University Press, 2006), 66–69; and in Ewan, Elizabeth, Rose Pipes, Jane Rendall and Siân Reynolds (eds), *The New Biographical Dictionary of Scottish Women*, 2nd ed. (Edinburgh: Edinburgh University Press, 2018).

Herries, W. M., *Report of the Stewartry of Kirkcudbright Agricultural Society for the Year 1810* (Dumfries: Geo. Johnstone & Company, 1811).

Hyde, Matthew, and Nikolaus Pevsner, *Cumbria: Cumberland, Westmorland and Furness* [*The Buildings of England*] (New Haven: Yale University Press, 2010).

Jones, Robert W., 'Notes on *The Camp*: women, effeminacy and the military in late eighteenth-century literature', *Textual Practice*, 11.3 (1997), 463–73.

Keown, Kathleen, 'Recent Scholarship on eighteenth-century women's poetry', *Literature Compass*, 18.8 (September 2021), online.

———, 'Eighteenth-Century Women's Poetry and Feminine Accomplishment', *Review of English Studies*, n.s. 73 (2022): 78–99 (online from 23 August 2021).

Kerrigan, Catherine (ed.), *An Anthology of Scottish Women Poets* (Edinburgh: Edinburgh University Press, 1991).

Kinsley, James (ed.), *Poems and Songs of Robert Burns*, 3 vols (Oxford: Clarendon Press, 1968).

Leask, Nigel, 'Bruce, James, of Kinnaird (1730–1794)', in *Oxford Dictionary of National Biography* (2004; entry revised 2006).

Levy, Michelle, *Literary Manuscript Culture in Romantic Britain* (Edinburgh: Edinburgh University Press, 2020).

Livingston, Alister, *The Galloway Levellers: a study of the origins, events, and consequences of their actions* (unpub. M.Phil., University of Glasgow, 2009).

Love, Harold. *The Culture and Commerce of Texts* (Amherst, MA: University of Massachusetts Press, 1993).

Mackay, James, *Burnsiana* (Ayr: Alloway Publishing, 1988).

———, *RB: A Biography* (Edinburgh: Mainstream, 1992).

MacKerlie, P. H., *An Account of the Scottish Regiments* (Edinburgh: Nimmo, 1862).

Manley, K. A., *Books, Borrowers, and Shareholders: Scottish Circulating and Subscription Libraries before 1825* (Edinburgh: Edinburgh Bibliographical Society, 2012).

Mathison, Hamish, '"Out of tune": Sex, Death, and Gothic Disharmony in Eighteenth-Century Scotland', in *Sex and Death in Eighteenth-Century Literature*, ed. Jolene Zigarovich (London: Routledge, 2013), pp. 224–40.

McCulloch, Andrew, *Galloway, A Land Apart* (Edinburgh: Birlinn, 2000).

McMillan, Dorothy (ed.), *The Scotswoman at Home and Abroad: Non-Fictional Writing, 1700–1900* (Glasgow: Association for Scottish Literary Studies, 1999).

M'Dowall, William, *History of the Burgh of Dumfries, with Notices of Nithsdale, Annandale, and the Western Border*, 3rd ed. (Dumfries: Thomas Hunter, 1906).

Memorial Catalogue of the Burns Exhibition Held in the Galleries of the Royal Institute of Fine Arts . . . 1896 (Glasgow: William Hodge, 1898).

'Miscellaneous Dissertations on Rural Subjects' in William Kenrick (ed.), *London Review of English and Foreign Literature*, 1 (London: Cox and Bigg, 1775), 191–98.

Morton, Graeme, *History of Everyday Life in Scotland, 1800–1900* (Edinburgh: Edinburgh University Press, 2010).

Neilson, Rev. Edward, 'Parish of Kirkbean' in Sir John Sinclair (ed.), *Statistical Account of Scotland*, 15, no. VII (Edinburgh: William Creech, 1795).

Neilson, George, 'The Maid of Enterkin: Burnsiana 1', *Glasgow Herald* (8 March 1919).

———, 'The Social and Literary Circle, 1790–1793: Burnsiana 2', *Glasgow Herald*, 15 March 1919.

———, 'Old and New: 'A Monody' by Davie: Burnsiana 3', *Glasgow Herald*, 22 March 1919.

———, 'The Maid of Enterkin: Poems by Helen Craik and Burnsiana', *Transactions and Journal Proceedings of the Dumfriesshire and Galloway Natural History and Antiquarian Society*, 3rd ser., 11 (1923–24): 63–76.

Neiman, Elizabeth, *Minerva's Gothics: The Politics and Poetics of Romantic Exchange, 1780–1820* (Cardiff: University of Wales Press, 2019).

Niles, John D. and Eleanor R. Long, 'Context and Loss in Scottish Ballad Tradition', *Western Folklore*, 45.2 (2006), 83–109.

Norquay, Glenda (ed.), *The Edinburgh Companion to Scottish Women's Writing* (Edinburgh: Edinburgh University Press, 2012).

Novak, Maximilian E., 'Sex, Madness and Suicide in Sir Henry Croft's Love and Madness', in *Sex and Death in Eighteenth-Century Literature*, ed. Jolene Zigarovich (London: Routledge, 2013), pp. 165–82.

'The Old Stag of Arbigland', reprinted from the *Dumfries Courier*, in *Cumberland Pacquet, and Ware's Whitehaven Advertiser*, 3 December 1821, p. 4.

Packer, Ian and Lynda Pratt (eds), *The Collected Letters of Robert Southey*, part 6, 1819–1821 (2017), online at *Romantic Circles*: romantic-circles.org/editions/southey_letters/Part_Six/.

Parks, Stephen, 'The Osborn Collection: A Fifth Biennial Report', *Yale University Library Gazette*, 52 (January 1978), 101–21.

Parson, William, and William White, *History, Directory and Gazetteer of the Counties of Cumberland and Westmoreland* (Leeds: Edward Baines for William White, 1829).

Perkins, Pam, *Women Writers and the Edinburgh Enlightenment* [SCROLL, vol. 15] (Amsterdam: Rodopi, 2010).

Perry, Ruth, '"The Finest Ballads": Women's Oral Traditions in Eighteenth-Century Scotland", *Eighteenth-Century Life*, 32.2 (Spring, 2008), 81–98.

———, 'The Printed Record of an Oral Tradition: Anna Gordon Brown's Ballads', *Studies in Scottish Literature*, 38.1 (2012), 71–91.

Pevsner, Niklaus, *The Buildings of England: Cumberland and Westmoreland* (Harmondsworth: Penguin, 1967).

Phillippy, Patricia Berrahou, *A History of Early Modern Women's Writing* (Cambridge: Cambridge University Press, 2018).

Porter, Roy, 'Hospitals and Surgery' in Roy Porter (ed.), *The Cambridge Illustrated History of Medicine* (Cambridge: Cambridge University Press, 1996), pp. 219–20.

Postlethwayt, Malachy, *Universal Dictionary of Trade and Commerce*, vol. 2, 4th ed., (London: Strahan, 1755).

Purdie, David, Kirsteen McCue, and Gerard Carruthers (eds), *Maurice Lindsay's The Burns Encyclopaedia*, 4th ed. rev. (London: Robert Hale, 2013).

Rankine, John, William Harvey, and Robert Berry (eds), *Scots Revised Reports: House of Lords, Series I, 1707–1797* (Edinburgh: William Green, 1898).

Robert Burns 1759–1796, a Collection of Original Manuscripts, Autograph Letters, First Editions and Association Copies (Philadelphia: The Rosenbach Company, 1948).

Rollie, Chris, 'A Monody on the Fatal 29th December, 1789: A Rediscovered Poem by Burns', *Burns Chronicle*, 110 (1998), 62–69.

Ross, Ian Simpson, *Lord Kames and the Scotland of his Day* (Oxford: Clarendon Press, 1972).

Roy, G. Ross (ed.), *Letters of Robert Burns*, 2 vols (Oxford: Clarendon Press, 1985).

Russo, Stephanie, 'Domesticating Charlotte Corday? *Adelaide de Narbonne* and private vengeance', in Jarad Cogle, et al. (eds), *Portable Prose: The Novel and the Everyday* (Lanham, MD: Lexington Books; 2018), pp. 111–25.

Scott, Patrick, *Robert Burns, A Documentary Volume* (Farmington Hills, MI: Gale/Cengage, 2018).

————, 'The Missing Manuscript of 'A Red, Red, Rose'', *Editing Burns for the 21st Century* (Glasgow: Centre for Robert Burns Studies, September 23, 2020): burnsc21.glasgow.ac.uk/the-missing-manuscript-of-a-red-red-rose/

————, 'Burns and the mysterious "Authoress"', *Eighteenth-Century Intelligencer*, 37.1 (March 2023), 7–13.

Scott-Eliot, J., 'McCulloch's Castle, Arbigland', *Transactions of Dumfriesshire and Galloway Natural History and Antiquarian Society*, 3rd ser., 41 (1962–1963), 118–24.

Scottish Exhibition of National History, Art & Industry Glasgow (1911): Palace of History Catalogue of Exhibits (Glasgow: Dalross, 1911).

Shields, Juliet, 'How to become an "Authoress" in Provincial Scotland: Women's Poetry in Manuscript and Print', in Leith Davis and Janet Sorensen (eds), *The International Companion to Scottish Literature of the Long Eighteenth Century* (Glasgow: Scottish Literature International, 2021), 132–48.

Shirley, G. W., 'Two pioneer Galloway agriculturalists—Robert Maxwell of Arkland and William Craik of Arbigland', *Transactions of Dumfriesshire and Galloway Natural History and Antiquarian Society*, 3rd ser., 13 (1925–1926), 129–61.

Simpson, J. M., 'Kirkcudbright Stewartry', in *The History of Parliament 1716–1746* (1970), consulted online.

Shuttleton, David, et al. (eds), *The Cullen Project: the Medical Consultation Letters of Dr. William Cullen (1710–1790) at the Royal College of Physicians of Edinburgh* (Glasgow: University of Glasgow, 2012–2015): cullenproject.ac.uk/

Smith, D. B., rev. Hector L. MacQueen, 'Neilson, George (1858–1923)', in *ODNB* (2004).

Smith, Margaret, and Penny Boumelha, *Index to English Literary Manuscripts*, III.1 (London: Mansell, 1986).

Smith, Samuel, *A General Survey of the Agriculture of Galloway* (London: for Richard Phillips, 1810).

Smyth, Mrs. Gillespie (ed.), *Memoirs and Correspondence (Official and Familiar) of Sir Robert Murray Keith, K. B.*, 2 vols (London: Colburn, 1849).

Sorrell, Mark, 'Ryley [formerly Romney], Samuel William (1759–1837)', in *ODNB* (2004): doi.org/10.1093/ref:odnb/24422.

Sterne, Laurence, *A Sentimental Journey through France and Italy, by Mr. Yorick*, vol. II, 2nd ed. (London: for T. Becket and P. A. De Hondt, 1768).

Stones, E. L. G., 'George Neilson (1858–1923): memoir', *Miscellany One, Stair Society*, 26 (Edinburgh: for the Stair Society, 1971), 1–10.

Strachan, Hew, *British Military Uniforms 1768–1796: The Dress of the British Army from Official Sources* (London: Arms and Armour Press, 1975).

Tankard, Paul, *Facts and Inventions: Selections from the Journalism of James Boswell* (New Haven: Yale University Press, 2014).

Temperley, Alan, 'The Groom of Arbigland', in his *Tales of Galloway* (London: Skilton and Shaw, 1979), 266–68.

Tenger, Zeynap and Paul Trolander, 'Katherine Phillips and Coterie Critical Practices', *Eighteenth-Century Studies*, 37.3 (2004), 367–87.

Thomson, Andrea, review of Katherine Glover, *Elite Women and Polite Society in Eighteenth-Century Scotland*, in *Journal of Scottish Historical Studies*, 35.1 (April 2015), 115–17.

Thornton, Robert Donald, *William Maxwell to Robert Burns* (John Donald, 1979).

Truckell, A. E., 'Arbigland Accounts, 1751–59', *Transactions of the Dumfriesshire and Galloway Natural History and Antiquarian Society*, 67 (1992), 81–86.

Universal Scots Almanac for 1770 (Edinburgh: Ruddiman, n.d.).

Valuation Roll, Antient and Modern, of the Stewartry of Kirkcudbright (Dumfries: at the Courier Office, 1820).

Voltaire, *Le Siecle de Louis XIV* (London: Dodsley, 1752).

Walker, John, 'Account of the Irruption of Solway Moss in December 16, 1772 [November 1771]', *Philosophical Transactions*, 62 (January 1772), 123–27.

Ward, Richard W., *Print Culture, Crime and Justice in 18th-Century London* (London: Bloomsbury, 2014).

Webster, James, *General View of the Agriculture of Galloway* (Edinburgh: James Paterson, 1794).

Whatley, Christopher A., *Scottish Society, 1707–1830: Beyond Jacobitism, towards Industrialisation* (Manchester: Manchester University Press, 2000).

———, *Immortal Memory: Burns and the Scottish People* (Edinburgh: John Donald, 2016).

Wight, Andrew, *The Present State of Husbandry in Scotland extracted from reports made to the Commissioners of the annexed estates*, vols. 1–3 (Edinburgh: Willliam Creech, 1778, 1784).

Witten, Laurence, 'Contemporary Collectors, XXII: James Marshall Osborn', *The Book Collector*, 8.4 (Winter 1959), 383–96.

Wodrow, Rev. Robert, *History of the Sufferings of the Church of Scotland*, 2 vols (Edinburgh: Watson, 1721–22).

Wollstonecraft, Mary, *Letters Written During a Short Residence in Sweden, Norway, and Denmark* (London: printed for J. Johnson, 1796).

Wood, Henry Trueman, 'The Royal Society of Arts. V.—The Society and Agriculture (1754–1830)', *Journal of the Royal Society of Arts*, 59 (3 November 1911), 1108–18.

Wraxall, Sir C. F. Lascelles, Bt., *Life and Times of Her Majesty Caroline Matilda, Queen of Denmark*, 3 vols (London: W. H. Allen, 1864).

Wright, Angela, *Britain, France and the Gothic, 1764–1820: The Import of Terror* (Cambridge: Cambridge University Press, 2013).

————, 'Scottish Gothic', in Catherine Spooner and Emma McEvoy (eds), *The Routledge Companion to Gothic* (London and New York: Routledge, 2007), 76–86.

Zigarovich, Jolene (ed.), *Sex and Death in Eighteenth-Century Literature* (London: Routledge, 2013).

INDEX OF TITLES AND FIRST LINES

THE ASSOCIATION FOR SCOTTISH LITERATURE
ANNUAL VOLUMES

Volumes marked * are, at the time of publication, still available.